W9-AHB-890

La Toya Jackson was the first sibling to arrive at the hospital after Michael was rushed there. She noticed suspicious details and demanded a second autopsy. For the first time, she exposes what she has uncovered.

In her own words:

When I finally realized that Michael was dead, my immediate thought was not

How did Michael die?

BUT

Who killed Michael?

My mind leapt to the many times that Michael had predicted this moment to me in no uncertain terms.

"La Toya, I'm going to be murdered for my music publishing catalog and my estate," *he told me again and again.*

Michael believed there was a conspiracy, and I can't help but think his suspicions may have come true. . . .

This title is also available as an eBook.

LA TOYA JACKSON

WITH **JEFFRÉ PHILLIPS**

STARTING OVER

POCKET BOOKS

New York London Toronto

Sydney New Delhi

JA-TAIL PUBLISHING COMPANY

A Division of

Ja-Tail Enterprises, LLC

Pocket Star Books
A Division of Simon & Schuster, Inc.
1230 Avenue of the Americas
New York, NY 10020

Ja-Tail Publishing Company
A Division of Ja-Tail Enterprises, LLC
8306 Wilshire Boulevard, Suite #528
Beverly Hills, CA 90211

Copyright © 2011 by Ja-Tail Publishing Company

All rights reserved, including the right to reproduce this book or portions thereof in any form whatsoever. For information, address Gallery Books Subsidiary Rights Department,
1230 Avenue of the Americas, New York, NY 10020.

First Pocket Star Books paperback edition June 2012

POCKET STAR BOOKS and colophon are registered trademarks of Simon & Schuster, Inc.

For information about special discounts for bulk purchases, please contact Simon & Schuster Special Sales at 1-866-506-1949 or business@simonandschuster.com.

The Simon & Schuster Speakers Bureau can bring authors to your live event. For more information or to book an event, contact the Simon & Schuster Speakers Bureau at 1-866-248-3049 or visit our website at www.simonspeakers.com.

Designed by Jaime Putorti

Photo insert credits:
insert page 6 (top): © Retna
insert page 6 (bottom): © Corbis Images
insert page 12 (bottom) and page 13: Harrison Funk/Ja-Tail Enterprises
All other photos courtesy of Ja-Tail Enterprises

Manufactured in the United States of America

10 9 8 7 6 5 4 3 2 1

ISBN 978-1-4516-2059-7
ISBN 978-1-4516-2060-3 (ebook)

I dedicate this book to my brother Michael;
I love you with all my heart, I felt your pain,
and I lived your pain.

Michael, you are the epitome of Godliness.
You have been an inspiration to us all. You
have taught us all so much by your kindness,
your actions, and your love for mankind. You
cared tremendously for those who were sick,
spending so much of your personal time with
them just to put smiles on their faces and joy
in their hearts. Your many contributions to
so many charities throughout the world have
helped provide those less fortunate with food,
clothing, shelter, and life-saving medicine. Your
stardom was so profound and so overwhelming,
and your incredible talent brought us all joy
and left a mark on this earth. You are truly a
prime example to the world of what Godliness
is like. We can all take a lesson out of your
book of love and become a better person.
You were so gifted, yet very humble. With all
your accolades and accomplishments, you still
remained humble. People took advantage of
you, and you knew you were in danger, yet you
continued to remain humble. Michael, every

human being on this earth should learn from you. You only wanted to give us love and light.

I love you for your soul and Godliness!
I love you for being you!
I love you!

La Toya

I dedicate this book to anyone who has suffered any type of abuse in any form, be it mental, verbal, or physical. One strike is one too many. Stand up for yourself and your loved ones, and walk away. IT'S NEVER TOO LATE TO START OVER.

I would very much like to thank the fans for their undying love and continuous support. I want you to know that Michael loved you more than anything else outside of his family. You guys gave him life. I love all of you for being there for him. Let's continue to support the King and find out what truly happened to him, and let's keep his legacy alive.

CONTENTS

CONTENTS   i x

STARTING OVER

PROLOGUE

I never believed I would survive to write a second book, but by the grace of God, here I am. Twenty long years have passed since I wrote my first autobiography, *La Toya*. The truth is that I didn't want to author that first book. My ex-manager, Jack Gordon, made me publish the book and speak out against my will in its pages, just as he forced me to marry him in 1989 and made me make so many career moves that were contrary to my wishes and beliefs. For almost a decade, Gordon controlled me with a campaign of brutalization and manipulation, beating me several times a week, threatening my life and the lives of my family members, and proving he had the mob ties to carry out his most violent promises. As is common with abusers, he also isolated me from anyone I loved, who might have come to my aid or inspired me to rebel against him. By the end of his first year of management, I was so insecure and traumatized that I couldn't even look at myself in the mirror. I hated the person I saw there because everything about her was ugly to me, and I thought it was my fault.

I am thankful that, this time around, I have the freedom to write what I want, the way I want. It truly is the most wonderful feeling to finally be free from the misery of my prior life. I am absolutely overjoyed to find myself still here on this earth, experiencing the most extreme happiness every day, in the company of my dear family and friends. Believe me, this is no exaggeration. After the horrors I have lived through, and the despair I have felt, every breath is truly a gift. I am so grateful for my freedom and the person I am now, even if I had to endure such painful experiences to get here.

There was a time, before Jack Gordon, and all of the tragedy that befell my family, when I was extremely happy. I lived at Hayvenhurst, the family home in Encino, California. I traveled the world, making a good living as an entertainer. I spent all of my time with my family, who were my best friends, and the people I loved most in the world.

Every day was a blessing, and I couldn't wait to wake up each morning to hear my sister Rebbie singing Mandy Patinkin's version of the song "When the Red, Red Robin Comes Bob, Bob, Bobbin' Along." Even though my more famous siblings' performances were already filling arenas at that point, nothing made me happier than hearing Rebbie croon that special song just for me. It would put the biggest smile on my face. My brothers' fame, as well as the Jehovah's Witness religion with which Mother raised us, meant that we were isolated when I was growing up. This was especially true of Rebbie, Michael, and me, who were the most devout. I'm sure this helped to make Michael and me vulnerable to our eventual fates, as did our not really understanding the value of money, having always grown up with the ability to earn plenty. But as a child and young woman, I was cheerful and helpful, and I wanted for nothing in the world.

When Jack Gordon preyed on my naïveté and took me away from all of this, I could not understand why God had brought such dark forces into my life and allowed me to suffer so greatly. It wasn't until I escaped from Gordon on May 3, 1996, and spent many years making sense of what I endured that I realized why God put me in the worst possible situation. He did so to make me the strong person I am today, so that I could help other women to escape their abusers and also have the chance to start their lives over.

I assumed it would be easy. I thought I could just wake up one morning and say, "Today is the first day of the rest of my life. Today I'm starting over." I didn't realize all of the difficulties that life presents us daily, and that starting over isn't something that we do once in a lifetime; it's something we do continuously, by learning from our mistakes, until we eventually become the people we will be.

I had considered the possibility of telling my story in a new book. But I was embarrassed and frightened to share my true story with the world. I had no self-esteem or sense of self-worth. I couldn't believe I let someone take away my dignity and go against my beliefs, while my family was out there, creating beautiful, legendary music, and making the world a better place to live. And I didn't think people would believe my story or relate to it. I was the subject of sensational tabloid reports and late-night jokes for too many years to want to open myself up to ridicule once again. Also, Gordon had threatened me for so long about what would happen if I told anyone what he did to me behind closed doors that I was still terrified he might find a way to harm me, or my family.

For the longest time, I didn't understand that abuse is a universal horror that happens to women of every race, religion, and social class. Because I was ashamed that I let it happen to me, I tried to pretend it didn't. Then, on March 4, 2003, I was an invited guest on *Larry King Live* after a self-imposed seven-year hiatus from the spotlight in America. During our conversation, Larry made a comment that I will never forget. It all began with a question about Gordon, which I did my best to circumvent.

"I really don't wish to talk about it, Larry, because it's negative energy, and I don't like it," I said.

"But you've come so far," King said.

"I promised I wouldn't speak about this because it brings such negativity that I don't wish to go through again."

While that negative-energy line had worked on everyone else, it didn't work for Mr. Larry King, whom I've always admired for his ability to dig beneath the surface of a subject.

"But people appreciate more how you're doing when they know what you've been through," he said.

His words got through to me in a way that nothing else had. I didn't want to cry on international television, so I didn't admit how much his statement had moved me. But it changed my life. That was the instant I realized I was going to help other women in the same situation that I had faced in my past.

I was further inspired when I began receiving countless letters following a sit-down interview I did on *20/20* on January 21, 2005, which contained a detailed discussion of my abuse. Women began walking up to me, wherever I was, to congratulate me for getting away, and then they would tell me their own stories. The courage these women showed in opening their hearts to me, and the similarity of our stories, made me feel more comfortable about sharing my story. I started realizing, for the first time, that I wasn't alone, and that this is a major problem that needs to be addressed to the world. But I still didn't feel that I was the one to take on the subject.

Then, one day in 2007, I was at Neiman Marcus in Beverly Hills when a dignified, impeccably dressed woman approached me. I could hardly believe it when she pulled me into a dressing room and spent the next hour crying, shaking, and telling me her own story of domestic abuse, as a concerned saleslady knocked on the dressing room door.

"Ms. Jackson, are you okay?" the saleswoman asked me again and again.

"Yes, I'm okay," I assured her every time she asked.

As I said the words, I actually realized I was okay. Even more than that, I had grown strong from everything I had been through and now had the experience, knowledge, and power to help others.

Other women seemed to want me to help, too. The universal comment I heard again and again after women told me about their abuse was:

"You have to share your story with others, so abused women will gain the confidence they need to overcome their own situations."

I was so honored to be acknowledged by so many women in this way, but I was still afraid. As I do with everything in life, I began praying to God every night:

Please give me the strength to help others who are in the same situation that you helped me to escape from.

My prayers were answered. I finally made peace with the idea of writing this book and became excited to get started. My first thought was to tell my family before they heard about it in the media and got the wrong impression.

Then, before I had a chance to say anything, Mother came over to my house one day. We sat on the sofa in my living room discussing life, family, just our typical conversation we always enjoyed having, when my phone started ringing. It was Michael, and he asked to speak to Mother.

When they were done conversing, Mother came right out with it: "La Toya, Randy told Michael that you were writing another book about the family. Is that true?"

I feared my mother's reaction, but I knew I had to be honest. "Yes, Mother, I am writing a book, a self-help book."

As soon as I spoke the words, I instantly went back into my shell where I had hidden from Gordon and the tension he caused within my family for so many years.

"Oh," Mother said. "I told Michael not to believe Randy; that he's just talking."

Nothing more was said. I realized that I wasn't the only one whose wounds had been healed. The fact that I might write a book didn't worry her because she knew Gordon was no longer around to make me include whatever he wanted. The real La Toya would never write or do anything to purposely hurt her family.

I once again had that old happy spirit, and I looked forward to waking up each morning to hear the birds chirping and see the sun shining. I was rebuilding my professional reputation, making music, and living out my lifelong dream of becoming a businesswoman. Best of all, I had been reunited with my family, and we were closer than ever. I began writing *Starting Over* in February 2008. I had a good deal of it completed by January 2009, but I didn't know how I was going to end it, and so I put it aside.

Then, on June 25, 2009, I lost my brother Michael, and I knew that I had a second purpose in my life now, and with this book. Michael had confided in me years earlier that he feared assassination by those who wanted to steal his valuable publishing catalog and estate. I believed him because I had been manipulated and abused so that a greedy, heartless man could profit from me. And my brother was Michael Jackson, the King of Pop, beloved by millions of fans around the world, and head of a music empire that was valued at more than a billion dollars when he died, with the potential to earn billions more. If I had been a target, it was even easier to understand how Michael could be one as well. I was lucky enough to escape, and I decided I must investigate Michael's death and go public with what I found, as I do in this book, with the hope of getting justice for Michael by identifying those who really killed him.

Because I almost lost my life, I want to dedicate the life I have left to helping save the lives of other abused women. I know it's not easy, but it is possible. I am living proof. It's ABSOLUTELY WONDERFUL to have freedom, and that's what I want for everyone who reads these words. We *can* all start over, whenever we want, and as many times as we want. We just have to take that first step and then support one another to keep walking.

1

∞

HE'S GOING TO KILL YOU

I was lying in a pool of blood on the cold marble floor of my New York City kitchen on April 21, 1993. My heart was beating so hard it felt as if it were about to bounce out of my chest. Every inch of my body was in excruciating pain. I started thinking to myself, *This is it. I'm dying. What was my purpose here?* I then heard my manager/husband, Jack Gordon, somewhere above me, talking on the telephone.

"I've killed her," Gordon said. "I think she's dead. I've killed her."

As I listened to his panicked words, I recalled a conversation in which my brother Michael had warned me about Gordon a few years prior.

"You have to get away from him or he's going to kill you," Michael had said.

Not wanting to worry Michael any more than he already was, I didn't say anything to him about how right he was to be afraid, both for me and for him. Michael knew that Gordon was dangerous, from his then manager, Frank DiLeo, and he understood he was taking a great risk to warn me about Gordon. While we talked, Michael interrupted our conversation several times to ask me if Gordon was listening in on another extension. Although I assured him that Gordon was not eavesdropping because he was out of the house, Michael was still frightened. So I didn't tell Michael that Gordon had threatened to harm him on numerous occasions if I disobeyed the orders Gordon gave me or revealed my abuse at his hands to the world. Instead, I assured Michael, and vowed to myself, that whatever Gordon might do to me, I would never allow him to hurt a member of my family. Michael was relieved. But while my thoughts and voice were forceful, my conviction was meaningless in the face of Gordon's power, and the harm I knew he could easily inflict on those I loved through his mob ties. The truth, as I knew it, was that something horrible was destined to happen if I didn't follow his every order and work my hardest to earn him money. I know now that, in his mind, he thought he was my pimp, and I was his prostitute. To ensure my family's safety, I did everything Gordon ordered me to do, even sitting in a closet all day without moving sometimes. That's how powerful his control was over me.

I became a pro at anticipating what might set Gordon off. But I wasn't able to avoid being nearly beaten to death that night in my penthouse. He often invented excuses to punish me, but on this occasion, he didn't give me any reason or warning. When he came home earlier that evening, I was frightened by his behavior, which was strange. I retreated into the bathroom, and when I came out, Gordon was waiting for me with a look of pure evil on his face. Surely, I was looking the devil straight in the eye. I was terrified.

Although my body trembled and my knees buckled, I ran out of the room and down the hallway to the kitchen. I could feel the blood rapidly pounding, and creating pressure, in my ears. I felt as if I were moving in slow motion, even though I was hurrying away from him as fast as I could. I knew there was no escape, nowhere to hide, and no one to come to my rescue. Gordon hired all of our help from among his Mafia connections. They were paid from money I earned, which he controlled 100 percent and spent to help control and intimidate me.

I was certain this would be the end of my life. I could easily imagine the lies Gordon would tell the world to cover up my murder. The headlines that would probably have read LA TOYA JACKSON JUMPS TO HER DEATH FROM THE BALCONY OF HER NYC CONDO. Or Gordon would bring in a shady doctor to shoot me full of drugs and claim I overdosed. I had no doubt that he knew enough evildoers to help him avoid responsibility. I wondered if my family would investigate, or if they would believe what they were told and never know the truth.

As I was cornered in the kitchen, Gordon came up close behind me. I was so afraid that I could hardly breathe, but I knew better than to beg for mercy.

Without saying anything, he punched me in the face. At 110 pounds, I was no match for him and fell to the floor. I curled into a ball to try to avoid his blows, but they came at me from every direction. He kicked me and beat me with his fists, and it just went on and on. He then picked up a heavy wooden chair and beat my legs with it. This was brutal, even for him.

I couldn't understand why he was acting this way toward me. I wondered if it was because he had been diagnosed with cancer a few years earlier, and he was taking it out on me. Maybe he was angry that he was sick, or maybe he was afraid he would die. But, as far as I knew, he was in remission. And he constantly kept me working so he could afford to get the best medical care possible. So that couldn't be it. I knew he had good days and bad days. Maybe this was a bad day. Or maybe there was no explanation and he was just mean. I couldn't understand how he could live with himself after doing such horrendous things to me.

The beating went on and on. He kept kicking me until there was blood everywhere. I was bleeding from my face, stomach, and vaginal area. As the blood spread around me on the floor, I drifted in and out of consciousness. I came to when he finally stopped beating me. That's when I heard him talking about how he thought he had killed me.

My blood was everywhere. As I lay there, motionless, one of our staff got a towel and wiped up the evidence of what Gordon had done to me. She immediately washed the towel in the washing machine, so no one could see how badly I had been hurt.

I'm dying, and she's already helping him to cover up the evidence, I thought.

Gordon had hired this person to be my assistant and housekeeper, but the real purpose was to watch me for him. Still, we spent a great deal of time together, and I was always pleasant. What hurt me more than anything else that night was that this person did nothing to protect or help me. All of the other workers were Gordon's friends from Las Vegas, where he had a great deal of power. Before I met him, he served six months in prison for attempting to bribe the then chairman of the Nevada Gaming Commission, Harry Reid, and Reid later wrote that he suspected Gordon was behind a car bomb found on Reid's car. So this person was completely on Gordon's side and probably feared him as much as I did.

I was in so much pain that it was hard for me to focus. The next thing I knew, several policemen entered the room. That must have been the phone call that Gordon made. But I couldn't figure out why he called them when he would surely get in trouble. Then I became aware of an object in my hand. I had no idea how it had gotten there.

One of the police officers squatted down near me so he could check my injuries and question me. I tried to focus on his face as he spoke, but everything was blurred.

"Who did this to you?" he asked.

I knew better than to tell the truth because Gordon had often warned me that if I ever spoke of his abuse to anyone, he would kill me or, even worse, kill Michael.

But I didn't have to say anything.

"Who did this to you?" the officer asked again.

"I did it," Gordon said.

"Put your hands behind your back," one of the cops said to Gordon. "You're under arrest. You're going to jail."

They didn't know Gordon the way I did. He had prepared for this.

He pointed to the knife someone had put in my hand. "She came after me with a knife. It was self-defense."

I couldn't believe that after trying to assassinate me, he would try to assassinate my character in an attempt to avoid blame for his awful abuse, on top of everything else he had done to me that night. I would never have come after him with a knife, even to save my own life, and he knew it. I wanted to shout out that it wasn't true, but I could barely breathe, let alone speak. And of course, I would never have dared to disobey Gordon, especially in front of the police. Luckily, the cops weren't impressed with his story, and they handcuffed him and led him away.

Gordon knew better than to threaten me in front of the police officers, but he gave me a warning look that told me I'd better not say a word, OR ELSE. *Those of you who have been through abuse, or are going through it now, know what those unspoken words meant: I'd get a worse beating than the one I had just received if I didn't obey him.* Not that he needed to warn me. Like so many victims of domestic abuse, I always protected my abuser. Even after he left the room, it was as if he were still watching me.

I was certain I was dying. My ribs felt broken, and the pain in my sides forced me to take short, shallow breaths. Big chunks of blood were coming out of me and forming new puddles on the floor.

And still I was covering up for Gordon. I didn't want to answer any questions. I didn't want to go to the hospital. I just wanted everyone to go away so I could climb into bed and be alone with my pain, my shame, and my fear. But no matter how much I closed my eyes and wished them away, the cops wouldn't leave.

"You have to go to the hospital, whether you want to or not," a cop said. "You don't have a right to say that you won't go. You have to get checked out."

I must have drifted into unconsciousness again because I don't remember leaving my home, or what the bellhop or doorman must have thought as I was carried out through the opulent lobby of our building. I don't know whether the police officers called an ambulance or transported me in one of their squad cars, but when I came to, I was in Lenox Hill Hospital. And I wasn't alone. The person Gordon had hired to watch over me was looking at me with the same expression Gordon had given me when he was led away in handcuffs. I sank deeper into the emergency room cot where I lay, trying to avoid the menacing gaze.

"You'd better not say anything."

Tears welled in my eyes. I wanted to cry because of the terror I had just experienced, the pain that gripped me now, how alone I was, and how helpless I felt.

But I knew better than to show any emotion, and I was afraid that if I started crying, I would never stop. Before long, a young doctor came in. I immediately began lying because I knew that what I said would be reported directly back to Gordon.

"Oh, I'm fine," I said. "You don't have to do this."

The doctor clearly didn't believe me. He gently moved his hands over my torso and legs, trying to measure the damage. I kept myself from wincing at his touch.

"Does this hurt?" he asked.

"No. Don't touch me there. Please. It's okay."

"Well, we need X-rays."

"No, you don't have to do that," I said. "I'm fine. Can I go home, please?"

I forced myself to sit up, even though the pain was excruciating, just so the doctor would think my injuries weren't bad and allow me to leave. I checked myself out and refused to make a follow-up appointment. Once outside, the Town Car that Gordon and I kept for traveling within the city was waiting for me. The staff member and I rode home in silence. All I wanted was to get into bed before Gordon was released from custody and came home to torment me further.

The ordeal was not yet over. An assistant district attorney came over with several people the following day and insisted she be allowed to check up on me. Gordon's hired help refused. The assistant district attorney kept up until she finally got her way. When she first saw me, she gasped. I could understand her reaction. I felt like the Elephant Man. My left eye was swollen shut and my right eye was black-and-blue. My lips, which were the size of a saucer, were so big and swollen that I could not close my mouth. Saliva constantly dripped out, no matter how often I inhaled to try to keep this from happening.

"Would you like to press charges?" the assistant district attorney asked.

"No, thank you," I said.

No matter how painful and uncomfortable my injuries were, I definitely knew better than to do that.

"Can I at least take pictures of your injuries?" she asked.

The hired help intervened then, defiantly. "Absolutely not."

The assistant district attorney tried to convince her.

"No, no, no!" the woman said.

She knew that if pictures of my face got out, Gordon would be in a great deal of trouble, and she took her job to protect him seriously. As desperate as I was to receive help of any kind, I didn't dare speak up. I actually wished the people would stop trying to help me and leave me alone. I was still convinced that if I could just find the perfect way to behave around Gordon, I could make the situation better. Little did I know, it would only get worse.

2

I WISH I COULD
HAVE YOUR LIFE

During the time I was married to Jack Gordon, no one ever thought I was being abused or even saw me look anything less than perfectly happy in public. I was always so polite and full of smiles, how could anyone suspect what was happening in my personal life? To strangers, I looked like the perfect little wife with the perfect little life. I was a successful entertainer, born into the world's most famous musical family, who traveled the world performing and making appearances. I had the nicest clothes and jewelry, beautiful cars, homes in London, Paris, New York, and Las Vegas. Most could only dream of having this lavish lifestyle. Yes, it was a dream, all right: a total nightmare. Even though my surroundings were exquisite, I was living in what I called "a prison without bars."

It was easy for me to pretend in public that life was oh so grand because I knew if I didn't act right, I was going to get a good beating once I got home. I became such a skilled actress that I was actually envied, even by royalty.

Once, I was performing in Saudi Arabia when a king's daughter snuck out of her palace to see my show. After returning to my hotel, I was asked to please come see the princess at the royal palace. When I arrived, the palace was dark and quiet. I was driven to a guard booth at the back, where security met me and scurried me inside. Like the rest of the building, the room was dim and quiet, and I could barely make out the shapes of exercise equipment around me. Sitting in a corner, on a plush bench, was a young girl completely covered in a burka.

"Hello," she said in a faint, polite voice.

She introduced herself as the princess and told me she wanted to speak to me. As I listened, I wondered why I had been snuck in through a back entry, and why we were talking in such a dark room. I soon came to understand. The princess described how she hated her life because she wasn't allowed to leave the compound or have visitors. That night, she had been able to attend my show only because she snuck out with a trusted guard. She then confessed, with tears in her eyes, that she had never felt happier than she did watching my performance and seeing such freedom.

"La Toya, you're so lucky," she said. "I wish I could have your life."

I just smiled and accepted the compliment as graciously as possible. But inside I was thinking, *If you only knew what my life was like, you wouldn't want it*.

Of course, I was so miserable and worried about my own survival at the time, I didn't realize until many years later that she was suffering through the same kind of abuse that I was. Both of us seemed to live the most wonderful existences on the surface while hiding the most painful secrets beneath.

The princess and I had another similarity that I didn't see at the time. We were both raised in sheltered environments with strict expectations about what our behavior should be like and how obedient we should be. This made me the perfect target, although I didn't come to understand any of this until years later. Because of my upbringing as a Jehovah's Witness, at the time I met Gordon I assumed everyone was telling me the truth and everything was as it appeared.

When I first crossed paths with Gordon in 1984, it was no Romeo-and-Juliet story, and it definitely wasn't love at first, second, or last sight. But I had no reason to think he was anything other than what he seemed, which was a slightly older businessman who had suddenly taken an interest in me. Our paths crossed while I was attending the Grammy Awards with my family. He kept following us everywhere that night and finally approached my father, Joseph. He opened the conversation by flattering Joseph, as was his way.

"How did you have so many talented kids?" Gordon asked.

Soon after that, I was cohosting the popular eighties television program *Solid Gold*, which featured different established recording artists performing their latest hit song each week. As I smiled into the camera and read my lines from the cue cards, I could feel someone staring at me so intently that I couldn't help but look in his direction. There was Gordon, although at that time I didn't realize he was the same man from the Grammys. Our eyes met, and I gave him a friendly smile, just to be polite. He was small, neatly shaven, with close-cropped dark hair and an impeccably tailored suit. I wasn't sure why he was on the set that day, because he didn't appear to be doing anything. But I was busy with my cohosting duties, and he never introduced himself or spoke to me, so I didn't think too much about it. I later learned that the whole thing was a setup, and Gordon was there only because I was. He had set his sights on me specifically, and he wanted to meet me, so he could try to worm his way into my family.

Soon after, I was hired to host another show similar to *Solid Gold*. When I walked into my dressing room on the first day, it looked like a florist's shop. I had never seen so many beautiful flowers in one room in my life. I opened the many cards, and they were all from the same person, Gordon. I thought it was a nice gesture. But these kinds of gifts—admittedly, in smaller quantities—happen so often in show business that it's almost customary. When Gordon and I met again before the taping, I didn't recognize him as the same man from the *Solid Gold* set and the Grammy Awards. But he told me that it had been him, and that he later contacted my father, who was then my manager, to negotiate a deal to have me host this program, which he was producing. I didn't tell him that I didn't want to host his show and was there only because Joseph had told me to do it. The entire time I was there, I behaved with the courtesy and professionalism that my siblings and I had been taught growing up. When I was done with the taping, Gordon asked for my direct number. I declined because I didn't feel comfortable giving my number to a man I didn't know. I was a devout Jehovah's Witness at the time, and we had extremely strict rules about dating, and it wasn't something I was really interested in anyway.

Gordon kept in touch with Joseph and began working on my father's vast sympathy, calling him daily and finding ways to be around constantly. Gordon earned everyone's trust by being the nicest person in the world. He knew my mother loved board games, so he'd come over and play with her for hours. Every time my family had an event in another state, he would either just show up or say he was already going to be in that particular state while we were there. He hung around so much that, eventually, my father hired him.

Joseph has the biggest heart and can never say no to a person in need. When Gordon told him that he had fallen on hard times, my father found work for him in his own office. After that, Gordon quickly made himself indispensable. This was not unusual, as aggressive people who wanted to work with our family were always around. It used to be that anyone who hung around Hayvenhurst long enough would be given a job. But with all of the times my family's kindness and generosity have caused us to be taken advantage of over the years, and sued, we are all much more careful whom we trust now. Especially me.

In 1984, when I went on a ten-city radio promotional tour for my third studio album, *Heart Don't Lie*, I started receiving the biggest bouquet of flowers in every hotel suite, all from Gordon. At first I was a little uncomfortable that he might want to date me. Then, I started to fear that he was stalking me, which was not uncommon in my family. Screaming girls had waited outside the gates of Hayvenhurst for my brothers since the first day we moved in, and we once found an obsessed female fan who had been living in Michael's closet for three days. I was both relieved and upset when I later found out that my father had given Gordon my itinerary. If I had known the depths of misery he would later bring me to, I would have been even more afraid than I was at the time.

I couldn't wait to get back to Los Angeles from the radio tour because my mother and I were about to go on the road with my brothers for their "Victory Tour." Before we left, I had a doctor's appointment because I wasn't feeling well. The doctor had bad news: I needed an emergency hemorrhoidal operation. I guess that's what I get for my lifelong love of Tabasco sauce, jalapeños, and anything else that burns the stomach. The whole experience was so painful that I could barely walk, even after surgery. The doctor suggested I stay home and rest. I was devastated to miss the excitement of the tour, but I knew I didn't have a choice. My brothers were expecting Mother to be with them, so she went ahead without me. I was left home alone with only the staff and security.

Gordon made his move. He sent flowers, get-well cards, and candy. Every day a new gift was waiting for me. He kept calling the security booth, trying to talk to me. When I wouldn't see him, he tried another tactic.

"I have a gift for you," he said when he finally got me on the phone.

"You shouldn't have," I said. "But thank you. If you leave it at the security booth, they'll bring it to me. I really appreciate your generosity."

"No, this is something I have to give you in person."

I felt obligated to see him after everything he had done for me. I agreed to let him come into the house. It was incredibly painful for me to walk down the grand front stairway to where he waited in the foyer below. But I smiled wide, determined to hide my discomfort. Little did I know that this would become my standard role in years to come, only Gordon would be the one inflicting the pain.

When I started feeling better, Gordon invited me to lunch. As a Jehovah's Witness, I couldn't socialize with men unless a third party was there because we might have sinful thoughts. I declined as politely as possible. That's when the mental manipulation began, only I was too naïve to see it at the time.

"What's wrong?" he asked. "Are you too good to be with a normal person who's not a Jackson?"

His accusation wounded me deeply. I didn't want him, or anyone else, to think I was a snob when it wasn't true. And because he wasn't someone I wanted to date, I didn't think it would go against the rules of Jehovah's Witness.

"Of course I'll have lunch with you," I said.

"Great," he said. "Could you bring some money? I'm not doing very well financially at the moment, and I don't have any."

Rather than being put off, or suspicious, I actually felt better about meeting him. Here was someone who needed help. I could provide it and was more than happy to do so. This all made our lunch perfectly acceptable for me as a Jehovah's Witness.

Since it wasn't a date, I dressed as on any other day, in slacks and a blouse, and I wasn't nervous about seeing Gordon. As I drove to meet him at Gaylord's, an Indian restaurant on La Cienega Boulevard in Beverly Hills, I stopped at my bank and withdrew a thousand dollars.

While we ate, Gordon grilled me about my family, career, and income. Since I'd known only members of my family and my religion, it didn't occur to me to be suspicious, and I answered honestly. When the bill came, I didn't want to embarrass him, so I handed him the money under the table. He paid the bill and pocketed the rest. I was a little shocked by this, but I didn't say anything. I had never confronted anyone in my life, because Joseph or security always did so for me. Here I was alone, with a man I didn't know well, and I didn't want to be rude.

That was the first of many lunches over the next few weeks. Gordon had found an easy mark, and he knew it. At each lunch he asked me to, I handed him a thousand dollars. Looking back, I can't believe what a fool I was. But at the time, I was acting with the generosity I had been taught to show others.

After I had given Gordon about $10,000 at these lunches, he called to tell me that if he didn't have $15,000 by the end of the day, he was going to have to start sleeping in his car. I was startled by his implicit request and hesitated before answering.

"You wealthy people don't care about people in need," he said. "There's no way you would give me fifteen thousand dollars."

Just as he had intended, his words made me feel bad. "That's not true," I said. "You can come over and pick up a check at the security booth."

"Actually, I need it in cash."

And just like that, I went to the bank and took out the money for him. A few days later, he needed another $30,000. This time, he said he wanted me to partner with him in an investment. After that, he was always trying to involve me in some scheme. He wanted to buy several of those arcade games where players attempt to grab a prize with a mechanical arm. He needed $50,000 to open a souvenir store on Hollywood Boulevard. He even told me where the store would be, and Mother drove me by the space. Without thinking to ask him any questions about his plan, I gave him the money. When he later told me his business partner had stolen the money from him, I couldn't believe that the world was full of such crooks. The world was full of crooks, all right; I just didn't know how to spot them.

I was an exceptional target. Having grown up a Jackson, I wasn't just raised wealthy. I could earn a good income for myself from the time of my debut at the MGM Grand Hotel in Las Vegas when I was sixteen. As my manager, my father not only never cheated me, as sadly happens to so many child entertainers, but he never seemed to take a commission. I'm sure he did for the appearances he booked for me, but never from my royalties. I always had enough funds, and more coming in all the time, so money had no value for me.

Besides, I was raised as a Jehovah's Witness, which meant I had been instructed to never worship money; to avoid all sinful thoughts, actions, and people ("Bad association spoils useful habits"); to surround myself only with other Jehovah's Witnesses, who were just as good as I was; and to trust everyone. Although my mother brought up all of us children as Jehovah's Witnesses, and we never celebrated Christmas or birthdays, as the religion forbade it, only Rebbie, Michael, and I took these religious teachings to heart. Even after Michael was a mega pop superstar, he and I went door-to-door with *Awake* and *Watchtower*, spreading God's news. Michael wore a fat suit so no one would recognize him, but for some odd reason the littlest children could see through his disguise.

"Mommy! Mommy! That's Michael Jackson!" the children would say.

The mothers would never believe them, and Michael and I would walk away laughing about it.

My sheltered approach to the world was fine, as long

as Joseph and Mother were there to protect me. But Gordon was already pulling me away from my family. He made me promise I wouldn't tell anyone I was giving him money because it would have embarrassed him, and so my parents didn't have a clue about it. Gordon also began influencing my thoughts about my family and their relationship to my career.

"It's your money anyways," he said. "It's nobody's business what you do with it."

Because I didn't realize he had ulterior motives, I thought he was being supportive of my desire to gain greater independence.

He then started asking me about my banking information and offered to help me with my money. Again, he made it sound as if he had only my best interests at heart.

"Dealing with money can be a headache," he said. "It's something I don't think you should have to deal with."

I thought it was nice of him to be concerned, but I assured him, "It's no big deal. We have accountants who take care of that."

Without realizing it, Joseph soon set Gordon up perfectly by allowing him to start handling certain areas of my career. Up until then, I had been happy to have Joseph manage me, but I was becoming restless. Although I was twenty-eight, I was naïve about the world. I thought I should be on my own, even though my parents disagreed. I begged them to let me get my own place, but Mother and Joseph always felt it was too dangerous out in the world.

"You can move out when you're married," they told me.

I didn't want to be under my parents' control anymore. I wanted to grow up and do things on my own, and in the way I thought was best.

Back then, I didn't realize how fickle the entertainment industry was and how many people would love me and want to work with me while I was hot, only to drop me the instant some hot new act came along. But Joseph would love me unconditionally and want what was best for me. All I knew was that I wanted to be independent, and that meant I wanted out of my contract with Joseph. As soon as Gordon heard this, he did everything in his power to make the split happen as quickly as possible. Although I can't say Gordon was the reason I wanted to leave my father's management, I do know I would never have gotten up enough nerve to do it without Gordon pushing me daily. Finally, Gordon brought an attorney to see me who had written a letter stating that I was resigning from my father's management. All I had to do was sign.

As soon as Gordon convinced me to do it, I felt knots in my stomach as I thought about its making its way to Joseph's office, where he would open and read it. I was scared of how he would react, and every time I saw him for the next few days, I waited for him to explode. But he never said anything to me about it. I later learned from Mother that he had been upset by the letter, but I guess he accepted that all of his children had to grow up eventually. Now that I'm older, I look back at this moment with regret. I know now I didn't handle the situation properly, and I hate to imagine the pain I caused Joseph. I was his little girl, yet I wanted to leave his side, which was the only place he knew he could protect me from an industry that didn't care for me as he did.

Around this same time, I had to go to Japan on business. Mother often traveled with me when she wasn't with one of my siblings, and she was supposed to go with me, but she couldn't. Joseph was unable as well. Because Gordon had been working with Joseph for several months now, Joseph felt comfortable sending him to Japan to oversee my business during the trip. Joseph and I weren't close then the way we are now, and he didn't know Gordon had taken money from me and masterminded the letter severing our working relationship. If he had, I'm sure he would never have let Gordon anywhere near me, and he certainly wouldn't have sent him to a foreign country alone with me. Given what happened on that trip, I'm sure Joseph came to regret the decision greatly. But at the time, it was business as usual. Meanwhile, Gordon had hit the jackpot, and he knew it.

Gordon called a meeting with Joseph to let him know how I felt, and that he should let me go from under his wing. To my surprise, Joseph agreed. He told Gordon that he could manage me, and Joseph would stay completely out of my business. I was happy. I thought this moment was the beginning of my freedom. But, really, it was the beginning of the end for the La Toya Jackson whom my family, friends, and the world had once known.

3

~

ILLUSIONS OF FREEDOM

I left home for Japan on May 29, 1987. I'll never forget that day because it was my birthday and I was going to have two birthdays due to the time difference between America and Japan. I was happy to be personally handling my career for the first time ever. Although I was incredibly grateful for everything Joseph had done for me, I believed he was a good starter manager who had taken me as far as he could. I was ready to break away from the Jackson clan and become responsible for my own life. I was the last member of my family to leave Joseph's management. I'll never forget how hurt Joseph was when Michael originally stopped being managed by him, and then, in later years, he was even more upset when he heard Michael hired Frank DiLeo as his manager in 1984.

The trip began just like any other, except that I was traveling abroad without a parental chaperone for the first time in my life, which gave every moment a special thrill. As my manager, Gordon had arranged all of our transportation and accommodations, as was customary. When we got to Los Angeles International Airport, Gordon asked for my passport, so he could show it to the ticket agent, along with our tickets. This was common practice in our family, as we always had a security guard or assistant go ahead of us with our tickets and passport, so that all we had to do was board the plane. Gordon and I were traveling alone together, and so it made sense to me that he would handle my passport and tickets. The flight was long and exhausting, as flights to Asia always are, but it went smoothly, and we arrived in Japan without incident. Only when I was in Japan, now over five thousand miles away from my family, did I begin seeing changes in Gordon's personality that suggested he was a little more controlling than seemed appropriate. After we landed and were waved through customs without being questioned, which was one of the perks of being a recognized entertainer, Gordon was surprised by how easily I was able to get through without questioning. We got into the car that was to take us to our hotel. I realized Gordon still had my passport.

"May I have my passport back?" I asked.

"No, I'll hold on to it for you," he said.

This seemed like a thoughtful gesture, if a little overbearing. But just as when Gordon had surprised me by keeping all of the money I had brought to our first lunch, I didn't question his actions. As Gordon already knew, I was timid, and I hated confrontation.

My meetings and appearances in Japan went well, and although nothing about the trip was out of the ordinary, I felt excited the whole time for my newfound independence. Gordon didn't do anything else during the trip that gave me reason to think he was overstepping our appropriate professional boundaries. That is, not until the day arrived for us to leave for Los Angeles. I innocently asked about our return trip home.

"You're not going back home," he said.

"What do you mean?" I said.

"You're never going back."

Icy tendrils of fear inched through my bloodstream, and I had to fight to remain calm.

I couldn't go back, not without his approval, because he still refused to give me my passport. Although no bars were visible, I was effectively his prisoner. It had all happened so quickly that I still couldn't quite believe it was true. I know it may be hard to believe that I was so quickly at Gordon's mercy and that, being from such a tight-knit and powerful family, I didn't call home for help. I don't think it can be mentioned often enough how vulnerable I was to this kind of exploitation because of my extremely sheltered and religious upbringing. As I said earlier, I had always had security guards and my father to protect me. Also, I truly believed that we must all be good to each other, and I didn't have any experience with con men and their lies.

I barely knew this man, and suddenly Gordon controlled my every movement. My excitement about being on my own was replaced with extreme loneliness as I thought about how far away my family was and how little they could do to help me now. Always the good, obedient young woman I had been raised to be, I continued to treat Gordon with nothing but politeness and smiles while wondering what would come next.

Meanwhile, it was business as usual in my career. From Japan, Gordon took me to Germany. We lived there for a good while, recording new material and using the country as a home base from which I traveled throughout Europe, performing and making appearances, just as I had when Joseph was my manager. From there, we went back and forth between London and New York several times, then over to Paris. The whole time, Gordon kept me away from my family, but they didn't think anything was wrong at first because he always made the excuse that I needed to be traveling for business. He quickly tightened his control over me until my missing passport was nothing, compared to the many other ways in which he ruled me.

During a brief trip to New York City, he took me to my bank one afternoon and told me that we had an appointment to see the head of the bank.

"She wants to meet you," he said. "And take a picture."

When we were brought into her office, I smiled and shook her hand. We exchanged small talk and then posed for pictures. For as long as I could remember, people had wanted to meet my family and have their picture taken with us, so all of this was normal to me. She seemed nice enough, and I didn't think anything of the whole exchange at the time.

Soon after that, I returned home to NYC after a weekend of appearances.

"Can I see the books?" I said, wanting to know my earnings for that weekend, information that Joseph routinely shared.

Gordon grabbed my wrist and slapped me across the face. My head snapped back from the impact. I could hardly believe it had happened. He had bullied me before, but he had never struck me, and I was stunned that he would dare treat me this way. As much as the blow hurt, it was almost more upsetting that he had responded so cruelly to such an innocent question.

I was still recovering when he said, shocking me even more, "You're not seeing anything. Everything has been turned over into my name. You don't own anything."

"What do you mean?" I said, fighting back tears and a desperate panic.

"You don't own anything," he sneered.

I listened in stunned silence as he told me how he had turned all of my bank accounts and credit cards over to his name. I realized with horror that our trip to the bank wasn't just to make some fan's dream come true. I wasn't sure how Gordon had done it, but whatever lie he had told her had been corroborated by my happily visiting the bank with him.

By the time I realized how bad things had gotten, it was too late for me to escape because he watched my every move. He had instilled such fear in me, as all abusers do, that he destroyed my spirit to the point where I wouldn't have dared escape, even if I had the opportunity to do so. Years later, I would see the same scenario unfold with the people who eventually took Michael's life. I don't think it's any coincidence that Michael's religious beliefs were as deeply ingrained in him as mine. We grew up in the same family, under the same rules. But, unlike Mother and Rebbie, Michael and I left the religion and went out on our own into a world full of wolves, and that's when we both were targeted and exploited, although by different groups of people. Like me, without a strong and benevolent personality to watch over him, as Joseph had always done for both of us, it was almost inevitable that Michael became a victim, too.

4

❧

A SMILE FOR THE PUBLIC

Even the most ordinary daily occurrences were an opportunity for Gordon to dominate and intimidate me. He insisted that we stay together at all times, so he could keep an eye on me, and if the phone rang, it was enough of an excuse for him to bully me.

"Go ahead and answer that," he would say.

When I did, he would take my free hand and twist it as hard as he could. After that, I never wanted to answer the phone again. But, at the same time, I was too frightened to disobey him, so if he told me to answer it again, I would. I couldn't figure out why he would be so cruel, but I never fought back or even spoke up in my own defense. If he was testing how much he could get away with, he clearly saw he could get away with anything anytime.

The violence escalated, as did the mental manipulation that accompanied it. Soon, he was no longer twisting my arm when I answered the phone because I wasn't allowed to answer or talk on the phone at all. This was part of a long list of forbidden activities that included my not leaving the house without his consent and my not having any contact with my family. I was obedient, as I was raised to be, and because I knew he'd check up on me when I was gone. I didn't want to do anything to make him punish me for not following his commands to the fullest. Fear has a powerful way of making people listen. Yet, knowing I obeyed his every word, he still accused me of calling people or going out, even when it was impossible for me to do so.

Gordon would storm into the room, yelling about how I called the assistant district attorney.

"I didn't do it," I said, already cowering from his anger and the potential of a blow.

"Well, she told me you called her," he said.

"But she couldn't have."

"Yes, you did."

It would go back and forth like this until it was enough to make me think I had lost my mind. I knew I had not called her, but he seemed so sure that I had, and no matter how much I protested, he didn't seem to believe me.

As painful as the beatings were, I think Gordon's mental abuse was the hardest to bear. I had grown up in a bustling home with eight siblings; my older siblings' various significant others; the constant involvement of both my parents; a full staff of employees, many of whom were with us for so long, and are still with us today, that we developed close personal relationships with them; and an assortment of famous family friends, from Elizabeth Taylor and Cary Grant to Gregory Peck and Marlon Brando, who were always at our house for dinner or movie night. I was used to laughter, singing, and many, many jokes. When Michael and I lived at home, we were so inseparable for many years that our family started calling us "the twins," so Michael and I took it a step further and started dressing alike all of the time. It was an extreme shock to suddenly find myself alone for long stretches of time, or watched over closely by unfamiliar burly security guards. Even my assistants were hired by Gordon and made it known that his rules also applied on their watch. My primary companion was Gordon, who frequently made up reasons to beat me. Even worse, he made me feel as if I had really done something wrong by slamming doors, not speaking to me, and telling the help to ignore me. It was a terrible way to live, and I began to feel incredibly alienated. I have never been one who wanted pity, or even sympathy, from others, and so that wasn't what I wanted during this time. But not to have *any* kind of, or even just normal, human interactions was incredibly painful. I felt completely invisible.

To make matters worse, Gordon relished playing with my mind. After a particularly vicious beating, he would turn to me with an incredulous expression and say, "I never hit you. What made you think I hit you?"

I knew better than to answer, and so I simply sat there and cried from the pain.

"Why are you crying?" he would say. "I never touched you. Oh my God, you're losing your mind."

"How could you sit there and say that?" I asked.

"Let's go see a psychiatrist. I'll go with you."

It was incredibly hard to maintain my composure because I had no one to tell me that I *wasn't* crazy. I began to think that something was wrong with *him*, and that perhaps he really thought he had never touched me. After a while, I didn't know what to believe anymore.

When we lived in Paris, the doors locked from the outside, so he would literally lock me in the house all day. Not that he needed to do so, because his threats were enough to keep me from disobeying him. When he told me not to answer the door for anyone, I didn't. When he told me to stay in the closet all day, I did, without even checking to see if he had locked me in. When he told me not to look out the window, I sat completely still in the middle of the room, not daring to let my gaze drift for an instant. It was enough to tear me to pieces.

He even controlled what and when I ate. He would place an order with room service or with our help. When the food was brought in, he would order me into the other room: "Stay in there. Don't come out until I call you."

Of course I did as I was told without the slightest protest.

"Okay, you can come and eat now," he would say.

Then, and only then, was I allowed to sit down and begin dining. I always assumed this was another way to let me know I was his property. However, years later, when I was finally reunited with my family, Mother had another theory about Gordon's mealtime habit.

"La Toya, he was giving you mind-altering drugs," she said.

Mother went on to tell me that one of Gordon's doctors had told her that he had prescribed Gordon these types of drugs, and he believed Gordon had regularly given them to me. I don't know if it was true, but Mother's theory always made sense.

Gordon never explained anything to me. Many times he would stride in and start giving orders as I anxiously tried not to set him off.

"You're going to Europe for four days," he would say. "You leave in two hours."

"What am I doing?" I would ask.

"You're performing."

Once we were en route to an appearance, he would grill me. For television interviews, he told me what to say and how to behave. Mentally dismissing him was one way of keeping a small spark of self-confidence alight during those terrible years. Of course, I never dared talk back. If I had, I wouldn't have lived to set one foot on-stage.

The problem was, even the most seasoned and talented entertainers need to practice, especially when they're performing with dancers and a live band. But Gordon was so paranoid that I might confide in one of the dancers that he began limiting my time with them. After Joseph's legendary devotion to making us practice, I was used to spending weeks perfecting my material before performing it. At first, Gordon cut my rehearsals down to a few hours. Soon, I was expected to just get onstage and wing it. Not only that, but I didn't even get to choose my material. Gordon simply handed me a song list right before I was due to go on. If I suggested I didn't feel prepared, he laughed it off.

"You'll be fine," he said. "You're a Jackson. You're always prepared."

But as I've said, even Jacksons need to practice. Over the years, my live performances suffered *tremendously* because of Gordon's methods. I hated feeling that I wasn't doing my best and was devastated when reviews of my live performances suffered because no one knew why I wasn't performing well.

Gordon stayed close to me at all times so I could never ask for help. When he wasn't available, he had menacing security guards, hired from the Genovese crime family, stand in for him. I was expected to cover Gordon's abuse with makeup. But I was not permitted to go out and purchase my own makeup. I wasn't allowed to have a makeup artist or hairdresser. Gordon and his workers bought my makeup for me, and I did my best with whatever shades they picked out. When I did shows that provided a makeup artist and hairdresser, Gordon stood nearby the entire time so I couldn't make a peep. I tried to act relaxed as the girl touched up my makeup and willed her not to say anything. Even with heavy makeup, it was often possible to tell that I had recently been hit.

Soon Gordon realized that he couldn't strike my face anymore. My living—which meant his living—

was dependent on my being constantly camera ready. Although sometimes he couldn't control himself and would still hit me in the face, he began to beat mainly my body. Even then, he was paranoid. Sometimes he beat me so badly that I could barely sit because of the unbearable pain, and if I ever shifted my weight while on a TV interview, he accused me of trying to alert the public to my abuse. But as with all aspects of his control, he had no reason to fear that I would act out. I knew the rules, whether he repeated them to me or not.

5

A BRAVE VOICE SILENCED

In the beginning, I couldn't always remain quiet about how horrible my life had become. During the late eighties, whenever I was living in New York, I would often write songs with Amir Bayyan, one of the members of Kool and the Gang. I trusted him deeply and considered him a friend. Remarkably, Gordon would sometimes let me meet with Amir alone. As soon as I was away from Gordon, I would fall apart, crying and pouring my heart out.

"He's beating me," I said. "He keeps beating me, and I don't know what to do."

Amir became so angry that he made a plan to gather up reinforcements and come over to my hotel to rescue me. Only, when Amir showed up with a bunch of guys, I panicked and defused the situation before Gordon realized what was happening.

"Everything is fine," I said.

"That's not what you told me," Amir said.

"Please don't," I pleaded. "Please don't say anything. Everything's fine."

Amir finally left, but in the back of my mind I couldn't understand why I didn't use that moment as a means to escape what had become a miserable life.

The one other time I tried to reach out for help—to a well-known television personality—the response I got made me feel more isolated than ever. I made the call secretly from my bedroom, where I sat nervously on the edge of the bed, ready to hide the phone should Gordon or one of the workers suddenly return. As I dialed, my hands were shaking, and I had to take a few deep breaths to calm myself. When I got the person on the phone, I whispered a rapid description of what Gordon was doing to me. Then I got the response that most abuse sufferers fear most.

"Come on, La Toya, it can't be that bad," he said. "Your family has too much power, money, and fame for this to be happening."

I pleaded with him to believe me and help, but he just couldn't conceive that what I was saying was true and suggested that maybe I was just being a little oversensitive about a minor situation. I had found the courage to finally speak out to someone. I had risked a terrible beating from Gordon. I had forced myself to swallow the embarrassment I felt about my circumstances. And now, I was being accused of lying. This was particularly hurtful since I was always careful to tell the truth because of the way I was raised. My relationship with Gordon had already forced me to be dishonest more than I would have liked.

It got worse.

A few days later, Gordon answered the phone in front of me. After listening for a moment, he began watching me in that frightening way he had. I realized it was the television host, and he was reporting back to Gordon what I had told him.

"She's crazy," Gordon said with a laugh.

I knew better than to think that he was feeling the least bit amused, and I knew that I was due a beating. After that, I went into a complete shell. I realized this was my life now, no one would ever believe what I was going through, and I just had to accept the abuse, live with it, and hope that he didn't kill me. Eventually I learned to be aware of Gordon's every word. Whenever I did a television interview, Gordon watched with the utmost concentration. When the interview was over, I waited for the following words from him: "You did a good job."

If I didn't hear them, I knew I was going to get a beating. Imagining this while I was still on the set was absolutely awful, especially because I had to hide my anxiety after the show while smiling for pictures and thanking everyone backstage.

As I heard Gordon tell the host that I was crazy, I knew I had made a terrible mistake. My heart sank, and I felt sick at the thought of what was coming. I was beaten so badly that night I thought I was going to die. I never risked asking for help again. Unfortunately, that didn't stop Gordon from beating me within an inch of my life on multiple other occasions. Please don't misunderstand what I'm saying. After Gordon had me mentally trained, he didn't always beat me black-and-blue. Sometimes it was just one smack across the face, and that would be it. I used to be grateful for those days because I had learned how to endure that temporary pain, and it wasn't so bad. Other times, I would go a week or two without getting touched. I was so proud of myself at those particular times. *I've now learned what Gordon wants from me, and I'm being perfect for him,* I would think.

At the time, it was incredibly painful to have my one attempt to help myself be received in such a cruel manner. Eventually, I realized that the TV host didn't intend to hurt me. He simply had no idea that his actions were the worst possible thing he could have done in the situation. I'm sure he would have helped me if he had understood what I learned through Gordon's beatings: *It doesn't matter how rich or poor a person is, what gender or social class, or how much fame or education she possesses. Verbal, mental, and physical abuse can happen to anyone. It doesn't matter what a woman's ethnicity is because the only distinguishing color of abuse is black-and-blue.*

I came to find out, only in recent years, that this same television personality did finally try to get people to rescue me. I've never had a chance to thank him personally, but I hope he is aware of the gratitude and love I will always feel toward him. I know how difficult it must have been to even try to help me because of how Gordon always kept several armed security guards around me at all times. In his eyes, he owned a bank, Bank of La Toya, and he was the CEO/president, and the around-the-clock armed security men were his Brinks guards, watching over "his" money.

I was so terrified of further retaliation that I began helping Gordon shut out anyone who might have aided me. I remember the time when I learned that my brother Tito and his three sons, 3T, were performing near my home in New York at the Beacon Theatre. For some reason, Gordon actually let us go by and visit them.

I was so happy to see my nephews, who had grown up to become such fine young men, and was incredibly excited to see Tito. From the way he kept smiling, I could tell that he was even more excited to see me. He got Mother on the phone, and I was so glad to speak with her. I knew that doing so would get me into trouble, but I didn't care. At that moment, to hear Mother's voice was a gift from God. Of course, I couldn't tell Tito that I would get in trouble if I spoke to Mother, so I took the cell phone from him and went into the restroom.

Even though Gordon was in the other room, I could feel him listening to my every word, so I didn't speak to Mother for long. I was already afraid of the consequences that awaited me later, but I really enjoyed this moment as it was happening. When I walked out of the restroom, Gordon kept staring at me. I knew, and feared, that look. But I tried to continue acting normal. Tito wasn't fooled, though.

"I heard you've been hitting my sister," Tito said.

"Of course not," Gordon said. "Where did you hear that from?"

Tito turned to me. "La Toya, has he been hitting you?"

Gordon glared at me. I didn't know quite how to respond. A part of me wanted to fall into Tito's arms, cry, and tell him everything. I was so happy inside, thinking my big brother was there to save me. But, at the same time, I was so afraid of what could happen to me, and possibly Tito, if I spoke out and didn't answer the way Gordon expected me to. My thoughts about acknowledging my abuse were overruled by fear of not doing everything I could to protect myself, and my family.

"No," I said, unable to meet Tito's eyes as I lied on Gordon's behalf.

Tito then asked Gordon to go out into the hallway with him so they could talk in private. Even though a door was between us, I heard Tito's every word.

"If you *ever* lay a hand on my sister, I'll kick your ass," Tito said.

Tito's sons ran out the door just in time to prevent Tito from attacking Gordon. Tito's son Taj had to keep pushing his father away. I looked on, pretending to be concerned, while of course hoping that Tito would beat the mess out of Gordon.

Finally, Tito's kids broke up what would have been a fight. Gordon gave me a warning look.

"You have an early television show to do in the morning," Gordon said. "It's time for you to go."

But Tito wasn't done yet. He turned to me with concern on his face. "If he ever hits you again, just let me know."

As we said our good-byes, I could hardly face what would come next. Yes, that's right, even though it was already late, and I had to be up early in the morning, I got a beating. A bad one.

Of all the ironies, the next morning I actually had to appear on the program of the television host I had reached out to. I was in excruciating pain while I did his show, but somehow, I managed to get through it.

When the show was over, I was terribly nervous as I waited to hear what Gordon would say. Finally, he gave me his verdict:

"You did a good job."

I was so relieved. That meant no beating after the show, and hopefully I could survive the rest of the day without getting into any more trouble.

The TV host wasn't the only one who couldn't believe my relationship with Gordon was anything less than perfect. After the particularly brutal New York City beating, which was one of only three times that Gordon's abusive behavior was actually reported in his years with me, the police officers regularly returned to check on me. When the doorman called up to let us know the police were headed up, Gordon immediately started threatening me.

"You tell them nothing is happening," he said.

Of course, I did just as I was told. "Why are you

guys here?" I asked. "Everything has been absolutely fine."

Those same words again, and again, even though it couldn't have been further from the truth.

Gordon thought I was clever, which he disliked because it intimidated him, and he feared that I might someday outsmart him. But he frequently praised me for my intelligence in front of others. He was always saying that he had the most beautiful wife in the world—ironic, given that my face was often bruised and misshapen from his beatings. Because my nature was to be nice, even given the way he treated me, he would often describe me as such to others. But it was almost as if he were praising a luxury automobile or a thoroughbred horse that he owned, and I never detected any real warmth in his words.

While he was never pleasant to me, Gordon could be a lot of fun in the presence of others. We frequently went down to the lounge of our hotel to listen to the band or went to a restaurant that had a harpist or pianist because I love live classical music. Gordon was such a ham that he would often grab the microphone and begin singing and dancing. These moments always made me happy because I knew he was happy, and that meant I wouldn't get a beating that night. He even surprised me by getting onstage with me several times, taking the microphone and launching into his own rendition of the song I was singing, while dancing across the stage. Such moments were always awkward for the audience, but I never wanted to anger him, so I always played it off as if the whole thing were an amusing joke we had planned.

"Wasn't that funny?" I would say when he finally returned the microphone. "Everyone give Gordon a hand," I would add, just to play it off to the audience.

Sometimes I think Gordon beat me out of jealousy as much as his desire to control me.

"I'm a frustrated entertainer," Gordon sometimes said. "I just want to be a musician, and I want to get onstage."

He hated it when people asked me for autographs; he would abruptly step in and say I wasn't giving any. This would upset me because I was raised to never say no if someone asked for my autograph. But if anybody ever asked him for one, he would start signing everything in sight, and I found this hilarious. Here he was so starved for attention, and I would gladly have left the limelight behind forever, especially during this time when I had so much to hide.

I was like a child. Gordon held all of the funds. I never saw a penny during the years he controlled me. Gordon also made me believe that if I ever left him, I would walk away with nothing, and he would damage my reputation so badly that everyone in the world would hate me, and I would never be capable of earning another dime. This was all from the man who was penniless when my father first took pity on him and gave him work, bringing him close enough to allow him to prey on me. Even then, it had not been enough that I had sympathized with his unfortunate situation and gifted him hundreds of thousands of dollars before I hardly knew him. He went on to steal much more from me and nearly kill me to do it. By the time I left him, he had almost accomplished his goal of having everyone in the world hate me, and making it impossible for me to earn another dime.

6

THE MAN BEHIND
THE MONSTER

Gordon's background was in brothels, literally. He had been born in a brothel, where, as Gordon's uncle told me on many occasions, Gordon first discovered his inner ham while tap dancing on a pool table for the prostitutes as a little boy. He owned amusement arcades and brothels in Las Vegas, and a massage parlor at Sunset Boulevard and La Cienega in Los Angeles that offered much more than massages, as I later learned from the Los Angeles Police Department. When Gordon lost this venture, shortly before setting his sights on my family, he ended up with nothing. This is not particularly surprising given what a bad businessman he was. People who knew him hated him because he treated everyone like dirt. He could act pleasant, which made him seem much more likable and business savvy than he was. This is exactly how he conned Joseph and me when we first met him. Like us, anyone who knew Gordon for any length of time usually came to dislike him, often strongly.

Gordon had a brother whom he didn't speak to for many years, even though they both lived in Las Vegas for much of that time. And Gordon was estranged from his children, both from a previous marriage. Although, as I later found out, Gordon was generous to his ex-wife and children as long as I was footing the bill, even giving them (and other women) the gifts of diamond jewelry and expensive watches that I received from various royal families after performing in Europe and the Middle East.

I never spent much time around Gordon's family. But I did have a few interesting conversations with his son.

"Don't let Dad beat you," he once said to me. "He tried that on my mom, but she never allowed it. She grabbed a knife and threatened him with it."

Suddenly, I understood why Gordon had put the knife in my hand after beating me in New York City. But had I tried to be stronger with him at this point, he would definitely have killed me because he had control over me, and besides, I would never hurt a fly. He probably didn't know if his ex-wife would kill him or not, and so, once she threatened him, he left her alone. As far as I was aware, Gordon never knew about my little heart-to-heart with his son. But, of course, this was the very reason he didn't want me to talk to anyone, because he never knew who might see through his act and encourage me to break free.

At the same time that I was being made to fear Gordon's true nature in private, he was revealing more of his shady business connections to me. I had already known about his conviction for attempting to bribe the then head of the Nevada Gaming Commission, Harry Reid, who is now a senior U.S. senator. I soon learned that Gordon and the thugs he hired as security were tied to one of the oldest and most powerful Mafia crime families, the Genovese.

From our first trip to New York together, Gordon began taking me to Mulberry Street in the city's Little Italy neighborhood. It was just as I had seen in the movies. The narrow street was lined with small Italian restaurants. All of the men seemed to have their own little place that they owned, and they sat around all day, smoking cigars and yelling at each other across the street. Some kind of argument was always going on, about who made the best pasta, who was or wasn't speaking to whom, or who capped whom last night. Tourists clogged the street, stopping for a cannoli while trying to catch sight of Gambino crime boss John Gotti or one of the heads of the Lucchese or Genovese crime families.

As far as I could tell, these guys Gordon hung out with were the ones who went out and did what had to be done, even whacking people, which I regularly heard talk of from the first evening I was there. Of course, this casual disregard for human life shocked me, as did the incredibly foul language all the men used, as I've always been offended by swearing. What I heard made me even more frightened of disobeying Gordon because some of my security was from the Genovese crime family, and I believed they were quite capable of serious violence.

Gordon and I usually went to the same restaurant, often every night during our two-to-three-week stays in New York. I would sit in a booth with the men, bored out of my mind, while they spent hours discussing all of their various deals and plots and grudges. Even though murder was the ultimate sin, I became accustomed to talk of it, just like the abuse in my home. If I ever allowed myself to stop and think about my surroundings, I became incredibly despondent. I often wondered how my life had turned out this way and asked God what I had done to deserve this kind of punishment.

I was the only woman present during these nights, and I knew better than to ever speak or draw attention to myself. The men mostly ignored me, especially the ones on Gordon's payroll, although occasionally one of them worried aloud about revealing a crime in front of me. Of course, Gordon could assure them with confidence that I was no threat.

"The kid won't talk," Gordon always said, referring to me.

Occasionally, the men would delve deep into some plot they didn't trust me to hear, no matter how much Gordon reassured them. At these times, I would be led over to the nearby card room where they all gambled. It was supposedly some important Mafia hideaway, but as far as I could tell, it was nothing more than a smoky little hut. In the end, it wasn't such a well-kept secret because the FBI had it bugged for years and gathered a great deal of evidence to prosecute mobsters from conversations held there.

In spite of these occasional precautions, nobody seemed particularly bothered by my presence. Except for whenever John Gotti passed by while I was at the restaurant. For some reason, he liked me and often made a point to stop and have a friendly conversation. I always found him to be pleasant, and of course I knew who he was, but the whole thing didn't seem like a big deal to me. Of course, it drove Gordon and the other guys crazy that Gotti singled me out for special attention.

As he did with everything else in our life together, Gordon used our trips to Mulberry Street to further intimidate and control me. It worked. Nothing made me more certain that he could carry out threats to kill me, or Michael, than overhearing their plans to do away with someone who then turned up dead in the news the following day. On one occasion, I was traveling from New York City to Philadelphia in a car full of Italian men when they nonchalantly took one guy and threw him out of the car. I had never imagined I would see something like that in my lifetime. I was frightened for my life, and I felt so helpless. I wanted to tell the driver to turn around and go back, so I could jump out of the car, see if the man was okay, and get him some medical attention. But I knew not to say a word, or I could be next.

While Gordon usually didn't let me read the newspaper or watch the news, as yet another way to keep me isolated, he made a point to show me the news when it was reported that the guy had turned up dead. When he turned off the television set, he didn't say anything, but he didn't have to make a verbal threat for me to understand his message. Equally unsettling was the fact that I was occasionally picked up at the airport by men still disheveled from a sleepless night and splattered with dirt and what looked like blood.

When I later spoke to Mother about all of this, she always said she didn't believe Gordon was a part of the Mafia. In her opinion, he only made me think so to frighten me. But there was clearly good reason to fear him, whether he was working for somebody else or just for himself. I don't think that he was a main Mafia figure by any means, but I do know that what I saw and heard on so many occasions in New York made me believe he had mob ties. Gordon always told me that those who were Jewish, such as he, were the brains, while those who were Italian were the brawn. He frequently expressed his opinion that the Genovese were the nicest of the five mob families. As if being nice were something Gordon knew anything about.

My suspicions were confirmed years later, after I finally escaped from Gordon. Out of nowhere, the FBI asked to speak to me about Gordon and our visits to Mulberry Street. Of course, Gordon had literally beaten me into understanding that the kid didn't talk.

"You don't know nothing about nothing," he always used to say.

Even when I was out from beneath his reign of terror, I was too scared to say anything. Along with my attorney, Brian Oxman, I met the agents in a Las Vegas hotel room. They questioned me for hours in hopes that they could eventually break me down.

"Do you know anyone from the Genovese family?"

"No."

"Have you ever met the head of the Genovese family?"

"No."

"Have you ever met the head of the Lucchese family?"

"No."

"Have you ever met anyone from the Gambino family?"

"No."

"Have you ever met John Gotti?"

"No."

"Have you ever seen him?"

"No."

"Have you ever been to the card room?"

"No."

"Okay, that's fine," they finally said.

They asked me to return a few weeks later. This time, they had a stack of pictures.

"Here's a picture of you and John Gotti, right here," one agent said.

"And here you are in the card room," another said.

I looked at the pictures. I couldn't deny them, but I still knew better than to talk.

"We already know," an agent said. "We've had your phone bugged."

My stomach flipped. I hated that Gordon was continuing to plague me, even after I had finally gotten free of him.

"We know you have nothing to do with this," the agent said. "You don't know anything about it."

His words filled me with relief. Even so, Gordon had conditioned me so well that I was careful not to divulge any of what I had seen on Mulberry Street. But the FBI agents did reveal some mob secrets to me that I could hardly believe.

"We know that they had a code name for you that you didn't know," one of the agents said.

I stared at him, wide-eyed. This was news to me.

"Do you really want to know what was going on?" he continued.

"Yes, of course . . . what?" I asked, almost afraid to hear what he was going to say next.

"They were smuggling diamonds and drugs through you."

"You're kidding. How could they do that?"

The agent detailed an extensive scam that Gordon and his associates ran through me, throughout the world for years, without me having a clue: international smuggling and money laundering. As the FBI informed me, these men took advantage of how, in the days before 9/11, I could board airplanes without going through security or having my bags checked at customs. Because I was a known entertainer, officials would just let me pass through, thinking the same thought: *She's fine*. Often, I was driven right onto the tarmac and allowed to depart on my flight without ever setting foot in the airport. I suddenly recalled all of the times when Gordon had made me travel to Switzerland and Turkey for no apparent reason, only to stay for a few days, and we would be met by several men who then traveled back to America with me. I knew better than to ask Gordon anything about the purpose of these trips. I had always assumed that the men were there to watch over me, since this was such a common practice at that point. It had struck me as odd that all of the men carried these noticeably large bags with them, especially given that they had only been traveling for a day or two. But, of course, I never dared to mention my observation or ask what was in their bags. Apparently, their luggage was filled with drugs and diamonds, which they carried right through security because they were with me. I felt my breath quicken and my pulse race at this news, almost as if Gordon were in the room with me again, even though I had not seen him in years and had finally begun to feel safe. It was chilling to realize that I had been right in the middle of so much illegal activity, and the threat it posed to my life, without even realizing it. I'm sure if we had ever been caught, Gordon and his goons would have made me take the fall for everything, saying I must have known what was happening around me. Even I had trouble believing that I could have been so oblivious. But, somehow, I managed to remain remarkably naïve, especially given the corrupt schemes being perpetrated all around me.

7

❦

TORN FROM THE NEST

As long as my family was in my life, Gordon knew he would never be able to completely control me, and my money, or get away with the vicious abuse that allowed him to do so. Installing himself as my manager, in place of Joseph, had been a good first step. But Joseph still had strong opinions about my career, and he vocally expressed them to Gordon. I'm sure that's why Gordon took control of my passport as soon as he was given the opportunity to do so, essentially kidnapping me and keeping me hidden away in Europe for months at a time.

In the beginning, Gordon allowed me to maintain minimal contact with my family to create the illusion that everything was fine. However, I wasn't allowed to call them.

When Gordon first had me living in Germany, my mother often called to see how I was doing. After turning on his abundant false charm while speaking with her, Gordon would reluctantly hand me the phone, then watch me intently throughout our entire conversation. I felt incredibly awkward trying to be my normal self while he stared me down with vicious threats in his eyes. Gordon also tape-recorded all of these conversations, which made me even more uncomfortable. I knew I would be beaten if he had reason to accuse me of breaking his rules while I was on a call. And if I tried to alert Mother to what was happening, or even just let her know that she was being taped, Gordon made it clear that he would kill me. Or, even worse, he would harm my family. As terrified as I was for my own life, I took responsibility for what I believed was the mess I had created by trusting Gordon in the first place. But the thought that someone else might be harmed because of me was too much to bear. Somehow Mother knew to be suspicious of Gordon, but she didn't yet know just how diabolical he was. So, she unwittingly made my situation even worse.

"La Toya, is he recording this conversation?" she would ask.

I couldn't stand the thought of lying to Mother. Yet I knew I couldn't say anything even remotely affirmative, so I would be as vague as possible. I didn't want to speak to Mother for long because I hated for Gordon to record her saying anything he might be able to use against her. Even the most benign question or comment from Mother had to be navigated with the utmost care, especially because she knew me well enough to be able to detect if something was wrong. Although she never said anything directly to me about it, I think Mother knew fairly early on that things were far from all right in my life.

"Are you okay?" she asked.

My heart beat rapidly in my chest as I stalled for as long as I could. No answer seemed safe, especially with Gordon glaring at me from a few feet away. I knew how quickly he could cross that small space and knock me to the floor the instant I returned the phone to its cradle.

"What do you mean, am I okay?" I said.

Mother paused for a moment but didn't press the matter. "What are you doing?"

"Well, I just had a cup of coffee."

"Coffee? You drink coffee!" she exclaimed. "What are you doing drinking coffee?"

I'm not sure why I even mentioned it because I never drank coffee and had only had one sip that day. I suppose that, given the circumstances, it had probably seemed like a relatively safe topic. But this news was extremely upsetting for Mother. It made her wonder what other things Gordon might push me to do and how far I might fall under his influence.

In turn, Gordon was oversensitive about her response because he was so paranoid that my family might get me back before he could implement his master plan. He thought Mother was implying that he was creating a potentially troublesome situation that required further monitoring and possible intervention by her and Joseph. From that point on, Gordon became extremely upset by every little thing that Mother said to me.

I also think that, in some strange way, Gordon was jealous of Mother. Although he certainly didn't lead a virtuous life or try to make me like him, he hated to hear me speak well of Mother. Gordon felt that I praised two people excessively, and it drove him crazy.

"You act like your mother is a saint," he said. "It's like whatever she says is gospel in your whole family."

Gordon also despised that I thought Michael was gold. "You think your brother's God."

"Well, he's the closest thing to God I know."

"How could you praise your brother so much and think he's so great?"

"Because he is." Michael was. He really was.

"Your brother is nothing. You'll soon see."

Michael was a truly remarkable human being. He had an incredible heart, and incredible talent, the likes of which will never be seen again. His exceptional nature had nothing to do with the fame that he achieved, although this was certainly a result of the incredibly special qualities he possessed. I felt the same way about Michael when he was just five years old as I did when he became a megastar. The way he thought, even as a kid, was unique. He had the initiative at a young age to buy candy and sell it to the other neighborhood children, as if he were running some kind of general store. Even as the youngest member of the Jackson 5, he would always jump out of photo lineups, take one quick look at all the brothers, rearrange everyone, then hop back in before the picture was taken. His instincts were always right, every single time, and his photos were always the ones they ended up using. He could also watch any song or dance on television, and in two seconds he could copy it perfectly. The kind of incredible gift he had was clearly from God. From an early age, music and God were the only two things Mike cared about other than his family, and then, his fans. He didn't care about school. He cared about singing and his career much more. He was deeply devoted to his study of God and the Bible. While my brother Randy and the other kids played basketball during the breaks at the private school we attended, Michael and I would sit on the lawn together and read our Bibles.

I knew, even at a young age, that Mike was a child of God. Of course, we all are children of God, but I had no doubt that he was special. I would often say so to Mother. Having been raised as a Jehovah's Witness, we believed that 144,000 chosen ones will ascend into heaven from earth, just before the world ends. I always used to tell Mike that he was one of them because I honestly believed it to be true.

Michael could also show incredible sensitivity and compassion. Growing up, I was extremely self-conscious about what I saw as my big, ugly hands. I used to always sit on them or hide them behind my back, so no one could see them. Well, Michael had those same big hands, and he was quick to show me that they were actually our particular blessing.

"La Toya, don't ever be embarrassed of your hands," he would say, spreading his fingers as wide as he could for emphasis. "Look at Fred Astaire. It's a form of expression. When you dance, it looks great. And it feels good."

Michael then started dancing, to show me just what I could do with my hands, and how to use them to my advantage in my performances.

I watched Michael closely after that, and of course he utilized his hands constantly to create the most amazing movement and energy onstage. It could be felt even in the final row of the largest arenas in the world. And I was never ashamed of my hands again.

Of course, I never shared any of the specifics of my affection for my brother with Gordon. It would only have made him hate Michael more. The few positive things Gordon did hear me say about Michael were already enough to set him off in a way that terrified me. Gordon wanted to dominate me completely and have me place no one higher than him. So he set out to change my thoughts about my family. The first thing he did was to limit my contact with Mother and Michael. But as close as my family and I had been before Gordon came into my life, he wasn't able to completely cut them out of my life right away.

After Gordon had kept me in Germany for a few months, Michael managed to get a call through to me. He was shooting the video for his song "The Way You Make Me Feel" from his 1987 album, *Bad*, and he wanted me to come home to LA to appear in it with him. I had always loved collaborating with him and had been thrilled to sing backup on his 1983 hit "P.Y.T. (Pretty Young Thing)," and to lend my scream to the opening of the song "Heartbreak Hotel." We also had so much fun when he and Paul McCartney made a video that same year for their duet "Say Say Say." It had actually been Paul's suggestion that I star in that one, which meant that I ended up playing Michael's love interest. Not that Michael and I thought of it that way. We were both just playing parts in the story line. We did the shoot at a piece of property outside of Los Angeles called Sycamore Valley Ranch. Paul was staying on the grounds at the time, and we met at the small house to discuss the video. The entire time, Michael was enthralled by the wild landscape around us.

"I'm going to own this property one day," Michael whispered to me.

"You actually want this, Mike? It's so unkempt."

"You'll see."

I didn't say anything else because I didn't want to hurt his feelings. Michael always was a visionary. True to his promise, he later bought the land for $17 million and turned it into his dream home, Neverland.

When it came time to shoot the video for "The Way You Make Me Feel," I flew in from Germany to appear alongside Michael. I was so excited to see my family and have the opportunity to work with Michael again, but I was also nervous about hiding everything that had happened to me since I left home. Gordon was with me, of course, and watching me closely. Rather than wanting to tell my family about my abuse, I was so brutalized and fearful for Michael's life that I just wanted to get through the trip without anyone suspecting the truth.

When I got to the set on the first day, I learned that the video had been taken in a new direction. Initially, I was supposed to be the lead girl opposite Michael, which was what had allowed me to convince Gordon to let me fly halfway across the world to do it.

"Some things have changed," Michael said when we met in the trailer that served as his dressing room and office.

"What's changed?" I asked.

"You're not going to be the main girl."

"Oh, okay, that's fine."

Apparently, Mother thought it was inappropriate for me to play Michael's love interest again in his video. She was particularly worried that it might cause people to talk in the press, which was the same reason she had vetoed Michael's wish to have me play the lead girl in his "Thriller" video. I didn't care either way. With my family in the public eye the way we were, I knew that we had to be careful not to fuel the kind of rumors the media loved.

After returning to Europe and remaining there for the next few months, it was time for me to record my 1988 album *La Toya*. With Gordon dictating everything, of course, we moved to New York City for much of 1987 so I could record the album with hip-hop producers Full Force. Gordon and I first stayed at the Helmsley Palace and Waldorf-Astoria hotels, then moved into a gorgeous place in Trump Parc that had a breathtaking view of Central Park. I wasn't there all that much, though, as I spent most of 1988 traveling to promote my new album, and making television appearances in locales as far afield as the Netherlands and Venezuela. When I was home, I knew better than to think that being back in America would allow me any greater freedom from Gordon. But it did feel good to be living on the same continent as my family. At least it did at first, before Gordon stole this comfort from me, too.

The many exciting developments in my career at this time kept me incredibly busy. I was preparing to make my live solo debut at the Trump's Castle Hotel Casino in Atlantic City. This high-profile appearance was a major production. It boasted three backup singers and four dancers, an eight-piece band, and a dramatic entrance with me arriving onstage on the back of a motorcycle as lasers cut through a haze of smoke. I was elated about the shows, and just a little bit nervous, as Gordon gave me no time to prepare. But I threw myself into my few rehearsals, and the performances were well received and attended, with two shows being added to satisfy ticket demand. I couldn't have been happier about the reception, and it meant a great deal to me that Mother and my sisters traveled to Atlantic City to see me perform. It could be difficult to perform during a time when I was often demoralized and experiencing physical and emotional pain, but being onstage was liberating. I knew I was safe there from Gordon's violence. Even under the most adverse circumstances, the music could set me free. It also continued to be one of the main ways in which I connected with my family. Around this same time, Michael came to New York City to attend the 1988

Grammy Awards and perform three shows at Madison Square Garden. He was also continuing to declare his independence from the family, having just moved from Hayvenhurst to Neverland Ranch. He was still being managed by Frank DiLeo, whose controlling approach to management was much like what I was secretly experiencing from Gordon. DiLeo had been known to say of Michael, "All I have to do is wind Michael up, point him in the direction I want him to go, and he does it."

Gordon and DiLeo met several times to discuss how Gordon could help with a few small aspects of Michael's Madison Square Garden shows. I don't know the details. I can imagine that after an initial face-off to see who was the alpha dog, they probably got along famously as they merrily advanced their agendas. But this friendly working relationship between Gordon and DiLeo didn't last long. Donald Trump was interested in putting together a show featuring Michael at the Atlantic City Convention Center, and his entertainment executive Tom Cantone approached Gordon and me about helping to broker the deal. DiLeo was interested in having Michael do the show, but he made a surprising statement about the unlikelihood of its happening. "I'm going to have to work on Michael because I've really poisoned him against you," DiLeo told Gordon, at least according to Gordon. "But he'll come around."

Gordon claimed to have no idea why DiLeo would have done this. With what I know of Gordon's shady business dealings, I can only assume that the two men had gotten into a disagreement involving something it would probably upset me to know more about. This bad blood was making Michael hesitant to commit to the show. I honestly couldn't have cared less if Michael played the show or not, as long as it was the best decision for him. But Gordon was putting a tremendous amount of pressure on me to make Michael commit. As usual, Gordon was making me exploit my family to earn him a profit and make him feel as if he were in the big leagues. When Gordon forced me to speak to Michael directly about the concert, Michael seemed startled that the deal had not yet been completed and vowed to talk to DiLeo.

"I thought Frank had taken care of it," he said. "I'd love to do this for Trump."

After this, I could never seem to get Michael on the phone. Finally, to speak with him I contacted Mother, who was traveling with him at the time, and had her actually hand the phone to Michael. Again he said that he wanted to do the shows, and then midsentence the line went dead. The next thing I knew, DiLeo called Gordon and told him in no uncertain terms that Michael had never planned to play Atlantic City, and that we should have known this from the beginning. I never knew what really happened.

At the same time, it seemed as if Michael was also being isolated from the rest of the family. Like Gordon with me, DiLeo wanted to be the only influence in Michael's life. As Joseph used to say, all they want to do is divide and conquer my family.

Because of Gordon's role in my life, I had less and less contact with my family. I also noticed it was the same with Michael. It wasn't just me noticing, either. I later learned that several of my family members often complained about how it was nearly impossible to reach Michael on the telephone. We all had experiences that seemed to suggest that our longtime family security guard Bill Bray was following orders to keep Michael isolated. That isolation could have come from only one person, in my opinion, and it wasn't Michael.

Not too long after this, Michael started cleaning house because he felt many of the people who worked for him were trying to take over and rule his empire. On February 14, 1989, Michael fired Frank DiLeo, who had managed Michael for five years. Michael hired Sandy Gallin as his new manager. Michael never did tell me why he fired DiLeo, but he did tell me that he didn't trust him the least bit. After he was fired, DiLeo made the following statement about Michael: "I have a strong belief in what comes around goes around. It's called Karma, and I hope Michael understands what that means. If he doesn't now, one day he will." Michael told me repeatedly, throughout the years, that DiLeo was bad news and he would never work with him again.

In July 1990, Michael fired his longtime attorney, John Branca, after ten years of service and hired Bert Fields as his new attorney. Branca was instrumental in Michael's purchase of his ATV music catalog, which included many of the Beatles' hit songs, and his purchase of Neverland. Michael felt that Branca was trying to have too much control over him, his finances, and his overall business. It's interesting how, after many years of Michael's not seeing them, and telling me that he wouldn't work with either of them again, both Branca and DiLeo showed up in his life again just before Michael passed. But more about that later.

I was overjoyed in the summer of 1992 when I learned that Michael was performing in Hannover, Germany, just a few hours from where Gordon and I were staying at the time. I longed to be reunited with my family, but I was also fearful I might cause harm to come to them because of Gordon's threats. Mother was traveling with Michael, and so I asked her to come visit me for a few days. When she couldn't, Gordon grudgingly let me travel the short distance to see them. Of course, he wouldn't let me go alone, so we both traveled by car to Hannover. Gordon had his own reason for the trip, which was probably the only reason I was allowed to see my family. He was still trying to get Michael to agree to Trump's Atlantic City concert, so he could revive the deal. I'm sure Gordon believed he would gain money and prestige from the deal, so he was eager to make me convince Michael to say yes.

We arrived in Hannover and went directly to the arena where Michael was performing. We were escorted to the side of the stage to watch his show. It always felt incredible to sit on the side of the stage, only a few feet from where Michael was delivering one of the best shows on earth. Even though my brother weighed almost nothing, he danced with such energy that it literally made the stage bounce beneath his feet. It was almost enough to make me nauseous because I get terrible motion sickness.

After the show, we all drove to the hotel together. Michael and I could not get enough of talking to each other. Although Gordon had a close watch on us, Michael and I managed to get away to a room where we could be alone for a few minutes. I'm sure Gordon was expecting me to use this time to talk about the Trump show. But I didn't care about that show; what I was desperate to talk about was the increasingly brutal abuse I was receiving from Gordon, and how Michael might help me escape. But when given the opportunity, I just couldn't bring myself to say anything. The subject came up briefly, but I think Michael and I were both well aware that Gordon was nearby, and we were too afraid to say more. Also, my brother was still dripping with sweat, exhausted from the night's performance, and expected to leave in a few hours to travel to the next city. I didn't want to trouble him with my own problems, even though I knew he would have done anything in his power to help me. I knew the tremendous pressure that Michael was under, and I didn't want to put my worries on him, too. I just wanted to enjoy our brief reunion. We kept the conversation light, catching up about family and his tour, and then our time together was interrupted. Bill Bray started trying to get Michael to go to bed.

"Joker, you know you gotta get up early," he said.

"Oh, come on, Bill, I haven't seen La Toya in a long time," Michael said. "Let me spend a little more time with her."

That bought us a few more moments together.

Then Mother came in. "Michael, don't you want to get your rest?"

"No, Mother, I want to talk to La Toya."

It was so much like old times that I almost pulled together the courage to say something to Michael about Gordon. But, just then, Bill Bray came back.

"Joker, you really, really have to go now," he said.

Michael had to get ready to leave for the next stop on the tour, so we embraced and said our good-byes. I bid farewell to Mother as well, then Gordon and I left. I was so extremely sad to leave my family and go back to the reality of my life.

When we reached the car, Gordon asked me about the Trump show. He was angry that I didn't have an answer and forced me to go back upstairs to ask Michael about it. I felt awful about bothering Michael when I knew he was probably busy packing, but I certainly wasn't going to defy Gordon. When Bill Bray opened the door of Michael's hotel suite, I got him to get Michael for me.

Michael seemed confused, and I quickly explained, "Michael, I hate to bother you again, but Gordon wanted me to ask if you're going to do this Trump thing or not."

Michael gave me a vague answer having to do with competing egos, which didn't sound like him, but I had to accept it as the only information I was going to get for Gordon.

A few weeks later, Michael somehow managed to get through to me on the phone, and he gave me the real explanation behind his reluctance to do the Trump shows: "Frank says Jack is tied to a bunch of gangsters, and if just one of them doesn't get paid off, they'll kill me."

My heart raced when I heard his words. I had never doubted Gordon's threats, but it made them even more real to hear other people acknowledge his mob ties and violent ways. I hated to think that Michael had reason to fear for his life, at least indirectly, because of me. I felt even more determined to do whatever Gordon demanded to keep Michael safe.

About a week later, Michael reached me with one of the last telephone calls we would have for some time. In this conversation, he gave me the warning that would flash through my mind on the night in 1993 when Gordon almost killed me.

"I love you too much to see this happen to you," Michael said. "You have to get away from Gordon, La Toya, or he will kill you."

I knew that Michael might be right, but I didn't feel there was anything I could do. Because Michael also had such good reason to fear Gordon, he felt he couldn't help me, either, or he could be killed.

Gordon made his move to completely divide me from my family around this time. Part of his strategy was to begin a public campaign to make it seem as if my family and I had experienced a big falling-out. But this wasn't true at all; Gordon would not allow me to have any contact with my family. He began by telling me that I was not to speak with Mother anymore. Of course, I had two parents with strong personalities and eight siblings, so it was no small feat for Gordon to cut them out of my life.

Gordon and I went to our London home for a few months, and while we were there, my brother Jermaine somehow found the number to our flat and often phoned me. Of course, he had no idea that anything was wrong, so he was just calling to have our usual brother-sister chats. All I had to do to get in trouble when Jermaine called was to take the phone out of Gordon's hand and say "Hello" to my brother. Gordon's nasty look told me exactly what was going to happen to me as soon as I hung up.

"What's going on?" Jermaine would say in his distinctive Jermaine way.

It was impossible not to feel happy just to hear that familiar voice and know that he was thinking about me and had cared enough to pick up the phone and call.

"How are you?" he would ask. "What are you doing?"

I always managed to sound as upbeat as possible while we talked and to answer his questions in a way that wouldn't anger Gordon. But it didn't matter what I did or didn't say to my brother. Every time Jermaine called me, I got a beating. The whole situation was horrific because I knew Jermaine had no idea he shouldn't have been calling me, and he would have felt awful if he could have seen what happened to me as soon as our conversations ended. Knowing what was to come, I used to hate hanging up the phone with Jermaine, so I would try to drag the conversation on as long as I could. Before I even hung up the phone completely, I would feel a hand slap my face as hard as it could.

"That's for talking to your brother," Gordon said.

Soon, Gordon ended all contact with my family. He didn't feel that it was enough just to separate me from my mother. He told me, again and again, that she was trying to kill me, and that he was barely able to keep me safe from harm. Not only that, all of his security guards backed up his story. As I detailed from Gordon's point of view in my first book, my parents seemed to be trying to kidnap me away from Gordon. Under different circumstances, I might have been relieved to learn my family was trying to save me. But Gordon's mental manipulation was so successful that I started to believe my family was trying to harm me.

When we got back to New York for a brief business trip, I stepped into the hallway of my building with a security guard by my side. Just then, another panicked security guard rushed up, pushed me back into the apartment, and locked the door behind us.

"Get back in there," he shouted. "Your mother's down the hall with a knife."

At first, I couldn't believe it could possibly be true. This was my mother, after all.

"You're kidding," I said.

"No, we're not kidding," he said. "Oh my God, your mother's something else."

I fought the idea for the longest time. The thought of my own mother wishing to do me harm made me so upset that I used to cry and ask myself, *Why? Why would she do this?*

The men were incredibly convincing. Here were these big, tough mob guys who seemed to be terrified of my mother.

"You don't understand," they said. "You don't have a clue."

Such moments happened repeatedly with all of Gordon's different guards. He had isolated me so completely that I had no one outside of Gordon's circle to offer me any perspective. I began to believe them. Soon, I was petrified of my mother. Of course, with Gordon beating me two or three times a week, I knew that he was no protector. But, sadly, I had no place else to turn.

8

∽

AGAINST MY WILL

Gordon was greedy, and even with the excellent money I was earning for him, it just wasn't enough. He began searching for new ways to exploit my fame and my family name. In late 1988, Gordon told me that I was going to be appearing in *Playboy* magazine. At first, I didn't understand. I had seen a copy of *Playboy* once, when the magazine ran a story about my family, but I didn't dare look at a single picture. To do so would have gone against my religious beliefs and earned a meeting with the elders of the congregation. If I couldn't even read the magazine, I certainly couldn't appear in it. Many women I respected had appeared in *Playboy* and I would never judge their decision to do so, but I knew it was not for me. I began to cry as I begged Gordon not to make me do it. Of course, he eventually convinced me, as he always did, by beating me into it.

When the time arrived, in November 1988, for my

Playboy photo shoot at the Neil Simon Theatre in New York, I still didn't really fathom what was expected. When I walked onto the set, people literally gasped. All of the negotiations had been so top secret that many of the magazine's employees hadn't known they would be photographing me. The entire plan had been given the code name Toyota.

After greeting everyone on the set as cordially as I could, given how unhappy and nervous I felt, I asked what I thought was a totally reasonable question.

"Well, which nightgowns am I going to wear?" I said to one of the assistants.

They all stared at me for a minute, not sure if I was joking. When they realized I wasn't, they laughed. They probably thought they'd seen everything, but here was a surprise.

"You're not wearing nightgowns," the assistant said. "You don't wear anything."

I really started crying then. "You're kidding," I said between tears.

I had just assumed I was going to be wearing a nightgown or lingerie, and I had even been against being photographed like that. The thought of removing my clothes in front of the handful of people who were there for the shoot was enough to make me feel faint. It was too much to even consider my family seeing the pictures, not to mention the rest of the world.

I don't know how I made it through the three-day shoot. I insisted that everyone except for the photographer and makeup artist leave the room. Even then, not until my robe accidentally fell open, revealing part of my breast, did they get a single shot they could use. As I later learned, the magazine's editors had lined up Hugh Hefner's then fiancée, Kimberley Conrad, to stand by, in case she needed to be photographed in my place. Somehow, we all survived the shoot, and they finally got their pictures of me.

The magazine was due to hit newsstands in March 1989, and the three months before were excruciating for me. I didn't actually have to wait that long to find out how my photos would be received, as several members of my family found out in advance of the publication date. This was when Gordon was still occasionally letting me talk to my family briefly. First, I got a call from Mother and Joseph, asking if the rumor was correct, that I had posed for the centerfold of *Playboy*. Since this wasn't technically true, as I was not the centerfold, I said no. I didn't mean to mislead them. I just wasn't ready for them to know the truth yet.

When Michael called me around this time, I knew he had recently visited the Playboy Mansion while a meeting was in session about the issue featuring my pictorial. I had difficulty focusing on our conversation as I nervously braced myself that he probably knew about my photos and had an opinion about them.

"I saw your pictures," Michael said.

"No, you couldn't have," I said. "Everything was confidential."

"Yes, I did."

"Michael, you didn't see the pictures from *Playboy*."

When I still didn't believe him, he described the picture of me wearing a white robe and going "Shhhhh," and the image of me holding a snake. I was totally surprised.

"I just want you to know," he said, "I think they're great pictures."

I was so shocked that I didn't even thank him for the compliment, especially when he told me that Diana Ross had also seen and liked the photos.

I was incredibly relieved to find out that the pictures weren't going to make everyone hate me, and to also receive some positive feedback. I valued Michael's opinion greatly, especially because I knew his religious beliefs had always been as important to him as mine were to me. I would have hated to offend him, especially since I had been forced to pose.

"Thank you," I finally managed to get out, just before we said our good-byes.

When the issue finally hit newsstands that March, the other members of my family all had their own opinions about the photos, some very negative. Both Mother and my brother Jermaine were strongly against the photos and told me that they knew Gordon was to blame. It was a relief to hear that my family knew me well enough to see Gordon's influence at work.

But that didn't lessen the pain I felt at their reaction. Particularly upsetting were Mother's words to me.

"You're no longer my daughter," she said, before slamming down the phone.

Hearing her say that devastated me. Now that I'm

older and have better perspective on the situation, I can understand why Mother reacted so strongly. Being deeply religious, and wanting her children to grow up with her same strong faith, she was offended by the photos and that her daughter had turned against her teachings to pose for them. If I were that religious, I would probably feel the same way if my daughter did the same thing.

I felt even worse as other family members responded negatively as well, even though they were kind enough to try to say something positive. While Marlon said the photos were beautiful, he didn't like the snake picture and it was clear that he didn't agree with my decision to pose for *Playboy* in the first place. Jackie said he would never look at such pictures of his sister, but he offered his support for whatever decisions I made. That small affirmation helped so much. My main fear was that Gordon would make my family lose all respect for me, or even hate me.

Gordon forced me to act as if I had posed for *Playboy* to declare my independence from my family. When I wrote my first book, he made me describe this whole incident as if it had been an important part of becoming my own woman. Of course, this couldn't have been further from the truth. I was extremely embarrassed by the photos. I was upset that Gordon had been able to force me to do them. And I was hurt by my family's negative reaction, even if they were really mad at Gordon.

It didn't help that the pictures were extremely controversial because of my family's name and reputation.

I had to do a promotional tour for the magazine, including television talk shows such as *Letterman* and *Donahue*. Again and again, I had to go on television and talk convincingly about my choice to do the photos, or else get a beating when I got home.

Everywhere I went, everyone I spoke to wanted to know what my family thought.

"Some agree with it, some don't," I said.

While this was true, it did nothing to convey the discord that had been stirred up within my family as a result of these varied reactions. Soon after the pictures were published, Jermaine condemned me on *Entertainment Tonight*. His negative words were especially hard for me to hear because I knew he realized that I had been forced to do the photos. Yet he claimed I had done them to get attention, and I was insulted by his comment.

In private, Jermaine spoke out against Gordon. Jermaine and Joseph both threatened to have Gordon arrested, which did happen during a trip Gordon made to Los Angeles. He was nabbed at the Burbank airport for some unpaid parking tickets. Whether my family had anything to do with this incident, however, I'm not sure.

Jermaine also let it be known that things would get physical if he saw Gordon face-to-face: "I'm gonna kick Gordon's behind, then step on him like a cockroach."

My family also began waging a public war against Gordon in the press, describing him as a Svengali in one *People* magazine article. But the negative publicity did nothing to inhibit Gordon. He loved it when my family attacked him publicly. He began dreaming up even more sensational and controversial moves for me, so he could get even more of the media coverage he so desired.

The *Playboy* incident marked the beginning of an alarming new trend in Gordon's approach to my career, one I'm still living down today. At least once a month, someone approaches me with a copy of my *Playboy* issue that he wants signed. The whole memory is so upsetting for me that I usually try to convince the person to let me sign something else instead. And if the person insists, I turn my head away while I'm leaving my autograph because I can't stand to even see the photos. The experience actually makes me look back at the *Playboy* incident in a new light. Gordon set up the photo shoot and beat me to cooperate, but I can't put all of the blame on him. Although naïve, I was an adult. I should have done more to stand my ground, even if it meant additional beatings. If I hadn't given in, then I wouldn't still be living it down today, and I would feel better about myself.

The *Playboy* pictorial made Gordon even bolder. He used the controversy it stirred up to land me a high-profile deal for a tell-all memoir. As soon as this news reached my family, all of their many lawyers wrote threatening letters to Gordon and me. Individual family members called me directly to express their extreme discomfort and displeasure with the idea. It was falsely reported in *Newsweek* that Michael and I were feuding because of the book. While I did receive several phone calls from Michael, he was as sweet and gentle as he always was about everything. His own book, *Moonwalk*, had just been published, and he knew the publisher of my book would encourage me to reveal as many family secrets as possible. But his only direct mention of the subject was far from negative or confrontational.

"You know, I said all good things about you in my book," he said.

Gordon used the tension between my family and me to finally sever our relationship completely. His allegations of my parents' kidnapping attempts intensified. Gordon had convinced me they were intent on silencing me forever. In several harrowing incidents in New York City, it seemed as if Gordon's security guards just barely kept me safe. I have no idea whether Gordon was actually concerned that my family might be capable of liberating me, but he left no doubt in my mind that the threat was real. And he made a bold move to ensure I couldn't escape him.

9

~⁓~

IN NAME ONLY

In the late summer of 1989, I was scheduled to do a run of nights at the Bally Hotel in Reno, Nevada. Like my Trump's Castle debut, the show was an elaborate production with dancers and a full band. One of the performances was being taped for a pay-per-view special. After all of the emotional stress of the supposed kidnapping attempts in New York, and the grueling rehearsals and preparations that went into the show, it was a relief to actually arrive in Nevada. But when Gordon and I got there, he told me he learned how the police department had received a tip about three men who were planning to kill him. The whole time I was in Reno that summer, eight security guards watched over us, which was excessive, even for Gordon.

In the midst of all this, it was difficult to focus on performing. Luckily, Joseph had instilled such unwavering professionalism in me from such a young age that I was able to turn it on anyhow. The shows went well and were well received, and I began to put the anxiety of New York behind me. I should have known better than to relax for even an instant.

During an otherwise normal performance on September 5, 1989, I noticed from the stage that Gordon was up to something. He was in the sound booth at the center of the room, and he kept getting on and off the phone, as if he were making preparations. For the rest of my performance, my attention was divided between singing and my nervousness about Gordon.

What is going on? I kept asking myself as I watched him, while keeping my performance going.

The minute the show was over and I exited the stage, Gordon came rushing over to me, surrounded by our usual security entourage. He pointed to the guards.

"Pick a security," he said.

"Which one?" I said. "Why? What's going on?"

He didn't answer, and I could tell my questions were about to land me in trouble.

"Okay, you," I said, pointing to one of the guys.

Gordon hurried us through the backstage area and out a side door. A black limousine was parked outside. When the driver saw us approach, he opened the door for me.

"Get in the car," Gordon said.

I sat in the backseat between Gordon and the security guard, anxiously trying to figure out what was happening. Obviously, I didn't dare ask.

We arrived at a nondescript structure, and the limousine pulled up close to the entrance so that the car door practically opened right into the building. I had no choice but to go inside. Gordon and the security guard opened the door for me and gestured me inside. I was filled with dread, but I had no choice but to obey. I walked into an open building that was completely empty. They sandwiched me in between them as we walked across an old tan marble floor and followed a red velvet rope toward a woman at a small podium.

"What's your mother's maiden name?" she asked.

"Scruse," I said. "Why?"

"Sign this right here," she said, pushing a piece of paper toward me.

"Well, what is it?"

"Sign it," she said.

Gordon and the security guard were on top of me, letting me know without words that I'd better sign the document, and sign it quick. Or else.

"Now go over there, down to that door," the woman said.

Gordon and the security guard practically carried me to the door she indicated. My heart was racing, and I didn't want to go through, for fear of what awaited me on the other side. I had no doubt that Gordon was capable of anything, and I was terrified of what he would do to me next. Also, after everything I had just experienced in New York, I was still living in dread of potential kidnappers.

Inside this second room, nothing was scarier than an older woman who looked at us expectantly as we entered. Only when we stood before her and she launched into a stripped-down version of the traditional wedding vows did I realize what was happening:

"Will you take this man . . ."

"I can't marry him," I said. "Are you insane? I can't do this."

Normally, I never allowed myself to react to Gordon, even when he was beating me. I knew that any word or action he saw as rebellion would only inspire greater violence. But, finally, this was too much. He would undoubtedly have even greater control over me, *forever*. Plus, this went against everything I believed. Marriage was a sacred union between a man and a woman who loved each other and intended to stay together for the rest of their lives, undertaken in the eyes of God, their church, and family. I couldn't let him do this. I *wouldn't* let him do this. I fought back as best I could.

"You can't do this to me," I said to Gordon. "You're just my manager. I don't have feelings for you."

He responded by saying that the marriage had nothing to do with love. Much later, Mother said she thought he married me so I couldn't be made to testify against him if he landed in front of a judge. However, I have no idea if this was true. When we included this scene in my first book, Gordon made me describe him telling me that this wedding was the only way he could protect me from my family. If he and I were married, he reasoned, then he would be able to protect me. If I didn't agree to go through with it, he predicted that I would end up kidnapped, and he would end up dead.

Gordon didn't care if the world knew that we were married in name only, as long as I continued to lie on his behalf. He even allowed me to admit on the page that I started to cry and tried to run out of the room when I heard him say, "I do." The real story is that I must have run away four or five times during the short ceremony.

"I can't, I can't, I can't," I said again and again.

Each time I tried to escape, the security guard brought me back to stand with Gordon.

Finally, I left for the last time. When the security guard followed, I pleaded with him.

"Please don't let him do this," I said. "Please."

"There are certain things you have to do in life, whether you want to or not," he said.

The guard pushed me back inside, walking close behind me the whole way. Rather than having sympathy for me, and my obvious distress, the officiator had become impatient.

"I'm not going to go through this again," she said. "I pronounce you man and wife."

The dirty deed was done, but I still couldn't accept that it was true.

"I can't marry you," I said. "I don't even want that ring."

As my wedding ring, Gordon had pulled a tacky ring off his own finger and handed it to me. The last thing I wanted was to wear it at all times as a symbol of his domination over me.

"Don't worry about it," he said. "In six months, you can get an annulment."

"Okay, but don't think you're going to sleep with me. You're *never* going to sleep with me. And we're going to keep staying in separate rooms. And I want the original copy of the marriage certificate."

Of course, he never gave me the document. Our marriage remained in name only for as long as it lasted, but it wasn't the mutually agreed upon business arrangement that Gordon made it appear in public. And I wasn't angry with my parents for forcing me into the situation, as my first book made it seem. I blamed no one but Gordon. I trusted him less and disliked him more than ever, which was incredibly disheartening, given that he had just married me.

I was still upset as we returned to the waiting limo, but I quickly masked my emotions, as I was accustomed to doing. I knew I might well be beaten for the defiance I had displayed during the wedding proceedings, and I didn't want to do anything that would anger Gordon further. Having been unable to defeat him, I felt my brief flicker of independence falter. When we arrived back at the hotel, we had dinner with the performer Edgar Winter, who was in the Bally show with me, and his wife. As always, I put on a smile and made it seem as if I were happy to be there with Gordon.

But on the inside, I was still hysterical and distraught. I kept thinking, *I can't believe this just happened to me.*

The minute dinner was over, I went upstairs to my room. Gordon escorted me, along with the eight security guards. As we arrived at my suite and the guards took their posts, I watched Gordon closely to see if he would punish me. Then, a new fear gripped me. We were married in name only, but I didn't trust Gordon not to try to consummate our marriage.

I could not have been more relieved when Gordon suddenly informed me that he was leaving for Las Vegas. Without further explanation, he departed with seven of the security guards. I never fully relaxed during those years, but the only time I came close was when he was out of town and I knew I was free of his constant bullying and abuse.

The single security guard left behind with me was one of Gordon's guys, a muscular, bald man who looked like Yul Brynner. I called him Eagle Eyes, and with good reason. After I climbed into bed that night, he lay across the dresser in front of my bed and watched me sleep to make sure I didn't try to escape. This was a little extreme, even for Gordon. But I was so used to constant surveillance, and so exhausted from the night's extreme emotions, that I actually managed to fall asleep with him hulking over me.

Of course, Gordon made it a point to keep his business affairs secret from me, so I had no idea what he was doing in Las Vegas or how long he would stay. Years later, I found out that his trip had something to do with Mother and Joseph. To this day, I don't know anything more than that, but I've since suspected that he met with my parents and told them that if they even thought about coming to get me, Michael would be dead.

I did know at the time that the wedding was a disturbing display of bravado on Gordon's part that didn't bode well for whatever he planned to do to me next.

10

⁂

I OWN YOU

I never forgot Gordon's promise on our wedding night that we could get an annulment in six months. The days could not go by fast enough as I waited to be free. On March 5, 1990, the allotted time had passed, and it was time for me to tell Gordon that I wanted to get our marriage annulled. I knew this wouldn't be easy: I suspected it would be painful. I just didn't know how painful it would be. I decided to play it smart and to wait for the perfect moment to raise the subject. Each and every morning after March 5, I'd wake up thinking that this was the day to tell him, but he never seemed to be in the right mood. I knew he would smack me across the face when I brought it up. That was nothing. At that point, I could take a hit like a professional boxer. But I had to find a time when he wouldn't do much worse to me.

On the morning of June 12, 1990, after three months of waiting for the perfect moment, I woke up to the sound of Gordon singing "That's Amore" like Dean Martin. I knew this was the time to do it because he was happy and singing as if he were onstage in front of twenty thousand people. We were staying at a hotel in Italy, which was probably why he was singing that song.

I finally gathered up my courage and adopted a nice, innocent—almost whispery—voice. "Good morning, Jack. It's been more than six months, and I want to get an annulment."

He ceased singing abruptly, stopped dead in his tracks, and looked at me with that mean expression that I knew all too well. I was certain I had made a terrible mistake. But I couldn't take back my words.

"Are you insane?" he sneered. He grabbed me with such force that I was trapped. "I own you."

He took hold of a fistful of my hair and banged my head down, hard and fast, on the corner of a table.

"I own you. You're never getting away from me."

He banged my head again for emphasis.

"I own you. Don't you understand that?"

He banged my head once again.

"I own you. Are you out of your mind? I will never let you go."

Again he banged my head.

Every time my face or eye socket made contact with the table's hard wood, the pain was excruciating. My head was throbbing, and I could feel the swelling starting already. It was as if Gordon had been seized by some kind of madness.

He's going to kill me if I don't get away from him, I thought.

Using all of my strength, I fought my way out of his grip and ran for the phone. He was too fast and strong, and he got his arms around me before I could cross the room. He dragged me back toward the table, seemingly intent on beating my head some more, as I kicked and fought and tried to release myself from his grip. My will to live was stronger, even, than his cruel intentions. I fought him off with everything I had. Finally I broke free and raced across the room toward the phone. I stood there, panting and bloody but defiant and determined to save myself, as I dialed.

"I'm calling the operator."

I was shaking and desperate, willing the front desk to pick up before he could rip the phone out of my hand and then punish me.

I heard a woman's voice on the line. I had done it!

"He's beating me!" I said. "He's beating me! He's beating me!"

Just then, Gordon lunged at me, wrestled the phone away, and replaced the receiver in the cradle with a loud crash. Certain my life was in danger, I fought him off once again and managed to dial a second time. He hung up the phone before anyone answered.

I knew I should be quiet to save my life. But the annulment meant so much to me that I couldn't give up, no matter the consequences.

"What are you talking about?" I said. "You said we could have an annulment."

I never heard his response. But I felt it.

I didn't wake up until the next morning. When I did, my face was swollen and both of my eyes were black-and-blue.

There was a knock at my door. I sat up and felt dizzy and light-headed. But I knew I had to act as if nothing out of the ordinary had happened and I was perfectly fine.

I got out of bed and crossed the room, feeling the blood pound in my head. I opened the door, but only a crack, so my face was not visible to whoever was on the other side.

It was the girl who worked for me in London, who had traveled with us to Italy. "I need to come in and pack your clothes. We're leaving."

"Okay," I said.

"Is there anything you want?"

"No."

"Do you want anything to eat?"

"No, thank you."

"Gordon wants me to pack your clothes now."

"Okay, but I'll do it myself."

"No, I'll do it."

"No, no, no, I'll do it myself."

I was worried that this was some kind of trap, and that even though Gordon had sent her to my room, he would punish me if I allowed her to see how badly he had beaten me. I needed time to decrease the swelling before we had to travel later in the day.

"Wait one second," I said. "You can get something for me."

"What is it?"

"Can you please get me a bucket of ice and just leave it right outside the door?"

"Sure, I'll be right back."

I waited and waited, then I waited some more, just to be safe, until I thought enough time had passed for her to have left the ice and gone away. I opened the door to retrieve the ice bucket. She was standing right outside my door, looking at me. She winced when she saw my face, and I knew there was no hiding it from her now.

"Oh, I slipped in the bathtub."

I spoke the words without even realizing what I was saying. The worst part of the whole awful situation was that I felt bad. Not for myself, but for Gordon. I didn't want to tell on him and get him in trouble. As I later learned, this was quite typical of abused women. I did everything in my power to protect the very person who was harming me.

Now that she had seen me, I decided it would be all right for her to come in and pack my clothes. While she did so, I went into the bathroom to ice my face and put on makeup.

I was able to hide only so much, so I wore the biggest, darkest sunglasses I had. When I got into the car with Gordon to go to the airport, he wouldn't speak to me, as if I had done something wrong.

"I don't want to have anything to do with you," he said.

Even though I hated him, and he had just beaten me so terribly, he was all I had. I always did my best to please him, and it felt awful to be treated so coldly by him.

The whole trip was incredibly uncomfortable and awkward, and I was feeling sad and low by the time we arrived in London. At the time, I lived at 55 Hyde Park, which was right next door to the Dorchester Hotel. Right across the street from the Dorchester was the Hilton Hotel, and as we were pulling up in front of my building, I noticed they were having an event at the Hilton, as they so often did.

Gordon dropped us at the house and went off on some business of his own. The woman let me in with her key because Gordon didn't allow me to have keys or anything of that nature. When we got upstairs, she set about trying to make me comfortable.

"Would you like something to eat?" she asked.

"No," I said.

"I think you need something to eat."

When I finally agreed, she formulated a plan: "We're going to go to the Hilton to eat."

"Is it okay?" I asked.

I was concerned because Gordon never let me leave without permission.

"Yes, it's okay for you to go to the Hilton," she said.

So I put on my big, dark glasses, my white sailor coat, and a sailor hat to match, and we went down the street to the Hilton. A cluster of photographers were waiting outside the front. I tried to run to the side door and hide, but they spotted me and surrounded us before we could get inside. Joseph had taught us to always be gracious to the press, as well as to our fans, and so I felt bad keeping my head low in such a rude manner. But I knew better than to allow them to photograph my bruised face. Even with my head down, they'd noticed me right away.

"La Toya! La Toya!" they shouted.

They began asking me questions, but I didn't dare answer them. They couldn't photograph me because I was walking briskly and my head was down.

Then, from all the pushing and shoving, my glasses slipped off my face. I was filled with a terrible panic.

"Oh my gosh," I said.

I quickly picked up my glasses and put them back on, but it was too late. The paparazzi were already shooting pictures of me just as fast as they could. They got several of me without my glasses on, as well as several of me returning my glasses to my face.

The pictures left no doubt that I had been beaten, and beaten badly. I had two black eyes and scratches all over my face. The next day, these photos were not only all over the London papers, but also in newspapers throughout the world. Photographers camped out in the street in front of our building, trying to catch another glimpse of me. I don't know how they got our number, but reporters were calling nonstop to get a statement about the domestic-abuse rumors. Although I was scared, I was thinking, *Great! Now that the world knows I'm being abused*, somebody *will finally help me to get out of this horrible situation.*

Of course, Gordon was furious. His anger made him particularly cruel. I was afraid in those first days after the beating that something was terribly wrong with me. I could feel something bubbling inside of my skull constantly. I begged Gordon to let me see a doctor, any doctor he chose, or even to have one come to see me at the apartment. But he refused.

"No, you're not sending me to jail," he said.

At the same time, I was waiting for the arrival of the cavalry to finally rescue me and take me away. I don't know what I was thinking, though, because Gordon was too slick, and he knew how to twist any story so he wouldn't receive any blame. As the press continued to hound us, Gordon accused me of giving them our number. No matter how much I denied his allegations, Gordon's rage only grew.

"This is it," he said, pacing around the room. "I am so sick and tired of you. You did this purposely. You went there to show them that I beat you."

"No, I didn't," I said.

"Didn't I tell you that I could go to jail for this? I'm on probation."

"I didn't. I would never do that."

"You're a liar. I'm going to tell them that you had plastic surgery."

Gordon thought he had concocted the perfect lie, and he released the story to the press. I'm sure the world would have believed him except for one small detail. When I reached down to put on my glasses, the photographers got pictures of the bruises up and down both of my wrists. This was pointed out in subsequent news stories, along with the opinion that these injuries couldn't possibly have been caused by plastic surgery. When Gordon realized that his lie wasn't going to work, he quickly thought of another story and called our publicist, Rubenstein & Rubenstein, in New York. This time, he acknowledged that I had been beaten but said my parents had hired thugs to pretend they were room service, enter my hotel suite in Italy, and attack me with metal pipes. He also claimed that the intense media presence outside my London home had prevented me from seeking medical treatment, when, of course, he was the only one keeping me from a doctor. The story of the Italian attackers was released to the news agencies and went around the world.

The *Los Angeles Times* headline read LA TOYA JACKSON BEATEN IN ROME. The story that followed read:

"La Toya Jackson . . . was beaten by a gang armed with metal pipes who broke into her Rome hotel suite, her manager said today. Jackson, 31, was badly bruised in the attack and is resting at her London home, where she returned after the incident, said her manager, Jack Gordon. Gordon said by telephone from the star's apartment he believed the attackers had been trying to abduct her. A group of men carrying metal pipes entered Jackson's hotel suite in the early hours Tuesday after she called for room service, he said, declining to give any more details. . . ."

A magazine ran the headline LA TOYA JACKSON ATTACKED BY FOUR MEN IN ROME, ITALY. The story said:

"Sultry entertainer La Toya Jackson was beaten up by four men in her hotel room in Rome, Italy. . . .

Ms. Jackson and her manager Jack Gordon ordered room service at 4 a.m. and were greeted by four attackers when they opened the door [according to her publicist]. . . . Gordon was slightly injured. Neither were hospitalized, he said.

"Ms. Jackson was visiting in Rome after appearing in concert in a show in Switzerland. 'She does not want to talk about it,' said [her publicist]. 'She really did not want to elaborate on it.' No arrests were made and no further information was available. Ms. Jackson currently lives in London."

Not that I knew that any of this was going on throughout the world at the time. As I've already said, I wasn't allowed to read newspapers or watch news reports as long as I was with Gordon, unless he wanted me to see something. At the time, it was upsetting to feel so isolated from the world. But it was probably better for my mental well-being that I wasn't able to follow the news. If I had, I might have learned about some of the increasingly bizarre and sinister actions Gordon was taking, often in my name, or while pretending to be me. The knowledge would have devastated me at a time when I was already incredibly demoralized and despondent. It could well have been too much for me to bear.

I later learned that in the same month, June 1990, my brother Michael believed he was suffering a heart attack and checked himself into St. John's hospital in Santa Monica to undergo tests. I never knew about black roses being sent to Michael in my name until years after the fact. When Mother eventually told me about them, I felt awful that he might have thought they were from me. It made me even more certain that I would never understand what made Gordon such a treacherous, conniving person. It was one thing to be so evil for my money, but many of his actions were unnecessary. Once again, that was just Gordon's way of trying to get my family and the world to hate me. I was told, at this same time, that Michael was under a great deal of stress because he was unhappy with his deal at Sony, which was then called CBS Records. He had threatened to leave them, but it had all worked out by March of 1991, when Michael renewed his contract with Sony in a record-breaking deal that gave him possible earnings of $700 million.

11

~❧~

A FAMILY FURTHER DIVIDED

My book *La Toya* was published on September 12, 1991, and my family was extremely unhappy about much of what it contained. Although they knew that Gordon was behind every word, they still had to live with the attention it received. It didn't help that Gordon beat me to do *Playboy* a second time that November, to promote the book, and also began having me film an embarrassing series called the Interactive Exotic Club Tour. After that, I embarked on the book's publicity tour. During interviews, I had to say that the book had been my idea, and that every word it contained was true. After this, it was a relief to return to Europe.

In early 1992, Gordon signed a deal for me to have my own show, "Formidable," at the Moulin Rouge in Paris. He continued to keep me ignorant about my business, so I didn't know I had just signed a $5 million contract. What I did know was what he was constantly bragging about in the press. This included that my book had become a best seller, and my Moulin Rouge agreement made me the highest-paid act in the cabaret's history. Such distinctions meant nothing to me, as I cared more about performing at my best and being well received by the fans and the public, but Gordon just loved to brag.

My agreement with the club had me performing for two thousand people a night—with two shows nightly, six nights a week—for a year. These weren't small shows, either. I had eleven costume changes during an elaborate extravaganza that found me singing nearly a dozen songs, many of them in French, while performing elaborate dance routines, backed by ninety showgirls and men. Not to mention the live crocodiles, acrobats, and topless snake charmer.

It would have been a feat to pull off, even under normal circumstances, and we had only two weeks to rehearse. The first time I ever actually performed together with my backing dancers was onstage during opening night. I knew I had big shoes to fill at the iconic cabaret, which once featured legendary performer Josephine Baker. It was a thrill to sell out the thousand-capacity theater most nights and release a live album of the show, *Formidable*.

The evenings that I performed were usually a bit of a blur. But one night stands out vividly in my mind because I received a surprise visitor who meant the world to me. I was in my dressing room when there was a knock at the door. There, to my wonderment and joy, was my brother Jermaine. I could hardly believe my eyes. But, yes, it really was him. He had decided to surprise me while he was in Paris for business, and he attended the show with Minister Louis Farrakhan's son. As an aside, I must say that it was always easy to tell when Americans were in the audience, simply because those American eyes were always fixed on the topless showgirls the whole time. The Europeans were so used to seeing breasts that no one usually bothered to glance at them twice.

After the show was over, I couldn't have been happier to visit with Jermaine. Gordon became so friendly that he actually suggested I ride in the car with Jermaine and Minister Farrakhan's son when we went out to eat afterward. This was unusual for Gordon. But I knew that he was playing the good guy only to make it look as if I weren't being held against my will. Plus, Gordon knew he had me so well trained that I would never say anything to Jermaine. Gordon was right, because I didn't say a single word, and his plan worked because Jermaine thought everything was just fine. This was a relief for Gordon, who had heard while we were in Belgium that Minister Farrakhan was looking for Jermaine to bring our abusive relationship to an end. I knew Gordon was afraid of Farrakhan and the power he held with the Nation of Islam. So Gordon went out of his way to make everything look great, just in case Farrakhan's son reported back otherwise to his father. Gordon even asked them over to the house after dinner, which was absolutely unheard of, and we all sat around talking and laughing.

When it was finally time for Jermaine to leave, I could hardly bring myself to say good-bye, and I cried like a baby. For the first time since Gordon had taken me away from my family, I saw signs of freedom. Seeing Jermaine, and enjoying all of the great memories of my family that came with him, made me feel alive again. When he said good-bye, I felt as if I were dying, knowing I was going back to Gordon. I wanted so badly to go with Jermaine, but I could only think of what Gordon promised he would do to Michael if I didn't follow orders. As I watched Jermaine walk away, it was as if he were a life raft that had suddenly appeared at my lonely island of abuse and shame, and there he was, returning to my old life without me.

That was one of the only times I got to see any member of my family during those years. But the period during which I performed at the Moulin Rouge was actually relatively social, compared to my normal life with Gordon. He was still careful to keep me isolated as much as possible, but because I had to spend so much time at the theater with the other performers, inevitably I sometimes socialized with others. I kept most of our conversations on the surface because I knew I was not to confide in anyone. But those French dancers were so spirited and bold that even a casual conversation could be quite revealing. One day, one of the dancers mentioned that the prostitutes who worked behind the theater were always talking about how Gordon frequented them all the time.

I was shocked when I first heard this, not only because of my religious beliefs and lack of life experience, but also because I was with Gordon constantly. It was hard to believe that he could have indulged in this habit without my knowing anything about it.

Then, my mind flashed back to something that had begun happening regularly after we moved to Trump Parc in New York. The back of the building was a regular gathering place for prostitutes, so we always walked by them when we were on our way out. Almost from the first day, they greeted us like old friends.

"Oh, hi, La Toya," the girls said to me.

"Hi, Jack Gordon," they said to him.

"How are you?" they asked.

"I'm fine, thanks," I said. "How are you guys?"

I wasn't exactly comfortable around prostitutes, but it's in my nature to be friendly to everyone. Besides, they were being so pleasant to us, and I didn't want to be rude.

"How do they all know you?" I asked Gordon.

He mumbled something that did nothing to answer my question, then changed the subject. Looking back, of course I can see what an idiot I was. But at the time, I was still so sheltered that I didn't know any better. Not until people started telling me that Gordon frequented prostitutes daily did I believe what I had seen with my own eyes. But up until the moment when I was forced to acknowledge what was really happening, I didn't have a clue.

I think my response to the dancer's gossip must have disappointed them.

"Oh, really?" I said.

It truly meant nothing to me. Better them than me, as far as I was concerned. The only time this revelation caused me concern was a few years later, when Gordon was in the hospital. He had first been told he had cancer early in his time as my manager, and he was always going in and out of remission. But any more than this, I didn't know. He was using my money to pay for the best possible treatment, at a cost I once heard estimated to be around $3 million. This was not a surprise to me, since he insisted on a private room with two twenty-four-hour security guards outside his door. Yet I was never allowed to go see him in the hospital. Everyone else in our world could, but not me. And I was not supposed to speak about his illness. It occurred to me on many occasions that if his condition was so serious, I should probably have been told more about it. Over time, I found myself wondering if Gordon really had cancer, or if maybe he had AIDS, and that's why he was so secretive.

Life in Paris settled into something like a normal routine, then, four months into my one-year contract, Gordon developed a new scheme for which I needed to go to America. This meant breaking my agreement with the Moulin Rouge, which of course infuriated them. It also caused them to come after me in court to try to recover the $550,000 they claimed to have lost because of me. Gordon didn't allow my name to be on any of my own bank accounts, but he certainly made sure it was on all of the contracts. This meant that, although I personally had no money, I now was legally responsible for

Gordon's debt. Years later, I learned that he had me declared bankrupt to avoid having to pay back the money to the cabaret. Again, sometimes it was probably best that I wasn't allowed to read the newspapers or watch the news.

Once we were in America, Gordon revealed that he expected me to film more specials for the Interactive Exotic Club Tour series. This experience was always extremely uncomfortable for me because I was so against what he was making me do, yet I had to act as if I couldn't have been happier as long as the cameras were on.

That fall, I did have the opportunity to make several appearances that were meaningful for me, when my old friend Bob Hope asked me to be a part of his USO tour to entertain troops fighting in the Gulf War. Even though it was difficult to hide how much my life had changed, and for the worse, since I had first come to know Hope when I was a young woman, it was wonderful to be reunited with him. Performing for the brave men and women who were risking their lives for our country was an honor.

However, while I was in Bahrain as part of this trip, I received a severe shock. As I was being escorted down a long, marble corridor on the way to my dressing room, I looked to my right and noticed a newspaper and magazine shop. I saw a familiar face on every magazine and newspaper and backtracked to take a second look. I couldn't understand why every publication had my grandmother on the cover.

"That's my grandmother!" I shouted.

I knew something had to be terribly wrong, and my stomach dropped. It was the strangest thing to see her picture like that, in a foreign country, when I was least expecting it.

"That's my grandmother," I said again.

I ran over and picked up one of the publications. Of course, it was written in Arabic.

"What does it say?" I asked.

The translator read the headline, then looked at me for a long moment before translating it for me. My grandmother had died, and this was the first I was hearing of it. She had been an important part of my childhood, and I was devastated by the news. It made me feel even further away from my family. Gordon softened in the face of my grief and actually allowed me to make one phone call. But he had made me so afraid of Mother that I didn't dare call her. Instead, I called Mother's friend Louise. She confirmed that the news was true and promised that she would tell Mother I had called. After that, I wasn't allowed to make any more calls. I later asked Mother about the incident, and I was glad to learn that Louise had in fact let her know about my call. But Mother also then gave me some disturbing news. Apparently, the family had called Gordon to tell him that my grandmother had passed, and he had hung up on them and never given me the message. Gordon also knew from them when my maternal grandmother died during these same years, but he never told me. I believe he kept this from me because he didn't want me to go back home to unite with my entire family during a time of such strong emotion. The reunion would have been too powerful, and he would have lost his control over me. Not to mention that they would have beaten the slop out of him. He knew that, too.

Gordon was already scheming to further exploit me and divide me from my family, which would bring me to one of the lowest points of my life.

12

⌘

THE PUPPET MASTER
AT WORK

Remarkably, even with everything Gordon had done to me in the nine long years since he had kidnapped me from my family, I never thought of taking my own life. To do so would have been a sin in the eyes of my religion. Thanks to my constant prayers, I kept myself alive. The only time my will to live was truly weakened was when I believed Gordon was going to harm someone in my family because of me. Or when he used me as a weapon against my family to put forward one of his terrible plans.

Through just such a plan, Gordon brought me lower in 1993 than he did at any other time. On August 17, 1993, Gordon briefly dismissed his ban against me watching television.

"They got him!" Gordon said. "He's not so great now, is he? Turn on the TV."

I didn't know what Gordon was speaking of, and I

thought this was another of his tests to set me up for another beating, so I didn't follow his instructions.

"I said turn it on, La Toya!"

"I don't want to get beaten," I said. "You told me to never touch the TV."

"You're right, kid, don't ever touch the TV. I'll turn it on. Sit!"

He turned on the television. I saw on the news that the LAPD had officially opened a criminal investigation against Michael because of Jordy Chandler's allegations of child abuse.

"This isn't fair!" I said. "None of this is true. Someone is just trying to frame Michael for money. Michael would never do anything like this."

"You still think this molester is great?" Gordon said. "They're taking him down now. I knew they would. I just didn't know when."

"Who's taking him down?"

"Shut up and don't ask any questions."

I was lucky I didn't get smacked for asking a question, but Gordon was too focused on the TV, just smiling at the negative story about Michael on the news.

Gordon stayed glued to the television all day, every day, following all of the news about Michael, but after that first time, he wouldn't let me watch. I was extremely concerned about Michael, and how he was feeling, but I couldn't do anything about it. I wasn't even allowed to call him, or my family members, to see exactly what was going on. So I just kept praying that everything would be okay for him because I knew he was completely innocent.

Gordon allowed me to once again watch television, on August 21, 1993. Again, he was as cheerful as he could be.

"La Toya, get in here," Gordon said. "You have to see this!"

On the television, I saw the LAPD raiding Neverland and Michael's Century City condo. I was devastated!

"I guess he won't be throwing parties there anymore," Gordon said.

He was really getting a kick out of all this. The phone started ringing like crazy. Finally, Gordon tore himself away from the TV long enough to pick up.

"You guys did it!" he said. "This is great, isn't it?"

He looked at me then and motioned me to go into another room until he told me to come out again. From that day on, Gordon stayed on the phone from morning until night. I didn't have a clue what he was doing. But I knew that he was always plotting and scheming something bad. And those words always stuck with me: "You guys did it!"

What could he have possibly meant by that, and is Michael being set up by someone? I thought.

I had to do something to help my brother and prove his innocence, but I was powerless because of Gordon. I started staying up all night, thinking of how I could convince Gordon to let me do or say something that would help the situation. Then, I got it! I didn't care if I got a beating for bringing it up, either. I was going to at least try.

"Gordon . . . can I go on TV and protect my brother by saying how I personally feel about the situation?" I said.

As he thought about my question, I was nervous, not knowing if I was going to get a backhand across the face or an angry "*No!* Go back to your room."

"I think that's a great idea," Gordon said. "I'll schedule something."

I was shocked. That was the first time Gordon had ever let me do anything I wanted to do. I was *extremely* happy. I couldn't wait to help Michael. But I did worry that there might be something behind this. Gordon instantly started making phone calls again. He sent me to another room, so I didn't have the slightest clue as to what those calls were regarding. About two weeks later, I was able to go on TV and speak out on Michael's behalf.

As happy as I was to do so, I knew that Gordon hated my brother, and that all of this kindness he was letting me display toward Michael was bound to have a cost. But, for the moment, I just allowed myself to enjoy speaking highly of Michael in public.

I suspected that Gordon was up to no good when he suddenly told me that we were going on a vacation. This was unusual because, first of all, I worked all the time. I had not taken even a short break in all of the years Gordon had managed me. Then, he told me that our vacation would be in Israel.

When we arrived in Tel Aviv on December 8, 1993, I wasn't any more convinced that we were on the verge

of a relaxing vacation. Because of Israel's political insta-
bility, we had to go through an extensive security check
in New York before we could even get on the plane to
leave.

*This is strange, out of all the places, why are we going
to Israel?*

But, of course, I kept my mouth shut, as I had been
trained to do.

When we landed in Israel, we exited the airport
and found a limo waiting to take us to our hotel. As we
pulled up to our hotel, I was alarmed to discover what
I thought was an awards show in progress. Swarms of
press were everywhere. I wasn't wearing any makeup.
Before we got out of the car, I quickly put on some
bright red lipstick and my big, black sunglasses.

Gordon handed me a piece of paper.

"Here, you're reading this," he said gruffly.

"What is *this*?"

All of a sudden it dawned on me: that press was here
for me, and I didn't have the slightest clue until just that
moment. I felt the world close in around me as I was
filled with rising panic. That was the kind of life Gordon
had me leading. He was always forcing me to do things
in the public eye without preparation or warning, and
with the constant knowledge that if I didn't perform impeccably, the consequences would be swift and painful.

"What is this?" I asked again nervously. "Can I go
to the ladies' room?"

"*No!* Read it."

Before I had time to even collect myself, Gordon

pushed me out of the car into an explosion of blazing flashbulbs as eager paparazzi jostled for position and shouted my name.

"La Toya! La Toya!"

I couldn't even imagine what terrible words I was about to be forced to speak. But I knew there was no getting out of it, so I pulled myself together. Joseph had taught all of us children that whenever we did something, we should do it professionally and with as much enthusiasm and energy as possible. I didn't want to be filmed looking down, with my face hidden in the piece of paper Gordon had given me. So I was trying to read words that I had never seen before, through these enormous sunglasses that obstructed my vision, while keeping my head held high, as if I were expressing my own thoughts. Even as I began to read, I still didn't know what I was saying, but I did know that, whatever it was, if I didn't read it properly, the way Gordon wanted me to, he was going to hurt me.

Then, with horror, as I was speaking, I realized that the statement was about Michael. It wasn't the positive message I had been preaching in public about the allegations against Michael. It was the worst possible thing I could say about a person who was innocent, and I *knew* Michael was innocent. But Gordon didn't care. He was thrilled to see Michael's image sullied in this way. He was making me say just the opposite of what I had been saying. Back then, I didn't know why he was making me do this, or who had put him up to it, but it was horrible.

Not only that, Gordon was making me speak out in

front of a mob of news cameras, which would broadcast the statement around the world. I knew better than to display any emotion on my face, but my heart was breaking as I spoke the words he forced upon me.

I truly believed that if I didn't say what I had been told to say, Gordon and his mob buddies would surely kill Michael. Gordon had drilled this threat into me, again and again, until I knew it to be true. So, although it was an excruciating choice, I decided that it was better to continue reading and do whatever it took to save Michael in the moment. I figured, afterward, when I knew Michael was safe, Michael and I could discuss what had happened, and I could try to make him understand how I had been forced to say such things. At the time, this reasoning allowed me to endure what was an impossible moment. But now that I look back from outside Gordon's control, this press conference is among the biggest regrets in my life. I can't stand to see the footage because it makes me so sick with remorse. I honestly think that I would rather have let Gordon kill me than make me say those words.

When I was finished reading those awful words from the piece of paper Gordon had handed me, he immediately took over the microphone. His words were meant to keep me convinced, and make the public think, that my family was trying to kidnap and kill me, so I wouldn't try to escape or speak to my family, and no one would try to reunite me with them.

"There's been two major kidnapping attempts on La Toya . . . that were stopped!" Gordon said to the media. "They were paid and financed by Michael Jackson."

I later learned that Gordon had attempted to extort money and favors from Michael's handlers by telling them that if they didn't comply with his demands, he would have me make this very statement. I was horrified to discover this plot and just how much thought Gordon had put into planning the whole awful event. I had been set up to commit a terrible transgression against my beloved brother so Gordon could profit.

Even more disturbing, I also discovered, long after that awful day in Tel Aviv, that the allegations against Michael had been just as manufactured as my press conference was, and with a similar goal in mind. Much like Gordon with me in that moment, evil forces were surrounding Michael. They wanted to tarnish his reputation to impoverish him and break his spirit, and perhaps force him to sell his valuable music catalog. At the time, Gordon was secretly meeting with Michael's former manager Frank DiLeo and Michael's attorney John Branca, whom Howard Weitzman had brought back into the picture in November 1993 to work on the case on Michael's behalf. Weitzman was enlisted by Bert Fields, Michael's lead attorney at the time, in around September or October of 1993. Bert Fields, as well as Michael, and the private investigator on the case, Anthony Pellicano, wanted very much to fight to prove Michael's innocence. Michael was actually looking forward to his court date, which would have been March 21, 1994. According to Michael, it was John Branca's idea not to take the case to trial, but to settle it instead. Michael always regretted that, because the settlement made Michael appear guilty of those horrific charges.

What I didn't know then was that, at the same time, Branca's law firm also represented Michael's label, Sony, which was desperate to get its hands on Michael's music publishing catalog. That seemed like a clear conflict of interest to me. As Michael's music publishing started to grow, everyone wanted a piece of it, and how convenient would it be if Michael was convicted of the child molestation charges? He would not only serve prison time, but his damaged reputation would ruin him, bankrupt him, and make it likely he would have to sell his prized possession, his music catalog. Obviously, because I was his sister, if I came out in support of the allegations, it made them more likely to stick. And even without a conviction, his ruined reputation could still have forced him to sell. I later came to believe that, because Gordon controlled me, he tried to earn favor with these powerful men by helping ruin my brother in a way that was likely to benefit them. Gordon would have been glad to do this because he hated Michael's success.

In the moment in Tel Aviv, though, all I knew was that I was in hell. Finally, the ordeal was over and Gordon led me away. The crowd pressed against me as reporters shouted questions, and their flashbulbs blinded me. My knees were weak, and I felt so nauseated I could barely walk. At the same time, we couldn't move fast enough because all I wanted was to get away from the pandemonium that surrounded us. But even later, when we were finally on the plane, there was no escaping what

I had done. At this moment I began to wish that I would die, so all of this anguish would be over. I prayed the entire flight that our plane would crash. I know this is awful, given all of the innocent passengers who would have perished as well, but I was so distraught that I couldn't think of anything but finding an end to my pain and shame.

The repercussions were just as bad as I had feared they would be. The news reports of my press conference went around the world. This was at the height of Michael's fame. He was a superstar of the highest magnitude, but he was also gravely misunderstood by much of the world after decades of false stories that made him seem eccentric and unstable. News of the allegations against him had already created a media frenzy. Now, the fact that his own sister had spoken out was a huge news story. This negative press was just what those working against Michael wanted. Since Gordon was jealous because he said I thought Michael was the closest thing to God, and he hated the way he felt that I worshipped Michael—even though it wasn't worship, it was love— Gordon was happy to see Michael's name tarnished, as others were, too. Everyone in the situation won, except for Michael and me. The disdain Michael's fans felt for me following the press conference could never equal that which I have for myself. If I could go back in time, I would prefer to have died at Gordon's hand than to have given in to him.

In the immediate aftermath of the press conference, my mother, father, and siblings were angry, but they knew I was probably forced to say those things. Even so, they had no choice but to condemn me harshly, and publicly, to minimize the damage to Michael as much as possible.

"La Toya is lying, and I'll tell her to her face she's lying," Mother said in one television interview. "She knows it."

In another interview she said, "I'm going to tell you something, which was never brought out, and all these people know it. That's not La Toya talking. That is Jack Gordon. . . . I think he has brainwashed La Toya, and when La Toya gets up there on TV, she is like a crazy person. She is not the same girl."

Joseph also said this during an interview: "He's manipulating her and he's doing everything he possibly can to get into her family and keep the family all messed up. . . . All these accusations she's making never happened. None of this. That's why we didn't understand it . . . It's like a different La Toya."

Even though their words were true, it was painful to hear their anger. But I did understand why they spoke in this way, and it even made me happy to think that their statements might help Michael in some way and diminish what I had been forced to do. Mother was torn because she knew what Gordon was doing to me, yet she also saw that he was trying to destroy Michael, and she had to protect him as well. Because she didn't know what else to do, she had no choice but to discredit Gordon and me. Not only did she hope that her words would protect Michael's innocence in the face of Gordon's lies, but she also hoped that if she disgraced me, Gordon would no longer be able to earn a living by exploiting me. Maybe then he would finally let me be reunited with my family.

But Gordon was far from done with me. He made me start appearing on television shows to speak about Michael. Gordon was intent on exploiting the misfortune that had befallen my brother to create a scandal from which he could profit. Even now, just thinking back on that time is difficult for me because every moment of it was so incredibly painful. I knew that it had to be even more upsetting for Michael. My heart went out to him in his time of need, but obviously I wasn't allowed to have any contact with him. After leaving Gordon, I found out that he made statements in the press that suggested I had evidence that proved the allegations true and demanded $500,000 in payment for what I claimed to know. It was absolutely horrible to me that he would profit off my brother, and particularly during such a low point in Michael's life. Gordon's dream deal fell through after a brief bidding war between several UK and American tabloids when they realized Gordon was lying and had nothing to reveal.

I couldn't stand to think of what Michael must have been feeling when he heard about the press conference. I wasn't aware that Michael had canceled the remainder of his world tour a few weeks earlier and made a public statement that he was checking into a drug rehabilitation center for a dependency on painkillers. When I later learned that he saw the press conference with his good friend Elizabeth Taylor, who was visiting him in the treatment center, it hurt me even more.

I knew how upsetting it must have been for Michael to admit he had a drug dependency, since his faith as a Jehovah's Witness had made him refuse to take so much as an aspirin throughout his life. I hated to think of adding extra emotional stress at such a difficult time. My only comfort was the memory of my earlier conversation with Michael, in which he had warned me that Gordon was no good. When I thought back to Michael's words, I was reassured that maybe Michael knew that Gordon was to blame for everything that had happened.

Thoughts of the press conference and how it had affected my brother plagued me constantly. I couldn't eat or sleep for thinking about it. I could barely drag myself out of bed in the morning, especially because I was expected to do whatever Gordon had set up for me that day. I wanted to die. I really did. If I didn't believe it was a sin of the gravest magnitude to commit suicide, I would probably have done so during the weeks that followed my trip to Tel Aviv. I thank God that I didn't, because even though I still had much to endure in the following years, my survival meant that I would eventually be reunited with Michael and my family.

❦

LIVING IN HELL

Rather than being nice because he was pleased with my obedience, Gordon just pushed me harder. It was as if he wouldn't be satisfied until he had wrung every penny out of me, or killed me, whichever came first. In the spring of 1993, he almost did the latter when he beat me nearly to death at our home in New York, which I have already described. Although the publicity that surrounded Gordon's arrest on two counts of second-degree assault brought my abuse out into the light, this did nothing to improve my life. Gordon continued to block my exposure to news of any kind. I had no idea that my family was so concerned about my safety after the beating, they had a spokesperson issue a statement: "They are very concerned about La Toya's mental and physical health and she is always welcome to come home."

Not only that, but Michael reportedly offered to fly me anywhere in the world for a private heart-to-heart, a

gesture that clearly showed Michael's generous and loving spirit. Jermaine and Jackie were rumored to be on
their way to New York to rescue me. Had I learned any
of this, I would have been extremely happy, knowing my
family had publicly forgiven me and opened their arms
to me.

All I knew was what Gordon told me, and that was
more threats and lies. At his bidding, I dropped the assault charges and didn't pursue the matter further in
family court.

At least for a time, Gordon took a short break from
tormenting my family and turned his attentions back
to me. He told me on several occasions that he would
not rest until he succeeded in making me the most hated
woman in the world. He eventually ruined my reputation so badly that he nearly succeeded. When I finally
got away from him, it took me years to repair the damage he did, and I'm still repairing it to this day. I continued to make music and perform around the world.
But Gordon no longer seemed to care if these ventures
advanced my musical career, or if they made me the target of more ridicule and hatred.

He forced me to become a spokesperson for the Psychic Friends Network, and to film commercials where I
promised to divulge Jackson family secrets during the
calls. Then, he started forcing me to make appearances
at strip clubs.

He had again beat me in 1991 to make me disrobe
for *Playboy*. Because the sales of the magazine were so
good, and Gordon was getting an excellent payday from

them, he had an even better idea than demanding I undress for the print magazine a third time.

"I know how much you hated doing *Playboy*, so I'm not going to have you do that again," Gordon said.

That was the best news I'd ever heard. I was so happy, until he went on . . .

"This time you're going to do a *Playboy* video."

I was devastated! I didn't know exactly what I would have to do, but I knew I didn't want to do it, so I tried to protest once again. Well, you can easily guess what happened after that.

In March 1994, they shot the *Playboy* video *Playboy Celebrity Centerfold: La Toya Jackson*. When we were on the set the first day, Gordon became extremely angry and ordered me to my trailer. As he walked in, he was already screaming. He pulled back to hit me, but then stopped himself in midmotion because I needed to go back in front of the cameras. I was already topless, but that wasn't enough for Gordon. He wanted me to show my private parts and kept yelling to try to force me.

"No, no, I'm not doing it," I said. "I can't do it."

I kept crying, and crying. The more I cried, the more he tried to convince me. My makeup was dripping down my face, until I had completely cried it off.

"No, I can't do it, and I won't do it," I said again.

I was defiant. It made Gordon go insane. It took everything in his power not to hit me. He couldn't, and we both knew it, because the only thing I was wearing on the set was a G-string, and the entire crew would notice bruises anywhere on my body. So he shook me.

"You have to do this," he said. "You have to do this. There's nothing wrong with it."

"No."

Gordon turned to his friend Lacresia, who was just entering the trailer. "Tell La Toya there is nothing wrong with her exposing her vaginal area for the cameras," he said.

Even though she wouldn't get involved, Gordon continued to hound me. But there was no convincing me. I was lost and hurt. I felt disrespected and, most of all, violated. But I wasn't about to perform nude in front of a crew of thirty, or anyone else. Finally, I got called back onto the set by one of the producers. I had won the battle, at least for the moment. The following day, Gordon continued to try to convince me to get completely nude on the set. I continued to refuse. Finally, he offered to help me by trying to pull my G-string down.

"Look, it's easy," he said. "This is all you have to do."

"No," I said.

"Just do it for two minutes. Then, you won't have to do it again."

He had stripped me of my pride, my dignity, my self-worth, and now he was trying to literally strip my clothes off me. I saw him as Satan and felt sure this was hell. I continued to pray to God in silence. As the days went on, I successfully held my ground. I was still disturbed that the video was going out into the world, but at least I had defeated him once.

Even when Gordon allowed me to do music, his decisions about the direction my musical output took were often bizarre and doomed from their inception, such as the country-western album *From Nashville to You.*

Throughout all of this degradation, I approached each new job with the professionalism that was instilled in me, no matter how little I wanted to do it. I also continued to be as obedient as ever, if not more. I had been deeply shaken by that terrible beating in New York. If he could beat me that badly, then nonchalantly lie about the whole incident to police officers, I knew that he could just as easily kill me. I had never doubted his threats because I had seen proof of just how far he could go, and how little remorse he felt. But I was reaching my breaking point. I don't think I even realized it at the time because I was still too frightened of Gordon. But I could take only so much, and he was coming close to helping me discover what that point would be.

Without ever making a conscious decision to do so, I dared my first small act of rebellion. I was in South America, where I have always performed a great deal, to appear on a television show. Of course, Gordon was there, keeping a constant watch over me. When he left me alone in my dressing room before we taped the show, I was sure he had only left on some small errand and would soon be back. I knew from experience that the television programs in this region could be extremely casual. Sometimes, I found myself waiting in my dressing room for several hours while the crew went off to enjoy a leisurely lunch and siesta. So I was waiting patiently to go to the set when there was a knock on my dressing room door.

"Yes?" I said.

It was one of the producers from a children's show that was being filmed on a television set right next to where I would soon be taping my segment.

"Can we do a quick interview with you?" he asked.

"No, I can't do that," I said.

"Please, we're dying to do an interview."

"No, I can't do that. My manager isn't here, and I'm not really allowed to do anything like that."

"Please, we're the same company as the show you're already filming. And it will only take three minutes, five minutes at the most."

"I'm very sorry," I said. "I just can't."

"We have one hundred thousand dollars in cash that we'll give you if you agree to do it."

I hadn't had a single cent in my possession since 1987, when Gordon had seized control of all my assets. If I could earn this money, which was a standard television appearance fee for me, and keep it a secret from Gordon, the funds would go far toward financing my eventual escape. That was enough to convince me to take the risk because I wanted so badly to leave him.

I agreed to do the interview. The studio was connected directly to my dressing room. The producer simply opened the door, and I was in front of the camera, although I'm not sure how I got through it. I was shaking the whole time, convinced that Gordon would storm onto the set at any instant and take me away to beat me.

When that didn't happen, I became certain that he was lurking just beyond the studio lights and would punish me as soon as I had finished the interview. It was difficult to appear relaxed as I answered the host's questions. But I managed to act as if nothing were out of the ordinary, as I had become so accustomed to doing during my time with Gordon.

Even after I returned to my dressing room and prepared for the show that I had originally been asked to tape, I was sure that I was about to be caught. When Gordon returned from wherever he had been, I could barely look him in the eye. As nervous as I was, a part of me wanted to tell Gordon what I had done. I knew I had broken the rules, and I felt guilty.

What if he really knows and he's just testing me?

But Gordon didn't seem to notice anything. Now, I had to figure out what to do with the money, which, as promised, was all in cash. I was nervous because I had never disobeyed Gordon before. I knew how important this moment was because I wanted to someday escape with this money. As soon as I could, I pulled aside one of the crew who had traveled to South America with me and gave him all of the money.

"Please keep this for me, please," I begged. "Do not tell Gordon. Do not let him know that you have this."

The crew member agreed. I gave him all that cash and trusted he would do the right thing. When we finally got back to New York, I arranged to get my money from him at our next rehearsal. But, as he was giving it to me, I became frightened that Gordon would find it and confiscate it from me. So I only took back about $30,000 and asked the crew member to hold on to the rest for me. I didn't particularly like this arrangement, especially as my years with Gordon had finally made me less trusting, but I had no choice.

I hid the stack of bills in one of the vanity cases I had at our New York home. I piled makeup on top of it and left it mostly untouched for probably about a year. I knew that, for my plan to work, I had to take my time and make sure I didn't do anything to make Gordon suspicious. Given how paranoid Gordon always was, this was no small feat.

Somehow, just knowing that the money was there made me feel a little bit better about myself. After all of those years, I had successfully gone behind Gordon's back and done something for myself. By this point, my self-esteem was as battered as my body, mind, and spirit, but this small act of rebellion helped a great deal.

My secret also inspired me to disobey Gordon a second time. In recent years I had managed to make one friend, which was incredibly exciting for me because of how isolated Gordon kept me. I had been looking for an assistant to help me with my wardrobe on the road, and I was introduced to this woman by one of my dancers. He told me that he knew a girl, Tania, who made incredible clothes. She came over and began fitting me for clothes, and I soon saw that the dancer had not been exaggerating. She was a fantastic designer and went on to make costumes for several of the top Olympic figure skaters who have won gold medals in recent years.

Because Tania was technically an employee, Gordon allowed me to spend time with her alone. He probably assumed by now that I would never dare to break any of his rules. Well, she ended up being a bad influence on me when it came to Gordon's rules, which was just what I needed. She was a true New Yorker in spirit, a native of El Salvador who had fought her way to her current success, and she was outspoken. Even the little bit she saw of how Gordon treated me always made her so angry on my behalf, and she asked me why I couldn't be more forceful the way she was.

"You just don't understand," I said.

"No, I don't understand," she said. "Why are you this way? Why are you so afraid of him?"

Even after I had worked with her for years and considered her a friend, I didn't know her well enough to trust her with my secret. I was never able to tell her he beat me because no matter how irreverently she spoke out against him when she and I were alone, I feared she would betray me.

Perhaps because she didn't know how serious the consequences would be if I got caught, she became convinced that what I really needed was to get out and go antiquing with her. Just the thought made me extremely nervous, but she was so sweet about the whole thing.

"You don't have to worry," she said. "I'll get a car. We'll get in the car. Nothing will happen."

And that's exactly what we did. We left my apartment, got in the car she had arranged for us, and went antiques shopping in Manhattan. As much as I was beginning to dare small moments of independence, I was still terrified of Gordon, and not just for myself, but also because of Michael. I was a wreck while we were shopping that day. I don't know if the excursion was worth it because I was so anxious the whole time.

While we were antiquing in Manhattan, I came across a clock, a Louis XV, which is a period I've always adored. I had brought some cash from my small stash of money, and my heart sang at the idea of actually buying something for myself with money I had earned. I couldn't bring home a clock. Gordon would know I had left the house, and that I had money hidden. But the allure of the clock was simply too great, and I couldn't bring myself to walk away from it.

"I love this clock so much," I said. "And I have to get it. But I don't know how."

"Well, just say I gave it to you," Tania said.

"No, I can't say that because he's going to see it."

In the end, I decided to risk Gordon's rage. We brought the clock home, and when he asked about it, I told him the story she and I had made up. Gordon was absolutely furious, and he called her right up. She later told me how their conversation unfolded, word for word.

"How could you do this?" he screamed. "You're not allowed to come over or speak to La Toya anymore."

"You know what?" she said. "You don't control her. Who do you think you are? I told her she needs to get out of the house, and she needs to be independent. And she does. I'm so sick and tired of your mess. I'll report you to the government."

She said all of the things I would never have dared to say, and I was so incredibly happy when I heard this. Finally, someone had stood up to Gordon on my behalf.

Of course, Gordon wasn't going to let that happen, and so he tried to poison me against my friend, just as he had poisoned me against my family. As soon as he got off the phone with her, he gave me some news that I'm sure he thought would devastate me.

"I want you to know, I've been sleeping with her almost every other night."

"Oh," I said. "Well, I don't care." Meanwhile, I was thinking what I didn't dare to say out loud: *Good, she can have you.*

I'm sure he was lying because she always struck me as having had better taste than that. But, either way, she was a good friend to me, and I wasn't angry with her if what he said was true.

After Gordon unleashed his fury on her during that telephone call, I think she had a better sense of what my life was really like, and why I was so afraid of him. Not long after that, she began planting an even more serious seed of rebellion within me. She began saying that I needed to leave Gordon. When I did get free, I would need something to help me start over in my new life. She told me that I had to secretly begin copying down the contact information from Gordon's Rolodex. This way, I would have the valuable industry contacts I would need to manage my own career when the time came.

Everything about the scenario she described seemed difficult and scary to me, and I didn't believe it was possible. But that small flame of hope I had somehow kept alive inside me responded to her words. I knew she was right. Whenever she came over to fit me for a costume, and Gordon wasn't there, she would lead me into his office. Once there, we would quickly scribble down a number or two in my address book, which I began hiding. As the months went by, I amassed quite a collection of contacts. Not that I thought I would ever have the courage to get free and use them. But, again, even just copying down the numbers was enough of a rebellion that it strengthened me and gave me a dream.

14

⤺

THE BEGINNING
OF THE END

Finally, about a year after I had earned my secret stash of money in South America, Gordon's son was in town visiting us, and I knew that he was going back to Las Vegas.

"Could you please take a vanity case of mine back to Vegas with you and leave it at our condo for me?" I said as innocently as possible.

"Sure," he said.

I carefully wrapped in towels all of the money I had left from the original $30,000, then put makeup and other things on top of it, so nothing appeared out of the ordinary. When I was sure the money was well hidden, I locked the case. After double-checking the lock, I gave the case to Gordon's son, and he took it back to Vegas with him.

Meanwhile, Gordon and I went to Argentina for an appearance, and then, from there, to our Vegas condo. After we'd been there a few days, I checked for the vanity case, and it was gone.

I kept waiting for Gordon to mention the money and dole out my punishment. But days, then weeks, went by and he didn't mention it. I never found out how Gordon found out about the money. Obviously I couldn't ask him. I think he chose not to say anything as some type of subtle psychological torture.

After this setback, I tried to muster up the strength to leave Gordon on several occasions, but I could never do it. I wanted to be courageous, but Gordon really had me trapped. Even if I had been able to find a way around the security guards, and my having no money or cell phone, his mental control was absolute. My biggest fear was that if I tried to escape, Gordon would catch me and beat me to death. I couldn't bring myself to risk it.

But at the same time, I was finding it increasingly difficult to act like the docile woman I had been for so long. My nerves were shot from years of intimidation and abuse, and I was losing my ability to function in a normal way. I wasn't able to read. I wasn't able to focus on anything. Even if Gordon had still been booking me prestigious appearances, I don't know if I could have maintained my Jackson professionalism.

In early 1996, Gordon left for a three-week business trip in Branson, Missouri. Before he left Las Vegas, he beat me, giving me a black eye, as was his usual way of reminding me who was boss before he left me on my own.

Of course, I wasn't alone. As always, Gordon had arranged for a security guard to be at my side around the clock. This guy wasn't from the Mafia contingent, though. He was one of Gordon's associates from Las Vegas, where he had lived in a trailer as part of the circus that he ran. He was sort of a hillbilly compared to what I was accustomed to, different from the other security guards, and I noticed it right away. On his first day he made a surprising comment.

"What did you do to deserve that?" he said, indicating my swollen eye.

I thought he was teasing me. "Please don't say that to me," I said.

But then I realized he might be sympathizing with me, and I just couldn't tell because it had been so long since anyone had done so. Either way, at least he had acknowledged that I had been beaten. After years of living near people who ignored Gordon's abuse, it was a relief to finally have someone see what Gordon was doing to me. Just that one little statement from him made me feel less worthless.

After that, the man came to the house first thing every morning and stayed until around eleven o'clock every night. We spent a great deal of time together during the day, and he even cooked for me. I wouldn't say that I trusted him completely. But we had a friendlier relationship than I'd ever had with any of the security guards before him. I could tell, somehow, that he saw that I was an innocent person in a bad situation.

Finally, after about a week of this arrangement, I decided to be brave and ask him to help me do something that had been on my mind for several years. As much solace as I got from praying on my own, what I really wanted was a Bible. But I couldn't get out to a Kingdom Hall to retrieve one for myself. I pleaded with him to help me.

"Please, please, please, can you just do this one favor for me?" I asked.

I could hardly breathe as I waited for his answer. I was terrified that I had been wrong about him, and he would tell Gordon.

Finally he said, "Okay, but don't tell him I'm getting it for you."

What a relief! I knew I could trust him not to tell Gordon.

A few days later, when he arrived in the morning, he handed me a Bible. I was incredibly moved by his kindness. Of course, he was still one of Gordon's goons.

"I want you to know, when I went there, I was drunk," he said.

Oh, God, I thought.

But at least he had gotten me my Bible. As soon as I held it in my hand, I instantly felt fortified. Now I just had to make sure Gordon didn't find out that I had it.

"Please, please, don't tell Gordon I have this," I said. "Please."

I figured I was safe because he couldn't tell Gordon I had the Bible without getting himself in trouble. I was almost too happy to care who got in trouble because I had my Bible. That's how much it meant to me to have a Bible of my own once again. I acquired it just in time, too, as I would need the strength it gave me to face what Gordon had in store for me next.

Gordon left Branson, Missouri, and had one of his guys fly down with me to meet him in Florida. I hid the Bible in my luggage, then took it out in my hotel suite. I hid it out of sight, and just in time, too.

Gordon came into my suite and started in on me right away. "I want you to do your own strip clubs. You're gonna strip at your own club."

I felt sick. It had been bad enough to be forced into staying overseas and alienated from my family back in 1987. It had been bad enough to be forced to pose for *Playboy* magazine in 1989, and then again in 1991. It had been bad enough to be forced into doing several Interactive Exotic Club Tour videos in 1992. It had been bad enough to be forced into speaking out against my brother in 1993. It had been bad enough to be forced into doing a *Playboy Celebrity Centerfold* video in 1994. It had been bad enough to be forced into doing a psychic hotline in early 1995. It had been bad enough to be forced into getting onstage and having him try to get me to strip at a strip club in Reading, Pennsylvania, in late 1995. It had been bad enough to hear that Gordon was planning to force me into spending the evening with Mike Tyson. Yes, he had solicited Mike Tyson to have sex with me for an evening, as if I were a prostitute. How embarrassing! It angers me to this day to think about it.

I learned this from Majestik, a family friend of thirty years, who told me that he and my mother had gone to visit Mike Tyson at his home in Las Vegas during the peak of his career, which was also during the time when I was with Gordon. Gordon always knew that

Mike Tyson had a crush on me and wanted to marry me before he married Robin Givens. Afterward, Mike even conveyed to me that he had made a mistake, and he wished he had married me instead. Mike told Mother and Majestik that Gordon had approached him.

"Hey, Mike, I know how much you like La Toya," Gordon said. "You give me one hundred thousand dollars, and I'll let you have her for a night to do whatever you would like to do with her. A girl like her, I could easily get two hundred thousand dollars a night for, but because I like you, you can have her for a hundred."

I was livid when I heard this. Gordon was actually trying to prostitute me! Who knows whom else he tried to sell me to over the years. Now, remember that Gordon's background was in brothels, so he looked at all women as prostitutes, and that's basically what he tried hard to turn me into: a high-class, celebrity prostitute.

Tyson was upset when Gordon solicited him with this proposal, and he ordered Gordon to leave and never come back. Tyson said he wanted to knock him out. I wish he would have. I thank Mike for standing up for my rights as a human being.

While we were in Florida, Gordon continued to push me to strip. He had gotten this dumb "bright" idea when he forced me to show up at a strip club in Pennsylvania. It was so packed that the cops had to come handle the crowd. After seeing this, he figured that if he owned the club where he forced me to appear, he could make this kind of money every night.

"I'm not doing it," I said. "I'm not doing it. You've

already made me look terrible, continuously, in front of the world, and I'm not doing it. You're going to have to kill me."

Of course, Gordon assumed he could make me do it, as he always did. We had meetings with everybody, even the mayor of one of the cities in Florida. He was speaking to them about opening a strip club called The Jacksons' Strip Club. I was infuriated.

"You are not opening a strip club in my family's name," I said. "You have exploited me and my family enough. I am not going to stand by and allow you to exploit my family's name more than you already have."

Gordon was so full of himself, strutting around and telling them how sensational the show was going to be and how much money guys would pay to see me strip live. The men were all looking at me in a way that made me extremely uncomfortable.

"No," I said.

I don't know where the courage came from to utter that one word, but I instantly felt proud of myself for doing so, no matter what the consequences might be.

Gordon was furious, of course, but he could do nothing to me in front of these businessmen he wanted to impress. So he simply gave me that look, laughed off my comment, and assured them that I would strip as promised.

When we got back to the hotel, he beat me and beat me.

"Don't you *ever* say no to me in front of people like that, ever again," he said.

I didn't know what to do because I was determined that I was not going to do this strip show, but I knew he would just keep beating me until he got me to submit. At a loss for answers, I started keeping my Bible close to me, as much as I possibly could. I even started showering with it because that was one of the only times I could be alone. I would stand in the shower, holding the Bible outside the shower stall, gaining strength from having it in my possession. I wouldn't let it go, no matter what. That's how much I wanted God to hear me and be on my side when I needed his strength and guidance more than ever before.

Gordon and I flew to New York together. He was in a dark mood the whole trip. I could tell that our fight wasn't yet finished, and that something even worse was about to happen. My instincts were correct, only I had underestimated just how low Gordon would try to bring me.

Back in New York, we were staying at the Palace Hotel. After we checked in, Gordon went out without telling me where or why, as usual, leaving me alone in our suite. A few hours later, he came back in, only he wasn't alone. When he arrived at the door, he had a bunch of hotel security guards with him from downstairs.

I couldn't tell exactly what lie Gordon had fed them, but they believed he had a good reason to fear for his safety.

What's he up to now? I wondered.

Then, I saw the way the security guards were looking at me, as if this man had convinced them that all 110 pounds of me were dangerous.

"Are you going to be all right, sir?" they asked Gordon.

"Yeah, I think I'll be all right now," he said nervously.

"Are you sure?" they asked.

"Yes, thank you. But if I'm not, I'll let you know."

Then it dawned on me. He was building up some sort of elaborate story he had already worked out in his mind. I thought back to the time he had been clever enough to put the knife in my hand, so it looked as if he had struck me only in self-defense. I watched him carefully after that, fearing he was about to attack me and really kill me this time.

Then, once the hotel security guards left, he spoke words that might as well have been a blow to my face.

"Whether you like it or not, you're doing pornography. All you have to do is have sex with four men, and the fifteen million is mine."

After everything Gordon had done to my life at this point, and the years of misery I'd endured, I was *not* going to be forced into doing a pornographic film having sex with four men! That's where the line was drawn, and my strength was recovered.

This was it, I wasn't going to let him think I would do this, even for a second. I was going to fight for my rights, and my life. He was going to have to kill me because I wasn't doing it! No threats or beatings would break me now. He had forced me ONE TOO MANY TIMES. ENOUGH!

I was filled with panic. This couldn't be happening to me. I felt faint. Then, I heard one simple word in my mind: *No*.

He had found my breaking point.

"NO! ABSOLUTELY NOT!" I said. "You have exploited me and my family in every way possible. You've destroyed me. You've destroyed my life. You've degraded me. People hate me. I am not going to do this."

"You're doing it," he said. "I've used you up. I'm doing this last thing, and then I'm done with you. You're finished. Nobody wants you. You're a has-been. Go be a bum. I'm getting my fifteen million from this, and you're not going to stop me! You're doing it! You're doing it! You're doing it! That's final! And then, that's it. I'm going after your niece next. I'm going to get me another Jackson."

I knew he was talking about Jackie's daughter, my lovely niece Brandi, and he intended to do with her just what he had done with me. I had seen the signs that he was trying, desperately, to go after her. He had already promised that he could help her start a career. He had tried to bring her to Paris when we lived there, and he told me he wanted to introduce her to the modeling world. He started giving her money and buying her mother little things. I knew that he would never rest until he had carried out his plan, and it made me sick. I had to stand up to him, not only for me, but to protect my niece.

"I'm not doing it," I said. "And that's final."

"You will do it."

If I stayed, I knew he would make me do pornography. His power over me was so absolute that if I stayed, I could not resist what he wanted. It was all or nothing. He had exploited me to the end, and I knew I had no choice but to leave him.

Now that I was determined to get free of him, I was willing to do anything it took. He had promised on so many occasions to make sure my life was miserable if I left him, to make sure I never worked again, to make sure the world despised my family and me. But I didn't care anymore. I was willing to be homeless and live on the streets, just to get away from him.

My mind raced backward and forward, trying to think of what I needed in order to get away from him. Then, it dawned on me. I had to get my passport back. He had kept it since that first Japan trip, nine years prior to this. But I couldn't think of any way to ask for it without making him angry. So, finally, I gathered up all of my courage and just blurted it out.

"I would like my passport please."

Gordon just ignored me.

"I would like my passport please."

"No!"

I begged for my passport then, knowing I absolutely had to get away, and this document would be my only form of identification if I escaped.

He laughed right in my face then. "There's no way I'm giving you your passport. Do you really think I'm that stupid?"

I didn't care what he thought, or what he planned to

do to me. I needed that passport, and I was determined to get it back from him. I continued to beg. The more I begged, the more infuriated he became. He picked up a Coca-Cola bottle and threw it at me. He missed, but he didn't stop there. Next, he ran over and picked up the bottle. Before I could get away from him, he grabbed me by the back of my head and started beating me with the bottle.

I was afraid, but I also felt stronger than I had in so long, maybe stronger than I had ever been in my entire life. The more he beat me, the stronger I got. I truly believed I had the Bible to thank for this: both the power of the book itself and the fact that I had gotten a copy in my time of need and he had not discovered it and taken it away from me. I needed God in this moment, and he was there for me. I was filled with a remarkable vigor. I fought Gordon off, desperate and wild, knowing that everything was at stake in this moment. I ran to the telephone and began to dial.

"I'm calling downstairs and calling the cops if you don't give me my passport."

Gordon saw that I was serious, and realizing that I had a new resilience in me that I had never before had, he grabbed my passport and threw it at me. Of course, he called me every cheap name in the book after that. But I didn't care. His words just rolled off me. Even though he had just beaten me badly, I felt better than I had in years. I had to do this, and I *was* doing this. I felt as if I had nothing else left to lose. Gordon had done everything that he could possibly do to me. He had degraded me, abused me, exploited me, and used me. Now he was going to kill me. But if he was going to kill me, let him kill me trying to escape. Gordon knew at that moment I had changed. My strength now weakened him. I didn't care if I didn't have a dime or if I had to live on the street. I was leaving him for good, and nothing else mattered.

15

RISKING IT ALL

The day after Gordon beat me with the Coca-Cola bottle, I could think of nothing but how and when I would escape him. I felt almost delirious with the idea that I might soon be free of him. But my excitement was tinged with fear that something would go wrong, and I wouldn't make it out alive. Gordon was acting as if nothing were out of the ordinary, and I'm sure that everything in our life was business as usual as far as he was concerned.

He knew he would get his way, as always. I would do his awful strip shows, and his pornographic film, and he would steal the money I earned from doing them.

Or so he thought.

What he didn't know was that, as far as I was concerned, his regime of terror was over. I would never allow our life to go back to the way it had been. Throughout that long day and night, however, I never saw an opportunity to attempt my escape. I was disappointed, but I wouldn't give up, so I went to bed determined to try again in the morning.

May 3, 1996, dawned just like any other day for me, but I could already sense that something was different, and special, about this day. I lay in bed listening to the street sounds below my suite at the Palace Hotel. I could hear the cars, the taxis, all of the hustle and bustle of another typical big-city morning. How I longed to be down there, to be a part of life again. Maybe, just maybe, if all went as I hoped in the next few hours, I would be free to rejoin humanity by the end of the day.

I knew I had to do everything absolutely right for my plan to work. So I lay in bed, pretending to be asleep. But the whole time, I was talking myself into what I had to do next. Now was the chosen time. This was the day that would change my life forever in one of two ways: either I was going to escape Gordon's torture and take back my future, or I was going to die trying. But I had no doubt in my mind that something historic was going to occur in my life that day. However it happened almost didn't matter to me anymore. I had reached my breaking point. I was incredibly frightened, yet a little part of me was happy, thinking I might successfully get free. If he caught me, he would have to kill me to make me stay. I have no doubt, to this day, about that. The thought was preferable to being forced to star in a pornographic film. Either way, Gordon would know that he no longer had control over me. Finally, I had found the strength that I had been trying to gather for so many years.

Without letting him see that I was awake, I watched Gordon get up and order his coffee. I knew that this was his routine; every morning, he had to have his cup of coffee before he did anything else. I had it all planned out in my head: the minute he went into the bathroom to take a shower, I was going to make my move. I was shaking like a leaf. Gordon stalled in the room, finishing his coffee and reading the paper. I couldn't stand it.

Is he going to leave the house today?

It would be just like him to stay home on the one day that I absolutely needed him to leave. Finally, Gordon walked out of the bedroom and went into the bathroom. As soon as I heard the water turn on, I was filled with relief.

Good, he's leaving! My dream is now becoming a reality.

I leapt into action. I knew I didn't have much time. As frightened as I was, I had never been so determined to do something in my entire life.

I eased out of bed and grabbed my phone book. Running quickly on the balls of my feet so I couldn't be heard, I made my way to the phone. I reached for the receiver and stopped. I knew I would only have enough time to complete one call, just like a prisoner. I had to make it count. Without thinking, I opened my phone book to the *J*'s, for the Jacksons. I hadn't been in the same room with, or spoken to, some members of my family in years. I had been forced to do things that embarrassed my entire family greatly and to tell the worst possible lies about them. I had been told even more lies about them and their evil intentions toward me. Yet, in my time of greatest need, there was nowhere else I would have turned. I was still a Jackson, and no matter what had happened over the years, I knew that we were still family, and I was ready to go home.

The first name my eyes gravitated toward was that of my brother Randy. I knew all too well that he never answered his phone, making him one of the hardest members of my family to contact. But, for some reason, I was absolutely certain that he was the one I should call.

I took a deep breath to steady my nerves, and shaking even harder than I was before, I picked up the phone. All I could do was hope Gordon wouldn't notice that the red light on the bathroom phone had just lit up. If he did, he would know I was using the other extension.

As I dialed, I had a single thought that was more like a prayer.

Oh, God, please have Randy answer the phone.

While I listened to the phone ring on the other end, my fear of discovery was so great that I was tempted to hang up. But I had already gotten this far, and I couldn't go back now.

God answered my prayer, and even though everyone in my family had complained for years that they could never seem to get him on the phone, Randy answered. To this day, I still believe this moment was God's way of telling me that I was doing the right thing, and he was right there, carrying me.

I was frantic, crying, daring only the faintest whisper as I spoke. I didn't even waste the time to say hello or tell Randy who it was. I was sure he would know it was me.

"Randy, please come get me. I can't take this abuse any longer. He's going to kill me."

"Calm down," he said. "Let me get Mother and Joseph on a three-way call."

I tried to stop him and tell him we didn't have enough time. That Gordon would be climbing out of the shower any second and storming in to rip the phone out of my hand. But Randy was already gone, setting up the three-way call. Fortunately, it didn't take long, even though it felt like an eternity to me, given how sure I was that I was about to be caught.

Once Randy got Mother and Joseph on the line with us, I told them that they had to help me. I couldn't take Gordon's abuse any longer, and I knew he was going to kill me if I didn't get away from him as soon as possible. They reacted with the utmost urgency.

"Randy, get on a plane *now*!" Joseph said. "Go to New York, and bring your sister home."

I had never felt so much love and support from my family as I did in that moment. It was as if they lifted a huge burden from me, which I had been struggling to carry on my own for so long. For once, I didn't feel so alone. I hadn't been this happy in many, many years.

Quickly, I told Randy where I was staying and warned him of my circumstances. I knew that if he tried to call me directly, Gordon could easily intercept his call.

"Don't contact me," I said. "I'll call you."

I managed to replace the receiver in its cradle, hide

my phone book, and climb back into bed, all before Gordon got out of the shower. I was exhausted from all of the morning's fear and stress, but I was also elated that I had accomplished even this much. At the same time, I was terrified of the moment that Gordon came back into the bedroom, in case he had heard me on the phone. I understood that it was important to act as normal as possible. This was an effort, given everything I was feeling, but I managed to do so. As Gordon got ready to leave, I said as little as possible.

Finally, Gordon left for the office, and I could tell that he hadn't suspected a thing.

"Put the dead bolt on the door," he said, as always. "And don't open it for anyone."

Yeah, whatever, I thought. "Yes, Gordon" was what I actually said.

I couldn't believe I had made it this far without his knowing anything, but I was not free yet. I had to be cautious until I actually left the hotel. Until then, there was a risk that Gordon might come back at any moment, since he never told me his plans. I stayed in my pajamas all day, so he wouldn't think anything was up, in case he did return.

There was nothing to do but wait, which was excruciating. I knew the flight from Los Angeles to New York took about five and a half hours, but it seemed like a lifetime to me.

Randy, hurry up, please hurry up, please, I kept saying to myself.

When I felt as if enough time had passed that he

should be well on his way, I dared to make one more phone call to Randy. He told me that he and our cousin Tony Whitehead were en route, and that he had a plan. In case Gordon came back before they could reach me, Randy would have a girl contact the suite when he was downstairs, so Gordon wouldn't hear Randy's voice on the line and suspect he was there to rescue me.

"If he's not there," Randy said, "I'm going to knock like this." He made a sound that mimicked the pattern of the knocks, so I would recognize it. "Open the door, and we'll have an elevator waiting, and a car downstairs to take us back home to Los Angeles, where you belong."

I was so excited that I could hardly stand to wait. Every time I thought I heard a noise outside, I was convinced that it was Gordon coming home, and my terror deepened.

Finally, the girl called, just as Randy had said she would. I told her that Gordon was not home, and it was safe for them to rescue me. Then, the knock came.

When I heard the sound, my heart began to beat almost as loudly in my chest. For a brief moment I didn't think I would actually be able to go through with it. Then I forced myself to move through the fear, said a quick prayer, and got ready to move.

Okay, it's time.

I jumped up, put on some pants, but didn't take the time to change out of my pajama top. I grabbed my purse, which contained no money or credit cards, and nothing more valuable than a lipstick, except for three possessions that were priceless: my Bible, my passport,

and a DAT recording, which contained all of the music
for my live show, which I had thought to grab. I'd re-
trieved it from its hiding place and put it in my bag,
knowing that it would help me rebuild my career.

This is it! I'm making a clean escape.

I was terrified that I would leave, only to run into
Gordon in the hallway or the lobby. My adrenaline was
racing, and my nerves were so frayed that I was almost
hysterical as I reached the door.

"I'm here," Randy said from the hallway.

Just hearing my brother's familiar voice, and knowing that he had my family's support behind him, added
to my strength. I opened the door to my hotel room and
breathed the first air of my newfound freedom.

I could hardly believe that this was all happening.
Randy was standing just outside the door, and Tony
was in the hallway, holding the elevator for us so I could
make a quick exit. I hugged Randy and closed the door
behind me. It made only a faint click when it snapped
shut, symbolizing all of the doors that Gordon had
locked me behind over the years. I froze for a moment,
right there outside my prison, unable to believe I was
really free.

"Come on," Randy said. "Come on."

Even though I hadn't seen either of them for years,
I wasn't thinking how great it was to be reunited with
them. All I could think of were the basics of my escape:
*Is the elevator open? He can't catch me. Is he going to be
waiting in the lobby for me? He can't catch me. Am I really
escaping? He can't catch me.*

The elevator seemed to take forever to descend to the hotel's ground floor. I was sure that when the doors slid open, Gordon would be standing on the other side. But the lobby was clear. I felt as if my legs were going to collapse beneath me, but they held me up, and I ran as fast as I could. It was hard to hurry because I was weak. I felt as if someone were taking my breath away, and as if my stomach were about to fall out of my body, all at the same time. I couldn't speak or even catch my breath. But, somehow, we made it out onto the sidewalk.

As promised, Randy had a limo waiting. I jumped into the car, Tony and Randy on either side of me. The door closed, and we pulled away from the curb and into traffic.

As we made our way to La Guardia Airport, I kept thinking the same thought again and again: *Did I really escape? Did I really escape? Did I really escape?*

Even though I was in the limo with my brother and cousin, and Gordon was nowhere in sight, I couldn't believe I had actually gotten free of him. A part of me was ecstatic, as if this was the first day of my new life. But at the same time, I was still absolutely terrified. As we put greater distance between Gordon and me, a sense of euphoria filled me.

Wow! I did it! This is it, I finally took the first step, I thought.

But the shock of what I had been through, and the way that everything was happening so fast, were so intense that I couldn't be happy for long. I could barely focus on the words Randy was speaking as he tried to talk to me. I know that he told me it was good to see me, and that he asked me how I felt, and if I needed anything. But I can't recall the exact details of what he said during that car ride, except for the most important question he asked me.

"Are you okay?"

"Yeah," I said. "But I don't know if he's following us."

"No, no," Randy said. "He's not following us."

No matter what I said, Randy knew I wasn't okay. And now that I *am* okay, I can look back and see that I wasn't okay in that moment. Tony has since told me how painful it was to find me in such a state, shaking, afraid of everything—more than anything, afraid of Gordon, certain that he was going to find me and kill me.

I was also afraid of myself. I knew that if Gordon came after me, I probably wouldn't be strong enough to resist his demands that I return to him. Even years after I had freed myself from his hold and healed the wounds he had inflicted on me, I was aware that I was still at great risk of falling under his influence again. I went so far as to make my family and all of the people around me promise that if they ever saw me with Gordon, they would intervene on my behalf. I let them know that they must step in, even if I told them that I was fine and that I was going off with Gordon of my own free will. When Gordon was around, there was no such thing, and I knew that I could end up right back where I had been.

As our limo neared the airport, I kept looking out the window, expecting Gordon to be in every car that pulled up next to us in traffic. I was convinced that he had somehow known about my whole plan, and that he was just playing with me now, letting me think I had succeeded, only to come down on me, hard, in the final moments of my escape.

"How do you feel?" Randy asked.

"I don't know," I said. "I'll feel better once I'm on the plane."

Even at the airport, I didn't feel safe at all. I just knew that I was going to get caught, and that when I did, Gordon was going to take me back, and he was going to kill me. A new certainty was beginning to grip me as well. As good as it was to see members of my family, and as much as I appreciated what they had done for me, I also knew that I had to get away from them as soon as I possibly could. I couldn't put them at risk by getting them involved with my problems. No matter how fearful I was of Gordon, I was strong enough to take him on without endangering anyone that I loved. I had already decided to do the rest on my own.

I was well aware that I had a long battle ahead of me. But I was willing to face whatever was to come, simply because I had risked so much to even get this far, and I knew that everything was at stake—my pride, my career, my life, and the life of my brother Michael.

I also knew that Gordon wasn't just going to sit back and let me get away from him. I often wished that I could have been a fly on the wall when he got back to our hotel suite on that day and discovered that the impossible had happened, and I had actually broken free. But I didn't have to see his face to know most certainly that it was gripped with pure rage. I didn't have to speak to him to know that in that first moment he was already formulating a plan. He would come after me, and he would not rest until he had done everything in his power to get me back, or to destroy me in trying to reassert his power. He had always promised me that if I tried to escape, he would kill me, and I believed him. But another promise in my mind meant much more to me in that moment. I had promised God that if he helped me escape, I would never go back to that man. This was one promise I intended to keep, no matter what Gordon did to me.

16

~~~

FREE AT LAST,
FREE AT LAST

I thought that physically freeing myself from Gordon's control would be the hardest part of leaving him. But I was already beginning to realize that my psychological bondage was even more binding. Once Randy, Tony, and I boarded the plane together, I settled back in my seat and tried to comprehend that I was really and truly free. But my mind was too scattered and confused to hold on to any one thought for more than a few moments. I felt like a lost soul, jumpy and unsure of myself, nervously shaking at every little sound I heard around me. I kept looking over my shoulder, wondering if Gordon had boarded the plane without my knowledge and was sitting behind me, waiting quietly for the moment I got off in Los Angeles, so he could sneak up from behind and kill me.

Then, my thoughts went in the last direction I would have expected during these first precious moments of freedom. It was as if Gordon were still my puppet master, as he liked to call himself, pulling my strings, and controlling my mind. I began blaming myself for having left him, and thinking that my situation would have improved if I had only stayed and tried harder. Maybe he didn't mean to abuse me. Maybe it was my fault. Maybe if I had just done what he told me to do and never said anything, I wouldn't have given him a reason to beat me. I now know that these types of thoughts are exactly how abused women are conditioned to think by their abusers, and that they can be even more difficult to escape than the physical abuse itself. But at the time, I only knew that I didn't feel the least bit euphoric. I felt guilty, frightened, and ashamed, and I couldn't see a clear way forward to a better life.

We had taken a flight that was bound for Los Angeles, but midway through the trip, we were rerouted to Las Vegas. As far as I was concerned, God pointed the plane in that direction so I could get my divorce. But by the time we arrived, I was in worse shape than I had been back in New York. I tried to distract myself by looking out my window at the beautiful hotels below us as the plane began descending over the runway. But the closer we got to the ground, the more I noticed the hives that were breaking out on my arms, neck, and back. My stomach began cramping to the point where I thought I was going to pass out.

God, please give me strength, I kept saying to myself.

Behind me, I could hear all of the other passengers laughing and having so much fun, discussing their plans for their stay in Vegas, because of our detour. As I continued to look out the window, I saw the MGM Grand Hotel, which brought me back to my childhood. This was where my entire family had first performed together in our variety show in the seventies. I had given my debut performance there, and received my introduction to the family business, when I was sixteen. Back then, Randy was only eleven, and he was the baby boy of the family. As his older sister, I had always felt that it was my responsibility to watch over him and make sure he was safe. Now, more than two decades later, he was the one making sure I was safe and helping me to escape from the living hell of my life with Gordon. I loved Randy deeply in that moment for his act of selfless courage, and that he did exactly what Joseph asked him to do without thinking of the risk to himself.

I will always love Randy so much for that. Gordon always promised to kill me if I ever tried to escape, and Randy made sure that I had the courage to leave and didn't die trying. I thank both Randy and my cousin Tony for helping me get free of the man who not only brought misery upon me, but also my whole family, and threatened Michael.

While I was reminiscing, tears began pouring down my face. This was the first time I had cried since escaping Gordon. Much of this emotion was certainly the result of everything I had experienced that day. Part of me was overwhelmed that I was free, and that I could live a normal life and be myself again. Another part of me couldn't believe I could possibly get away with this and was imagining the consequences when he caught me. But I was also moved by just how much I had missed my family, and all the wonderful times we used to have together, before Gordon took me away. Even more than that, I was grasping for the first time just how much I had missed out on in my entire life. As a child, I had been isolated from the real world because I was raised a Jehovah's Witness in a famous family. As an adult, I had spent almost a decade hidden away from humanity because of Gordon.

I was also crying because, as reassuring as it felt to be reunited with my family, I knew that I was going to have to face Gordon's wrath and put my life back together on my own. I was determined to do so, but the thought of facing all of this by myself seemed completely overwhelming. Of course my family wanted to help me, and I appreciated that, but I refused to burden them with the pressures of my personal life.

When the flight attendant approached me and asked me to please move my seat forward for our final descent, I did so without looking at her because I didn't want her to see the tears that streaked my face.

"Ms. Jackson, I'm sure you're going to have a fun time here in Vegas," she said brightly.

I was so confused about my life that I didn't know how to answer her, so I pretended not to hear her.

I hated to be rude, but it was difficult for me to speak even a single word.

The plane finally landed. Here we were in Viva Las Vegas, Sin City, the destination to which people from around the world flocked to stay in the best of the best hotels, see the most dazzling shows, eat at the finest restaurants, and gamble their life savings on the chance they might hit the jackpot. As a nongambler, I had always felt removed from this aspect of Vegas. But in this moment I certainly understood what it meant to gamble. I felt that I was taking the biggest risk of my life just trying to make it through McCarran Airport without being killed by the man I was sure awaited me there.

Our flight was full, and I stood eagerly at the plane's door, waiting for it to open so I could be the first one off, just in case Gordon really was somewhere among the passengers. I didn't want him to have the opportunity to get off first and ambush me.

As soon as I left the plane, two airport securities escorted me through the airport. I was walking as fast as I could, with Randy, Tony, and the security guards surrounding me, when a couple jumped right in front of me. Because my nerves were already shattered, I screamed. They apologized for scaring me, then asked for an autograph. I wanted so badly to decline, but I couldn't disappoint them. All I could think of was Joseph saying to us again and again when we were children, "This is part of the business you're in. Expect it to happen. And if you don't like it, then get out of the business."

The problem was that, as every entertainer knows, if I stopped to sign one autograph and take one picture, it would attract attention to myself. Then, everyone else would see me and try to get an autograph or a picture from me as well. I tried to strike a compromise. I signed their autograph, but I kept walking quickly as I did so. The whole time, I was looking over my shoulder, wondering if Gordon was going to sneak up behind me and kill me right in front of everyone. I believed he was capable of it, especially in his town, Vegas. As the gathering crowd made me the center of attention, I became even more nervous.

If he sees me because of the crowd, I'm dead!

The people around me were asking me questions. In my panic, I couldn't focus on what they were saying. I tried to be polite, but it was becoming increasingly difficult for me. I just wanted to get out of there as quickly as possible.

Now, to make matters worse, the same couple who had originally requested an autograph asked if I would stop for a moment to take a picture with them.

I smiled, nodded, and tried to act natural as the husband hugged me and posed for a picture. All that the wife had to do was hit the button, and I'd be on my way. Of course, I had to get stopped by the one couple who didn't know how to work their camera.

"Honey, all you have to do is . . . ," the husband said, pointing at the camera.

Oh, boy, here we go, I thought.

Finally, he seemed to realize that his wife wasn't any closer to figuring it out. "Here, honey, you get in the picture, and I'll take it of you two," he said.

The husband stopped hugging me and switched places with his wife, taking the camera from her as he did so. While she hugged me and smiled for the photo, I began seeing people walk by who I recognized from my flight. I felt certain that Gordon was getting closer to appearing out of the throng and killing me, and I prayed that this moment would soon be over so I could finally make my escape.

Meanwhile, the couple with the camera were oblivious to my distress. They were just as happy as could be, laughing and chattering away to each other and to me.

Little do they know that they're about to witness my murder, I thought grimly.

The husband was still playing around with the camera. Now *he* couldn't get it to work either. Every second felt like an eternity as I stood there trying my best to smile, and feeling as if I were going to crawl out of my skin if I had to remain there with them for even one instant longer.

Finally I snapped. "I'm sorry, but we'll have to do it next time. I'm really in a rush."

As filled with panic as I was, I felt bad to disappoint them. I do realize that most people don't get to meet entertainers every day. When they do, they feel as if they will never again have the opportunity, so they want their moment to be special. Under any other circumstances, I would never have been so abrupt with them. Even on that day, of all days, I tried to be patient, but I just couldn't. I felt that my life was in jeopardy.

I was so grateful to finally start walking again, with the security and my family members closing in around me. I sped up my pace and finally made it to where the car was waiting for us outside the airport. I got into the car quickly, with Randy and Tony close behind me, and sighed in relief.

I had made it. I was alive.

The famous line from Dr. Martin Luther King, Jr. had never meant so much to me before: "Free at last, free at last, thank God Almighty, I am free at last."

The only problem was that now I was in Las Vegas, a town in which Gordon had a lot of connections. His brother, ex-wife, children, grandchildren, nieces, nephews, and many of his friends lived here. He had a great deal of power in the city. It might have seemed like an unlikely place for me to settle if I wanted to get away from him, but I had roots here of my own. I had a home that I had purchased a few years prior, or so I thought, and I just knew it was the perfect place to begin starting over. Of course, I soon learned that I didn't own my home in Las Vegas, as I thought I did. Gordon may have bought it with my money, but he didn't buy it in my name. So, technically, it didn't belong to me. It belonged to him. I had left him knowing that my situation would be difficult, but not caring, as long as I was finally away from him. Now I was finding out that my circumstances were even worse than I had expected because of the many underhanded things he did behind my back that I didn't learn about until I got free. And, of course, as I had feared, I still had to continue fighting for my freedom, because Gordon was not quite done with me yet.

17

BABY STEPS

When we arrived at my home in Las Vegas, it was just before dawn, and I was exhausted and emotionally depleted. With the time difference between New York and Nevada, it was now early morning, and I had been traveling all night with only two hours of uneasy sleep that I managed to catch on the plane. All I wanted was to get somewhere that felt safe and finally exhale and begin to process everything. But even at my comforting home, I felt that my life was in the gravest danger. Gordon had always told me that anyone could be convinced to commit murder for a certain amount of money, and I had no problem believing that he could easily find someone to take on such a job. Although it was reassuring to have Randy and Tony there, I didn't think that they would be able to stand up to Gordon.

Randy called Mother to let her know that we had arrived safely in Las Vegas. When he got off the phone, he had a message for me: "Mother wants you to come back home to Hayvenhurst."

After all of the evil stories about Mother that Gordon had planted in my mind over the years, this thought terrified me even more than the fear of being alone in my home. If I went home to Hayvenhurst, I was certain that she would kill me. I burst into tears.

As I cried, I could see that Randy was confused by my reaction, but I knew that I couldn't begin to explain.

"La Toya, what's wrong with you?" Randy asked.

"I just can't go back to Hayvenhurst."

Although I had wanted to stay in Las Vegas only long enough to pick up some of my belongings, I realized, once there, it was the place where I felt the most safe at that moment.

"I'll stay here in Vegas instead," I said. "Besides, this is the fastest place in the world to get a divorce, and that's what I need right now."

"Okay, if that's what you want, here's what we're gonna do," Randy said. "First thing in the morning, we're gonna go get you examined by a doctor so we can file a report of Gordon's abuse."

"Why?" I was still trying to make sense of all that was happening.

"Because you need a report. You need the records. And then, we're gonna take you right down, get a restraining order, and file for a divorce."

It was a relief to let my brother take care of me. I was still in shock, and I felt incapable of doing much more than sitting and worrying what Gordon might be planning to do to me next.

After the past twenty-four hours, everyone was exhausted. Randy and Tony lay down and napped for several hours. I went into my room, but was still far too nervous and worked up to even think about sleeping.

As soon as Randy and Tony woke up, Randy called Joseph, who lives in Las Vegas. When Randy told Joseph the news that he had rescued me from Gordon, Joseph wanted us to come over to his house immediately. I was excited to see Joseph after so many years, but we told him that first we needed to take care of some necessary business, and that I would visit him as soon as I could.

After that initial reconciliation with Mother and Joseph, I began hearing from other members of my family. Jermaine called with a suggestion that echoed Mother's request.

"Well, why don't you come live at Hayvenhurst?" He was living there at the time.

"No, no, no," I said. "I have to do this on my own. I need to be independent."

I knew that if I became reaccustomed to having people take care of me, I would lose my personal power and self-direction. It was almost as if I were being asked to pick up right where I had been—sheltered and naïve—when I got into this whole mess with Gordon in the first place. Now, after being under Gordon's thumb for so long, I really had something to prove to myself and the world. I was a grown woman. I was independent. I was strong. I knew that I was quite capable of taking care of myself. But I still had to prove to myself and everyone else that, even at the lowest point of my life, I was going to pull myself out of this situation without the continuing help of anyone else.

My first issue was money. Gordon had taken and controlled every single penny I earned. I was so desperate to leave Gordon that I had walked out with nothing, and gladly. No credit cards. No bank accounts. No credit. He kept me so isolated that I had no friends, and nobody outside of my family to approach for help. Now that I was free, I had to face that, at forty years old, it would cost money to start over.

Because I had worked hard and been paid well since the age of sixteen, I had always lived a lifestyle of diamonds and furs and multi-international homes, without thinking about the value of any of it. Now I didn't know how I was going to even feed myself or pay my most basic bills, which was also an unknown responsibility. I was determined not to take any money from my family, and I had just cut off my ability to earn money by fleeing from the person who had secured all of my work for almost a decade. I had absolutely no idea what I was going to do. Once I was able to start working again, I knew that I could bring in enough money to set up my household in Las Vegas. This was why I had thought to bring along the DAT in my otherwise empty purse. But I didn't know how long it would be before my return to performing could happen.

Then, as I was sitting in my room on that first day, a

memory surfaced. Years earlier, and long before I ever hid the money I was paid to appear on that children's show in South America, I had gotten my hands on a bundle of cash without Gordon's knowledge. I can't honestly remember how I even did it because he kept such tight control over me in those years. But, somehow, I had done it, and once I had the money in my hand, I knew that I needed to hide it in case I ever had the chance to get free of him. Back then, emancipation had seemed like an impossible dream. But I knew that I had stumbled upon a rare chance to help myself. I had been in Las Vegas at the time, so I had stashed the money somewhere in my condo.

The question was, could I find my hiding place again, and would the money still be there? I couldn't even remember how much it was. I raced into my walk-in closet and stood staring at row upon row of shoes. I've always had a particular fondness for boots, and dozens of pairs were all lined up neatly on racks. I ran my finger over their toes, selected a brown suede boot, and pulled it down. Then I turned it upside down and shook it over the floor. Nothing. I tried the other boot in the pair. Again, nothing. But after several tries, I found the boot that was my long-ago hiding spot. When I reached in, I pulled out the bundle of cash that I had forgotten about until just this day. I felt giddy with excitement as I held the $27,000 in my hand. My immediate financial problems were solved. Now I just had to make sure I kept myself alive long enough to spend it properly, at least until I could get myself back on my feet.

First, I had a locksmith come over and change the locks immediately. I knew Gordon would soon arrive in Las Vegas and try to get me back. He had already begun calling me almost as soon as I got there. I'm sure he would have been bombarding me even before then, but I didn't have a cell phone where he could reach me. Gordon had never allowed me to have one for fear that I would use it to devise an escape plan or communicate with the outside world. The phone system at my building in Las Vegas was such that any incoming calls had to go through the main switchboard, which then patched the caller through to my unit. Because of this, when the phone rang in my condo, I had no forewarning of who was on the other end.

I knew Gordon would call me, but it was still a shock to my system when I actually heard his voice. The first time the phone rang after I got to my Vegas condo, it was him. I was surprised by what he said to me instead of the threats I had expected:

"I love you. Come back. Get on a plane and come back. I'll give you all of your money and accounts."

Although I didn't anticipate hearing this from him, I wasn't fooled in the slightest.

"It's over and don't call me again," I said.

When the phone rang, I was always terrified. Gordon had made up some lie about me and given the condo's phone number to reporters from TV shows and magazines, who called constantly. Even after I hung up on Gordon that first time, he wouldn't give up. He began calling me nonstop with more of the same attempts at sweet talk.

"I am so sorry," he said. "I promise you I'll never, ever hit you again if you come back to me. As a matter of fact, I'll give you all of your money. I'll turn everything over to you. I promise you this. All I want is for you to come back."

"Gordon, it's over," I said. "I'm done with you. It's over."

"But I'll give you all of your money back," he pleaded. "I'll give you everything. I'll never hit you again. All you have to do is come back to me."

"It's over."

It felt good to hang up the phone on him and be able to shut him out of my life, even in this small way. But I knew better than to think that this would be the last time he would try to convince me to return, either with words or with physical intimidation and violence.

Hearing Gordon's voice was enough to fill me with dread and redouble my determination to do everything in my power to ensure that he would never recapture me. As exhausted and overwhelmed as I was, I got started on the list of things I needed to do right away. The first stop that Randy, Tony, and I made was the hospital. I had a doctor examine and photograph the wounds Gordon had inflicted on me with the Coca-Cola bottle just before I left him. Next, I went to the police station to file a domestic-abuse report against Gordon. Then, I went to the Family Courthouse and filed a restraining order. Again, I was asked to disrobe so pictures could be taken of my bruises. Afterward, I met with a police officer for three hours and answered all of the questions necessary to file a second abuse report.

After helping me during my first day of freedom in Las Vegas, Randy and Tony reluctantly went back to LA without me. I continued breaking away from Gordon. Although I started each morning early, the days didn't seem long enough. There was so much paperwork to be filled out, so much yet to fear. In the midst of all of this, I began to look for an attorney who could handle my divorce. I had physically gotten free of Gordon, but I was still his wife. I hated the thought of being linked to him in any way.

I knew Gordon was going to fight me with everything he had over the divorce, but I was planning to make it easy on my end. He could have everything he had taken from me, even though it was the culmination of my life's work thus far, as long as I could be done with him forever.

One by one, I approached all of the top divorce attorneys in the city, and one by one, they all turned me down. That's how well connected Gordon was in Las Vegas. He was even close with Oscar Goodman, who was a well-known and respected Mafia attorney, who even became mayor of Las Vegas in 1999.

None of the city's many divorce lawyers wanted to handle my case because they were either hoping to handle Gordon's case for him, or they didn't want to cross him. The few attorneys that seemed agreeable to working with me showed their true colors within minutes of our first conversation. As soon as we began discussing my case, I saw them siding with Gordon, and so I had to get rid of them immediately. Finally, I had gone through pretty much every viable attorney in Las Vegas without finding anyone I felt comfortable working with, and I feared I would never find anyone to take my case.

While on the phone with my brother Jermaine, I mentioned my inability to find an attorney who would approach my case with fairness and not side with Gordon.

"I know a great attorney," Jermaine said. "And he will not side with Gordon. He will definitely be for you. I promise you that."

"Are you sure, Jermaine? Because this is what's happening, and I don't like it."

"He's in LA. Give him a call."

I trusted my brother, and I didn't have any other options. So I called Brian Oxman, the attorney who Jermaine recommended. When I spoke to him, he didn't try to intimidate or manipulate me the way the dirty Las Vegas lawyers had done. He just got down to business and went through all of the initial questions that we needed to cover right away. I immediately felt that he cared about my case and was going to protect me. After everything I had been through, this was such a relief. I could not have been happier to finally get the divorce proceedings started. That first day, we stayed on the phone for hours and worked all night. It was the same thing the next night, and the next night, and every single night after that, until he understood my relationship with Gordon completely. I wasn't sleeping anyway, so I was happy to finally put all of my nervous energy to use in a constructive way. After having been belittled for so long and told I would be nothing without Gordon, I was so happy to see that I had managed some type of accomplishment on my own. Not only that, the achievement was going to ensure that I remained free forever.

Even with my separation from Gordon well under way, I was unable to sleep because of the manic energy that raced through me day and night, and because I was a bundle of nerves that jumped at the slightest sound or movement. As soon as I received the restraining order, I made a point to inform all of the security guards in my building that it was in effect against Gordon. I let them know that he, and anyone else I had named along with him in its pages, were not to set foot on the grounds or enter the building. Later I was told that the condo actually belonged to Gordon. But my attorney got permission from the judge handling my divorce case to let me stay there until the proceedings were settled, which meant that Gordon could not come into the building without violating the terms of my restraining order. This was a small relief, but it wasn't enough to allow me to get a single night's rest.

It didn't help that Gordon kept calling. I was through with him, but he wouldn't give up. He was done pretending to be Mr. Nice Guy. His mean and nasty ways returned.

"It's finished," I kept saying. "It's over. You just don't understand. It's over."

"It's not over," he said. "You'll see. You're coming back to me and you don't realize it."

"No, it's *over*," I said one last time before hanging up.

When he couldn't get to me through threats and intimidation, he resorted to his usual secondary approach. He expanded his threats to include my family. Because he continued to wish evil upon all Jacksons, he seemed to enjoy this tactic.

"I'm going to be the thorn in your family's side," he said. "Don't ever think that you're going to get away from me. I'm not done with you yet. I'm going to make the world hate your guts. You watch me. This is just the beginning."

I had many reasons to believe that he would keep his promise. He had already done a good job of ruining my reputation within the entertainment industry and making me a joke in the eyes of much of the world. There was no reason for it, either. At least when he was threatening and abusing me to keep control of my bank accounts, he was personally profiting from his actions. But he harmed me in these other ways simply because he was malicious and truly hated me, and by extension, all of my family, just because of the blessings we had received in life.

Soon, he spoke the words I feared most since I left him:

"Okay, I'm on my way out there. If you won't come home to me, I'm coming to you."

I didn't say anything in response to this, and I specifically didn't tell him that I had taken out a restraining order against him. I was hoping that when he arrived in Las Vegas, he would unknowingly break the rules of the restraining order and be arrested. Because I was sure that his first move would be to come after me, I knew I would have just cause to put the protective documents to work on my behalf.

Of course, in typical Gordon fashion, he didn't just come to Las Vegas to force me to return to New York. He also called a big press conference at the airport so he could tell even more lies and further attempt to destroy my family's name. As soon as I heard this, I called the airport directly and begged them to make sure that Gordon was served with his restraining order as soon as he stepped off his plane. The man I spoke with was not exactly helpful because he blamed me for what was turning out to be a circus at the airport. Apparently, Gordon's press conference had thrown the entire place into complete chaos, making it difficult for them to keep planes going in and out of the airport. Luckily, Gordon's flight was delayed, and he didn't make it to his precious press conference. Whether he successfully completed a second one, I don't know. Although I was free to watch the news for the first time in years, I was so beaten down by everything that I had been through that I could barely focus on the TV. Besides, I didn't want to know what was happening out there in the world, particularly when it came to any additional difficulties that Gordon was creating for my family and me.

18

STARTING OVER

Later I would spend a great deal of time thinking about my years with Gordon and everything he had done to me. The severity of what I had experienced made me analytical. I pondered what in Gordon's background had caused him to become such an evil aggressor, as well as what had made me so susceptible to his control. These reflections led me to understand a great deal about Gordon and myself. They also allowed me, years later, to observe manipulation and abuse in Michael's life. But it took ages for me to reach the level of healing where I was able to even think about what I had endured.

In the first weeks and months after I left Gordon, my mind was so discombobulated that I was not able to think about my freedom and how I felt about it. It was all I could do to make it through each day. I was such a nervous wreck that I was afraid of everything. I was afraid of my shadow. I was afraid of every sound that I heard. Even though I lived in a secure building, and I had security guards outside my door in my first days of freedom, I was convinced that Gordon was lurking outside my door. I was sure that he was coming after me from above. I lived on the twenty-seventh floor, and the only thing up there was a crawl space, the twenty-eighth floor, then the roof and sky. But I heard voices from above talking, and although I knew Gordon couldn't be up there, I was convinced he was. Even though, logically, I knew it was only workers doing their jobs, I couldn't shake my suspicion that Gordon was everywhere.

Other than the first few days when I went to the hospital and the courthouse with Randy and Tony, I didn't dare to leave my house for six months. I rarely even went close to my front door, fearing I was going to be killed. I was terrified to drive because I worried about what I would do if Gordon saw me on the street. I was afraid to even go down to the rubbish chute in my hall because I was convinced that someone would come out of another door and attack me. Not only was I afraid of Gordon, but also I was still afraid of Mother, whom I had not yet seen since leaving Gordon. I feared that she could be waiting down the hall with a knife, as Gordon's guards had told me so many times that she was.

For months, I stayed in every day and every night. It was almost as if I were hibernating. Finally, though, I knew that I had to start making myself leave the house as the first step in rebuilding my life. Every morning, I decided that this would be the day.

I have to get out of the house today.

I would get up, get dressed, and try to force myself.

You're doing it.

I would try, but I couldn't even make myself stand up and walk toward the door.

No, you can't do it, I would think, disappointed in myself.

The next day, I would get up, get dressed, and try to force myself once again.

But as much as I tried, the results were always the same.

Each day, I would progress a little farther, until I actually made it to the front door. I opened the door and willed myself to walk out. But I still couldn't do it. So I closed the door and accepted that I was still too afraid to leave the house.

I had no contact with people or the outside world. I didn't have a single friend or any staff, and my phone never rang unless it was Gordon. I would order food three times a day just to feel that connection with human life. This was the highlight of my day, and I couldn't wait for the delivery person to arrive, just so I would hear a human voice. I was still too afraid to let a stranger enter my home, so I would tell the person to leave my delivery outside in the hall. I would slide the money under the door, then, when the person left, I would open the door really fast, grab the food, and close it before Gordon or anyone else could ambush me. It wasn't much. But I felt that at least some kind of human interaction was happening.

I viewed the entire scenario with Gordon as cancer, and I told myself that I had to remove all of the cancer or else risk that it would come back. So I completely eliminated everyone from my life that had ever been involved with him. But then, when it came time to hire new staff, I couldn't bring myself to do so. I had no way of knowing if the person I employed might be someone who knew Gordon, especially as he had so much pull in Las Vegas. It would be so easy for any employees to go back and tell Gordon intimate details about my life. They could reveal my daily routine to him, or my whereabouts at any time. They could even make him a copy of my house keys. So I decided, as lonely as it was, that I could not risk bringing anyone into my home. It was an absolutely horrible way to live—all alone, no staff, no real knowledge of life, sitting in my condo, watching the sun rise and fall outside my bedroom window every day, scared for my life, wondering if today would be my last day on earth—but unfortunately, going through all of this was a necessary part of my healing.

Not only did my lack of staff add to my loneliness, but it also meant that I was learning to do even the most basic tasks for myself for the first time ever. For as long as I could remember, when I was growing up and throughout my adult life, I had always had people around to take care of my needs. I was eight years old when I moved from Gary, Indiana, to the Los Angeles home that my family bought in the wake of the Jackson 5's incredible success. I was too young to remember the hard times that came before that when Joseph and

Mother were trying to raise nine children on the money that Joseph earned at the mill. I do know that we were never hungry, and I was never aware of wanting for something. Although my parents have never discussed it, now that I look back on those days, I know it must have been extremely difficult for them at times. I'm so grateful for the childhood they gave me in spite of this, and that they never took their stress out on us children or even let us know how hard things were.

When I arrived in California with Mother, my sisters, and Randy, I was incredibly excited to be reunited with my other brothers, who had already been living in Los Angeles for nearly a year. It marked a total life change for my family, as we were not only moving to a new state, we were also moving into a bigger house, we were driving nicer cars, and we suddenly had a lot of people working for us. Because I was just a kid, I assumed this was how everyone lived in California. Our new family friends, such as Diana Ross and Berry Gordy, had a similar lifestyle. No tabloids or entertainment programs were on TV at the time, so I didn't know that my family had crossed into the territory of stars that lived with privilege. I soon forgot what it had been like before, when I was eight years old and living in Gary, Indiana.

Because I grew up with so much, and everyone that my family socialized with had just as much, my material possessions weren't significant to me, and money had no real value. I thought it was completely normal to attend private schools and have tutors, chauffeurs, housekeepers, cooks, personal assistants, full-time security guards, and gardeners, as well as private planes at our disposal, and every other luxury that people could possibly have. Naturally I took things for granted and didn't realize how truly blessed I was.

Having always lived in this way, when I finally left home, I immediately hired staff of my own. My siblings had all done this as well, and I was earning enough money to do so myself. I didn't think twice about it. I hired full-time staff, and they traveled the world with me. One of my assistant's jobs was to pack and unpack my luggage when we traveled. She ironed all of my clothes and put them all on hangers. Every day she also put a new set of clean satin sheets on my bed. My other assistant handled my day-to-day schedule and needs. My security guards never left my side and made sure I was always protected. My cook's only job was to prepare healthy foods that I liked and keep me eating on a proper schedule.

The only dose of perspective I ever got that this wasn't how everybody in the world lived was from Gordon when he first weaseled his way in close to me.

"Wow, I've never seen anyone live like this before," he said.

I had no idea what he meant. "Like what?" I asked.

"With a staff of people working for them like this. This is like royalty."

When he saw the lifestyle that was possible for someone who earned the type of success my family did from show business, Gordon wanted to live like royalty, too. Soon enough, my life became his life, and my staff became his staff. After that, my staff began to fear him and realize that I had no power in the household, so they listened only to him. When that wasn't enough control for Gordon, and he had all of my money in his power, he hired his own staff.

Now that I was living without staff for the first time since I was eight years old, I was facing a daily reality that was completely foreign to me. Feeling out of place in my own life only added to the already uncomfortable process of trying to discover who I was without Gordon or my family around to define me.

Gordon continued to torment me, even if he was only doing it from a distance for now. Any time he did get through to me on the telephone, he laughed at me, and that I thought I had won my independence from him.

"Don't worry," he said. "You'll be back. I'll get you back. You'll see."

Although I never said anything to suggest that I believed him, a part of me wondered why he was saying this again and again, and what he knew that I didn't. I was sure that he had an elaborate plan in the works. But I think the truth is that he spoke like this simply because he underestimated me and believed that I was weaker than I really was.

Well, I had gained strength.

The days passed one after the other, and still Gordon didn't get me back. I think this actually surprised us both. He wasn't as invincible as either of us had thought he was. I could also tell that he was not expecting me to get the restraining order and to set the divorce in motion as quickly as I did. But the law didn't matter to him. In his world, the rules were meant to be broken, and he was allowed to take whatever he wanted, no matter the cost to others or the commandments against his actions. So he tried everything he possibly could to get me back, or to at least ruin my life.

Gordon attempted to get me out of my Las Vegas condo, where we had both lived, which I thought I had bought with my own money. He told the building's manager that he owned the condo, not me. I didn't know anything about any of these matters until I got a call from the building's management company.

"You have to get out," the manager said. "You don't even own this place."

"But that's not true," I said. "I do."

What I didn't realize at that time was that I didn't technically own the condo because, without my knowledge, Gordon had bought it with my money, but without putting it in my name. Luckily, once the divorce proceedings began, all of our assets were frozen, and I was allowed to stay in the Las Vegas condo free of charge until it was decided who owned it. This meant no monthly mortgage payments during this period, which allowed me to save on a major expense and help me stretch my nest egg until I began working again. Otherwise, I don't know where I would have gone. Gordon had switched the deeds to my penthouse in New York and my homes in Europe so they were not in my name either. He kept my cars from me. He gave away all of my beautiful Louis XV furniture, which I had in storage. It just went on and on. Every day, I would find out some new and terrible scheme that he had put in the works to destroy me.

Another major setback occurred around this time. Gordon had been taking all of my album royalties. When I got free of him, I expected to have that money start coming to me again every quarter, for the rest of my life, as it should have been all along. I needed the income to help me get back on my feet, so I was devastated to learn that Gordon had fixed it so these earnings would not return to me for another fourteen years. Everywhere I turned, I faced setback after setback, and I had no solid ground on which to stand. It was a battle, and I fought all the way. Some moments I was deeply discouraged, but I never gave up. Slowly, I started gaining strength. The whole time, I kept praying to God to help me in my time of persecution.

Please give me the strength to endure all of this. I cannot let this man win.

When Gordon realized he wasn't going to be able to gain access to me directly, his attacks on me became more subtle and psychological. The phone would ring and I would hear his familiar raspy voice on the other end.

"I'm watching you," he would say. "I see you. You just walked into your kitchen."

My condominium had floor-to-ceiling windows in every room, so I believed him when he said he was watching me, and his words made me afraid. I was convinced that he might shoot me through the glass. I kept the lights off and walked around in my own home like a criminal, ducking behind pieces of furniture to avoid being seen from outside. This went on for months.

An acquaintance of mine called to give me a warning that frightened me even more.

"You know the building across the street from the building where you live?" he said. "Well, Gordon was over there, looking for a unit. And he insisted on getting a unit that was on the same floor as you, and facing directly into your unit, so he would be eye level, looking across at you."

I felt those same icy tendrils of fear creep through me that I used to feel when Gordon walked into a room with that look he got on his face right before he beat me.

"How do you know this?" I asked, panic in my voice.

"Because I know the broker in the building that Gordon was working with. And I know that he insisted and said, 'No, I want a unit that looks directly into her unit.' "

Even though Gordon wasn't ultimately able to make this plan come true, he did somehow manage to continue watching me, which scared me no end. One day, nearly a year and a half after I left Gordon, I actually dared to leave my condo. During that time my brother Jackie's wife had passed, and so I went to Joseph's home in Vegas to be with my family. As soon as I got back to my condo, the phone rang.

"You just came home," Gordon said. "I'm watching you."

That just frightened the daylights out of me because what he said seemed to be true. I had only been gone for a short while, and somehow Gordon knew.

Throughout all of this, I kept my family at bay to protect them from Gordon and prove that I was strong enough to rebuild my own life. Gordon had promised on so many occasions that he would kill my various family members, or at least destroy them, and I couldn't bear the thought of anything happening to them because of me. So I decided that this was my battle and I had to face it alone. Not that my parents and siblings didn't try to assist me in many different ways. Starting with the moment that Randy and Tony helped me to make my dramatic escape, my family quickly stepped up to offer support and show me, to my great relief, that the long estrangement that Gordon had caused between us was finally over. Before Randy flew back to Los Angeles, he took the important step of reconnecting me with Mother and Joseph. Because I still feared Mother in the wake of Gordon's many untruths about her, I needed some more time before I was able to leave Gordon's lies behind and enjoy a true reconciliation with her. But my reunion with Joseph was swift and emotional.

When Randy brought me to see Joseph on my first day in Las Vegas, I had not seen or spoken to my father in years. It was wonderful to be there with him because I finally felt safe. I knew that, if Gordon did try to capture me, Joseph would protect me.

My father greeted me warmly and gave me the biggest hug. "La Toya, I'm so happy that you're away from that guy. If he comes in here, I've got something for him."

These words were exactly what I needed to hear at this time of great anxiety and fear in my life. Although I had already decided to stand up to Gordon on my own, it soothed me to know that Joseph would be there to protect me if I needed him. It was incredibly reassuring to understand that, as much as Gordon had tried to turn Joseph and me against each other, he hadn't succeeded. That reconciliation between my father and me was unbelievably sweet for me.

Joseph was concerned about my safety, but I pretended to be much stronger than I felt at that moment. I told him that he didn't need to worry about a thing because I was going to be totally fine. I talked a good talk, but deep down, I didn't want to ever leave Joseph's side again because I knew he wouldn't let anything happen to me. Years later, when Michael's own life was being targeted like mine, he would use these same words to describe why he wanted Joseph near him. One of Michael's last phone calls, the day before he died, was to our father, asking him for protection against the people who were preying on him. Unfortunately, the forces at work against Michael were so great that neither Michael nor Joseph could overcome them, even with their combined strength.

I didn't take that same step of asking Joseph for help, even though I craved his intervention, because I didn't want him to worry about me. Also, I was more concerned about his safety than I was about my own.

In spite of my protests, Joseph was trying everything in his power to help me. But as soon as he made even the slightest effort, Gordon somehow found out and began calling Joseph and threatening his life. As with the rest of my family members, I couldn't stand the thought of any harm coming to Joseph because of me, so I again warned him not to try to aid me in any way.

"I don't want you involved," I said. "Joseph, please don't."

Although I didn't allow Joseph to help me directly, other than for the security he hired for outside my door, our relationship did flourish in all-new ways following my flight from Gordon. When Joseph had been my manager, we had spent a great deal of time together, but he was always the decision maker and I did what I was told, sometimes with a degree of resentment. Now that we were both adults, and I wasn't dependent on him for anything, I could be more objective about his personality and our interactions. I came to understand him and my feelings about his role in my life, and my family's life, so much better than ever before.

A lot of negative things have been said about Joseph, which hurts me deeply. Now, with greater age and perspective, and the freedom to finally think for myself, I have developed a great appreciation for everything Joseph did for our family, and all that I have personally gained from him in my life and as a person. As I had more contact with Joseph in Las Vegas, I came to see how deeply he loved me, and all of his children. I realized that he was a good, strong man who had raised us up the best way that he knew how and did everything in his power to keep us together as a family. We were his children, and he loved us more than anything else. He did everything in his power not to let anyone come between him and us because he knew that no one else in the world would ever care for us the way he did.

Finally, I concluded that Joseph's tough-love approach to parenting when we were kids gave my siblings and me the skills and work ethic that allowed us to find such great success in the entertainment industry. Sure, he was hard on the brothers when he was rehearsing them in the early days of the Jackson 5. But this demand for perfection was also a beautiful gift because it directly helped them to achieve everything that they did. It has often been stated that the brothers, and especially Michael, had an amazing discipline and maturity well beyond their years when they were starting out. I believe they demonstrated these traits because of the level at which Joseph expected them to practice and be serious about every aspect of their music and their careers. I know that everything I have accomplished as an entertainer was built on the foundation of professionalism and precision that Joseph drilled into me when he was first launching and managing my career. Even more than that, when I was at my lowest because of Gordon, I know that so much of the fierce spirit and strength that emerged in me and helped me to stay alive was both inherited from and learned from Joseph. I wasn't the only one to revise my earlier opinion of Joseph, either. I thought it was interesting that Michael, who had also spoken negatively about Joseph when he was younger, came to appreciate and understand Joseph in later life. Michael always used to say that he wished he had more of Joseph's strength in him.

In the months before Michael died, he called Joseph to his meetings. Michael wanted Joseph by his side because he knew our father would do everything in his power to protect him. On May 15, 2009, Michael called for Joseph to attend one of his last big meetings at the Beverly Hills Hotel. Michael was in talks with Randy Phillips and Paul Gongaware of AEG, with whom he had signed a deal to perform shows at the O2 Arena in London, and he wanted Joseph there because he believed he was being taken advantage of. Joseph was the only one Michael could trust to shield him.

As I eventually spent more time with my siblings and their children, I began to realize that we grew up in a different time. Spanking was considered an appropriate form of discipline when we were young, forty or fifty years ago, whereas now it is basically considered abuse. Yes, Joseph did spank us. He was a disciplinarian, and he had a great deal of discipline to dole out, especially in the early years when he and Mother were raising nine children in a small house in Gary, Indiana. He did his best, and not only did he end up raising nine great, polite kids, but also several of the greatest pop stars in the world. At a time when blacks received no respect in our culture and would never have dared to dream of achieving all that the Jackson 5 did, let alone what Michael went on to accomplish, Joseph had an incredible vision of what was possible. No other man, alive or dead, has done anything like what Joseph did for his family, and I thank him for it.

Joseph was also well aware of every potential risk in the world that he opened up to his children. After the brothers became as incredibly successful as they were, Joseph knew that someone would come in and try to divide his children and take advantage of them. He wasn't going to let that happen, so he had to be strict to keep his family together. He was protective of us because we were his children. But we couldn't understand this as children because we saw things quite differently then, and we just thought that he was mean. Even though we were raised in a sheltered way that meant we didn't know all of the evil lurking in the outside world, just waiting to exploit our wealth and fame, Joseph did. Now that I have been preyed on by the very type of man that Joseph tried to protect us from, and I have seen Michael likewise victimized, I understand what Joseph knew all along. And now Michael's no longer with us. The stakes were incredibly high, and Joseph had to be exceedingly tough to keep predators at bay.

I've often been asked if I blame Joseph for all I went through with Gordon because Joseph sent me to Japan with Gordon in the first place. *Absolutely not!* I'd be a fool to blame Joseph. Japan or no Japan, Gordon would have found a way to get me under his control eventually. Anyone who is as determined as Gordon was is bound to accomplish his goals. I'd decided at the time that I no longer wanted to be managed by Joseph, so I was just as instrumental in coming under Gordon's influence as anyone else. Looking back, I know that my father would have been the last man on this earth to align me with Gordon if he thought he was going to harm me. Knowing what I know now, I would have kept Joseph on as my comanager, rather than letting him go. And I believe, had Michael continued to be comanaged by Joseph throughout his life, he would still be here today. There's no doubt in my mind about it, and I think everyone in my family would agree.

Now I can see how much integrity and heart Joseph had compared to Gordon. And compared to so many people I've since met in the entertainment industry over the years, who maybe weren't crooks, but still wouldn't have looked out for me in the same way that Joseph looked out for all of his children. But, of course, we can't go back and change the past. All we can do is learn from it.

This is exactly the approach that I took with Joseph during our time together in Las Vegas. Even the smallest interactions between us were incredibly healing. Joseph knew that after I left Gordon, I was completely alone. Although I refused to accept his larger offers of help, he was always doing little things for me. I think these small acts of kindness did much to hasten our reconciliation, even though they might not have seemed like much to the outside world, especially compared to the elaborate gifts that were often exchanged in my family. Right after I left Gordon, Joseph gave me one of his sweetest gifts ever. He knew I was afraid to leave the house, and that I didn't know how to cook at the time, so he bought me a device I could use to make eggs in the microwave. I was still too fragile to receive many visitors in person, but any time Joseph did come to my condo, he would bring over some cute little thing of that nature, just to try to put a smile on my face. I was moved by the thoughtfulness of these gifts. But when it came to any assistance of a larger nature, I was determined to get by on my own.

"Do you need anything?" Joseph would ask me, time and time again.

"No," I always replied. "But thank you."

Even though I repeatedly declined his help, Joseph had the type of generous spirit that made him try to keep on giving. One time, he sent over a guy who was working with him to bring me an envelope of money.

"Tell him that's so sweet and kind of him, but I couldn't possibly accept it," I said, returning the envelope to the man who had brought it. "Please give it back to him."

I appreciated Joseph's generosity, which knew no bounds, even after so many crooks such as Gordon had tried to take advantage of him over the years. I learned around this time that Joseph had been approached by a young man who wanted to make a film and needed money to do so. Joseph believed in the youth and his project. Because he didn't have any liquid assets at the time, Joseph sold his Rolls-Royce and his boat to get money for the young man to make his film. The young man did make his film, but he pocketed more of the money than he should have. Although the film was completed, it was never released, so Joseph lost all of the money he had given this young man. To some people, this may sound as if my father is gullible, but I prefer to focus on his desire to give back after he had achieved so much for himself and his family.

I appreciated Joseph's generosity, but I knew that this situation I found myself in was something I needed to work out on my own. Just having my father back was enough of a gift. I'm so happy that we've remained extremely close since I left Gordon, and I love him dearly. He'll probably never forgive me for saying this, but as I've gotten older, I've come to realize that Joseph's bark is much bigger than his bite.

19

A FAMILY REUNION AND
A FACE-OFF IN COURT

I was overjoyed to discover an all-new closeness with Joseph and my siblings, especially Randy and Jermaine, who did so much for me in my first days of freedom from Gordon. Then I had cause to rejoice at the generosity and supportiveness of the entire Jackson clan. My whole family, except for Michael, who was in the midst of the *HIStory* tour when I first left Gordon, and whom I had not seen since then, assembled in Las Vegas to stand beside me on my first day of court with Gordon. I had met my attorney for the first time the night before, when he came into town and stayed in my building's guest quarters to prep me for the following day. Even with his excellent legal counsel and support, I was incredibly nervous about seeing Gordon for the first time since I had escaped from him. It meant the world to me that my family made such a grand show of love and encouragement.

I was so happy to see them, and so nervous because it was my first day in court. They had all driven out from Los Angeles together, and they arrived at my building just in time for us to leave and go over to the courthouse together. This was my first experience of having so much life in my home since arriving in Las Vegas, and it felt wonderful. Of course, we couldn't be late for court. So, while I was hugging everybody, I was also aware that we didn't have much time. It was all a rush.

The only person I had reservations about seeing was Mother. She had been my best friend for years when I was growing up, and so of course I was glad to see her. But I was also still afraid of her.

"Hi," I said uncertainly. "Um, it's good to see you."

Later, when Mother and I discussed this moment, she couldn't figure out why I had told her it was good to see her if I was still terrified that she would harm me. I answered as honestly as I could. I told her that I didn't know what else to say, and that it *was* good to see her, even if I was afraid. With so much going on between us, it was an intense, emotionally charged moment.

I found myself wishing that I had the time to savor my first moments with my family. But always, in the front of my mind, were thoughts of court and my curiosity about and fear of what was going to happen. This was all new to me. I had never been involved in court proceedings before or even been in a courtroom. Now I was not only going to a courtroom, but I was facing off there against a man whom I knew would stop at nothing to humiliate and destroy me, which caused me great anxiety. On top of this, I had been in seclusion for months, so even though my family was there with me, it was difficult to set aside the feeling that I was alone in the day's fight against Gordon. But because I was seeing most of my family for the first time in years and I didn't want to worry them, I did my best to hide my nerves and appear strong.

Still, it was a great feeling to see everyone. My brothers made me feel good, as only they could. No one, except for Randy, had been to my condo before, and they all wanted to explore the place.

"Yeah, sure, look around," I said. "Do whatever you want."

So they all walked around the space together, admiring it, exclaiming over what a magnificent view I had of the Strip.

"WOW, your place is beautiful," one brother said.

"Look what we have here," another said.

"This is great," said a third.

"Yes, it's yours," I said, so glad I was once again in a position to share what I had with my family. "You guys can stay here whenever you want."

All their words of praise and admiration made me start to feel better about myself.

"Wow, look at all of this perfume you have in here," one of my brothers said as he came into my bedroom.

In some ways, the small, insignificant moments such as this meant more to me than anything else during this period. Their words brought forth memories of old times when we had been a happy family, as well as new hope that we might be on the verge of being so again.

While I was enjoying this joyous reunion, my mind was still thinking ahead. *Oh my God, what's going to happen in court? What is Gordon going to do?*

I told my attorney the night before how worried I was. When he quickly brushed off my concerns, I tried to explain to him that Gordon wasn't the average disappointed husband who didn't want to grant his wife a divorce. My attorney was well aware of all that Gordon was capable of because of everything we had uncovered while preparing for the divorce proceedings, and he assured me that he wouldn't let anything happen to me. Then, just before it was time to face the man who had set out to ruin me, and my family as well, my attorney told me to ignore Gordon and to be strong.

To do so was easier said than done. When I walked into the courtroom, I made it a point not to look at Gordon because I didn't want my insides to twist and turn with fear as I relived all of the terror and pain he had put me through for so many years. I just couldn't take the intensity of those negative emotions any longer, and I didn't want to go through them again. Also, I was filled with a graver fear that, if I so much as made eye contact with Gordon, he might be able to worm his way back into my life. I had even told the people around me to keep an eye on me.

"No matter what Gordon does in this courtroom, please don't listen to me," I said. "If I say that he just wants to take me to the side and talk to me, please, don't let it happen. And don't let him say, 'La Toya, tell them it's okay.' Because that's what he would always do. No matter how much I tell you something like that, don't listen to me."

Gordon had exercised just that much control over me for nearly a decade, and I was terrified that a few months of freedom was not nearly long enough to undo all of the programming he had successfully done inside me. Because I wouldn't speak to Gordon or even look at him, he was left with fewer opportunities to intimidate me than he would have liked.

But he still found ways to show off his power. He and his attorney kept seeking the recusal of judges until he finally got the judge that he wanted. So I believed from day one that the judge was on his side. I wasn't surprised when people called me and told me that Gordon and the judge were friends.

Then Gordon began doing the legal equivalent of everything he had done to me in private for more than a decade. First of all, he was so angry and upset that I had my family there to support me. He absolutely could not stand it.

"This is unfair," he said to the judge. "I don't want them in the courtroom."

Unbelievably, the judge actually made my family leave. Even though they had driven all the way from Los Angeles to be there, and they were simply there to show their solidarity with me, they weren't even allowed to sit behind me.

After Gordon accomplished this first power move,

he sat there and lied about every aspect of the case he possibly could. He had always dressed impeccably the whole time that I had known him. Now, he came to court looking like a homeless man. Every day, he showed up dirty and disheveled in clothes that made it appear that he'd been sleeping on the street for days. In this elaborate ruse, he tried to appear broke so as not to have to give me back any of the millions of dollars that he had stolen from me. At the same time he was claiming to have nothing, he would fabricate stories about how I had millions and millions of dollars hidden away in bank accounts all over Switzerland. Not content to lie about me, he also tried to besmirch my reputation, so that any time I suggested he was lying, he could call my credibility into question.

"She's a sleaze," he said about me. "She's so rotten. She did *Playboy*. I tried to convince her not to do it, but she wanted to do it. You can get footage of her on TV saying this herself."

I couldn't believe what I was hearing. At the time that I had been forced to appear in *Playboy*, I thought of it as a temporary compromise of my beliefs and a source of shame that would eventually fade. I didn't realize at the time that Gordon was making me pose he was also telling the press that it had been my idea, because of the long-term repercussions it would have in moments like this. Suddenly it all became clear to me. He had every moment preplanned. He was looking far down the road because he knew exactly what he was going to do to me. He was going to use me, abuse me, and drop me. And that's what he did, at least until I escaped from him. Even then, Gordon tried every trick he could possibly think of to discredit and discourage me. He forced me to take a drug test, and when that, of course, came back negative, he made me submit to psychological testing.

No matter what Gordon pulled, the judge took his side over mine. The judge had frozen all of our assets for the length of the proceedings and said that neither of us could have access to them until the case was settled and it was determined what belonged to whom. During this time, Gordon went ahead and sold my penthouse apartment in New York and took the money. Finally, the judge had to step in. Rather than making him give back the money, which never happened, the judge just put him in jail for a few days. They handcuffed him right there in court and walked him away in front of where I was sitting. He looked at my attorney as the guards led him by us.

"You haven't heard the end of this, buddy," Gordon said.

As I sat there in court and listened to his many false-hoods, which I could only deny in my depositions, I came to understand exactly what I was up against.

It's going to be a battle, but I'm going to fight it all the way, I thought.

What he didn't realize is that, while he was playing all of these games just to keep the money that I had earned, all I cared about was getting free of him. I didn't want any one of those dirty pennies back from him. He

Michael and me at the Dominion Theatre
in London, 1983.

Janet, Michael, and me out having fun in the mid-eighties.

With Tito's son TJ.

My cousin Tony Whitehead and me at Tito's house.

With Michael's pet tiger.

On the set of "Say Say Say" with Paul McCartney and Michael.

With Cary Grant, Michael, Elizabeth Taylor, and Gregory Peck,
having dinner at Hayvenhurst.

With Jack Gordon in Germany.

In London, 1990, after Jack Gordon beat me.

Jack Gordon getting arrested after beating me in 1993.

On *Larry King Live* in 2003, after a seven-year hiatus from show business. This was my first interview since leaving Jack.

Michael and me in his dressing room at the 2003 BET Awards.

Thanksgiving 2003 at Janet's house in Malibu.

With my parents at the MGM Grand Hotel in Las Vegas in 2001, about to go to Janet's concert.

Having fun with my sisters at a family gathering in June 2004.

Gossiping with Janet at the Kentucky Derby in May 2004.

With my family at Jermaine's fifty-first birthday lunch in 2005.

Tito and his three sons, TJ (holding baby Dee Dee Dior), Taj, and Taryll (holding baby Bryce).

At Neverland after the first day of court for Michael's preliminary trial.

Back in the studio.

Patrolling the streets with my police partner, Officer Amy Kesler.

The last photo I took with Michael, at my parents'
sixtieth anniversary party on May 14, 2009.

With my sisters Janet and Rebbie, on our way to thank Michael's fans
after his memorial for their love and support.

At my family's private memorial for Michael on September 3, 2009.

Jermaine and me backstage at *Dancing with the Stars* in October 2009.

With my girlfriend since childhood, Kathy Hilton, and her husband, Rick, and Jeffré Phillips on Christmas Day 2009.

With my family at my surprise fifty-third birthday party.

Relaxing in Malta in 2010.

was greedy, and so, as with everything else he had done, he was driven by money. To me, it was dirty money because he had touched it, and so it held no appeal for me. All I wanted was to start over and live my life in my own way now.

My attorney vehemently opposed my stance on the whole proceedings. "No," he said. "Get what's yours. Get what belongs to you."

"Please, I just want out," I said. "I can start over again."

Finally, after months of this, the judge thankfully brought the proceedings to a close.

"You want out of this relationship, don't you?" she asked me.

"Yes, Your Honor," I said.

"How badly do you want out?" she said, giving me a long look.

I didn't say anything in reply.

"You know what?" she said. "Since you want out so badly, guess what? You're La Toya Jackson. You can always make a living for yourself. You want out? I'll grant you a divorce. You're out."

I was so ecstatic that I barely heard the bad news that came next. She let me go, but she let me go with almost nothing. Gordon was required to pay me a small settlement of $350,000, but of course, he never did. I got the place in Las Vegas, and that was it. Gordon got everything else.

I didn't care. It had been no understatement when I had said that I just wanted out. And more important than anything else, I had gotten out. Finally, more than a decade after Gordon set his sights on me at the Grammys, and still bearing the emotional scars from everything he had done to me in those years, I was free of the cancer that was Jack Gordon.

20

❦

REBUILDING A LIFE

By the time my divorce from Gordon was granted, I had even greater reason to rejoice than I had when I first went into the proceedings. During the many months that we prepared our case, my attorney constantly made horrifying revelations. Gordon had stooped amazingly low in his mission to take all of my money and destroy my personal and professional reputation. One of Gordon's workers took a computer from an office Gordon kept at the Waldorf-Astoria in New York City and gave it to my attorney.

"He has been treating her so badly," the worker said, "here's the computer."

As my attorney began pulling up documents from the computer and looking into the details of Gordon's financial dealings, what he found threw me into even greater shock. Seeing the proof of all that Gordon had stolen from me, and all of the lies that he had told in my name, was just awful. I was now facing dire circumstances as a result of his behavior.

Gordon's many threats to destroy me had clearly been absolutely sincere. He not only wanted to leave me with nothing, he wanted to make sure that when he was done with me, I would have no chance to make any money that he would lose out on stealing from me. He tried to make sure that everybody in the world hated me by making me a laughingstock, so that I was truly worth nothing, and I had the potential to earn nothing.

After claiming in court that he deserved $50,000 a month in alimony from me, not only did Gordon get everything and leave me with nothing in our divorce, he actually left me with less than nothing because of the huge debt that was now my responsibility. While he was taking all of the money for himself, he was putting everything I earned in my name. I was responsible for every penny, even though I didn't have any idea of how much was coming in, how much was going out, or what it was being spent on. I owed hundreds of thousands of dollars in unpaid taxes, as well as being responsible for purchases Gordon had made on credit in my name.

All the money that I possessed in the world was that $27,000 I had stashed away, which was already dwindling. It certainly wasn't going to begin to make a dent in the massive debt that Gordon had accrued on my behalf. Then I remembered the money I had earned for that South American television appearance without Gordon's knowledge. My former crew member still had most of it. I went to New York, called him, and tried to arrange a meeting so he could give me what was rightfully mine. But he always had an excuse for why he couldn't meet. At first, I remained optimistic. Having worked with him, I truly believed I could trust him. My first assessment of his character had seemed correct. After all, he had returned some of the money to me, so it seemed likely that he really was busy, and he would return the rest eventually.

But time went by, and the crew member was still evading my requests. Finally, I enlisted the help of someone I absolutely knew I could trust, my old friend and songwriting partner Amir Bayyan. I explained the situation to Amir and asked him to go speak to the crew member on my behalf, which Amir did.

"Here's the FedEx envelope that he gave me," Amir said.

When I opened the envelope, no money was inside. *How could people be so cruel?* I wondered.

This crew member knew what Gordon had done to me, and rather than feeling compassion toward me and a desire to help me, he felt inspired to exploit me himself. It was as if, after having watched Gordon abuse me and take advantage of me, the crew member felt entitled to do it, too. I was devastated.

I can't win for losing, I thought. *But I'm not giving up.*

My plan was to do what I had always done: to work hard until I had enough money to pay down all of the financial obligations Gordon had created for me without my knowledge. My attorney was a huge ally, and at my bidding, he began contacting television programs and venues in Europe and South America, where I had been performing for decades, with the intention of booking appearances for me to begin earning money and rebuilding my career. Now we made one of the worst discoveries of all, given how proud I was of the work ethic and professionalism that Joseph had instilled in me.

Unbeknownst to me, after I left Gordon, he was still booking shows for me in Europe. These agreements were made with his full knowledge that he was no longer my manager, and that I wouldn't be honoring any of them because I didn't know anything about them. He had been taking the money I was paid in advance for all of these performances that never happened. He was lying and stealing in my name. I didn't find out about any of this until I was suddenly facing lawsuits from a handful of disgruntled promoters around the world. My attorney and I had to travel to all of these places to address these lawsuits, because if we didn't, we would have had to automatically pay for them. Once my reputation was sabotaged like that, the promoters involved never wanted to work with me again, and they started telling other promoters that I would probably not show up. Well, how could I, when I didn't even know that Gordon was booking these appearances for me?

So when my attorney and I began trying to book new appearances, it was extremely difficult for me to get work because none of the promoters were sure if I would arrive as promised. Then, just as I was starting to repair some of the damage Gordon had done by going to Europe and delivering such professional performances that people began to have faith in me again, Gordon took his campaign to destroy me one step further. He actually started booking other girls, saying each of them was La Toya Jackson, even though they quite obviously weren't. He was doing anything to keep making money off of me.

It was actually easier to rebuild following Gordon's fraudulent activity than I at first expected because I didn't want to work with any of the people with whom he did business. I saw them as part of the cancer that I wanted to remove. So I began by thinking of people I had met and had a positive interaction with outside of Gordon's sphere of influence, which made me feel able to trust them. Slowly, I began working in Europe and South America, which is where I had always worked the most. The way I looked at it, Gordon had taken every penny from me, but he wasn't going to stop me from working now just because he was holding things up in court. At that time I could fly to Europe or South America, do a personal appearance or perform two or three songs on a television show, and easily earn around $50,000 to $75,000 per appearance. While there, I could usually book several weeks' worth of performances all at once.

Although I knew that I was being paid well for all of these appearances, I found it difficult at first to believe that this was my money, that I actually got to keep it.

"This is all yours," my attorney said when the money started coming in.

"Is it really?" I asked.

"Yeah, it's yours. You performed. This is your money."

"This is mine," I said, feeling a bit awed.

Once it sank in that I was earning my own money again, I became excited by how great it felt to be independent. My attorney took me to open a bank account in Las Vegas, and although I had a brief moment of sadness that I had been forced to start over again that completely at the age of forty-two, I couldn't have been more proud of myself or that money I had earned.

But there was another problem. Even with as much as I was earning, I was in bankruptcy as a result of Gordon's effort to avoid the Moulin Rouge when they tried to come after me for the money they lost because Gordon had made me breach my contract with them. Even with that, and everything he had taken from me in the divorce, I still had to pay back $850,000 of Gordon's debt after he was out of my life.

Sadly, even the *nice* people around me didn't always give me the best advice. My attorney recommended that I stay in bankruptcy, even though he and I were both aware that I could have gone out, worked, and earned that money quickly. And because I had been referred to him by my brother and he had always been on my side in the past, I began thinking that maybe I should take his advice. Because I was so intent on being independent, I didn't have anyone else to ask, and I was afraid if I talked to anyone in my family about it, they would try to pay my debt for me. With each new hurdle I encountered, I was more determined than ever to pull myself back up on my own.

"Well, you want to pay back all of these creditors, right?" my attorney asked.

"Yes, I want to pay back everybody," I said. "But I can work to make this money in no time."

"No, you should remain in bankruptcy."

So I did, not knowing that it was going to stick with me for seven years, and that in that time I wouldn't be able to get any credit to buy a house or a car. Of course, the news of my financial woes was all over the press. I was highly embarrassed by this because I wanted so badly to establish my reputation as a competent, successful career woman. I had grown up with everything I ever needed, plus the ability to earn even more money than I needed, to the point where money had no real value to me. To suddenly be forced to realize the value of money was a shock, and the difficulty of not having it once again was dramatic and upsetting. The worst part was, I had thought that, following the divorce, I was past all of the hard times. Here I was, brought up short once more. But I was more certain than ever that I needed to fight my way back to a place where I earned respect from myself and others, and earned my own money, completely on my own.

21

◦∞◦

LEARNING TO TRUST AGAIN

On March 3, 1998, I was granted my divorce from Gordon. It was the happiest day of my life. When I returned home from the Las Vegas courthouse, I sat on the balcony of my condominium and celebrated with my attorney, drinking champagne and eating caviar. I was so elated. I had come out on the other side of a fierce battle in possession of my own name and my own life. I had only been given my Las Vegas condominium and a $350,000 settlement, which I rightly predicted that Gordon would never pay. That was all, even though I had earned millions in the years that Gordon managed me. I didn't even have any of my family photos, which Gordon held on to and would not return. But I didn't care. *I was free!* And that's all that mattered. I was my own person again, with my own name back, La Toya Jackson ~~Gordon~~.

I wasn't bitter about allowing Gordon to walk away

with my money, and nearly all of my possessions. I was just glad to be liberated from him, and to have the right to work and earn my own money again. I quickly found that I needed to start working as much as possible. Once our assets were unfrozen following the divorce, I was immediately expected to deliver the mortgage payments that had been on hold for almost two years. And the many creditors who had led my attorney to advise me to stay in bankruptcy were still clamoring to be paid.

I went back to doing what I had always done, making appearances and performing around the world. It was the best and quickest way for me to make money, and the familiar routine offered some comfort. But now that I was free to make my own decisions for the first time in my life, I was beginning to think about making a substantial change. Although I enjoy performing now, which has been a major part of most of my life, I was always even more intrigued by the business side of the music industry. I had never wanted to be a performer, as I knew from an early age that I was much happier behind the scenes than onstage. When I was a young woman, I had planned to pursue a career in the music industry's business side, but Joseph wouldn't hear of it.

"You are a Jackson, and Jacksons are entertainers," he always said.

Even so, music was never my first love, and I never felt that I embraced it, no matter how many *Billboard* hits I achieved or how many decades I performed.

Now, though, there was no one to tell me what to do. When I was honest with myself about how I felt about music, I realized that I could now take it or leave it. Even more than that, Gordon had tainted the business for me. I didn't know that I cared enough to fight my way back. I realized that I wanted to pursue opportunities that would allow me to help other people. I thought about ways I might be able to manifest my lifelong dream to become a businesswoman, or an entreprenette, as I like to call it. I became interested in possibly becoming a manager or taking on another role that would allow me to use my lifetime of experience to help other artists advance their careers. I also realized that I no longer wanted anything to do with America. I set plans in motion to move to Europe, where I would divide my time between Paris and London. But I was not yet free to go, as I had to remain in America to deal with the bankruptcy and debt Gordon had caused in my name.

After my divorce was finalized, I retained a new attorney to help me reclaim my residual income, which had been designated to the trustees of my bankruptcy for seven years. This money was for all of the royalties I earned for my own songs and the hit song "Reggae Night," which I cowrote with Amir Bayyan for Jimmy Cliff. It equaled about $200,000 a year and would have gone far toward helping me to get my financial life in order. When the seven years of my bankruptcy were up, I was so relieved I would begin receiving the money again. My attorney told me that I didn't have to go to court to petition for the money because the trustees were not extending my bankruptcy for another seven years. As I soon found out, that was wrong, and because

I didn't know to send someone as my representative to the court proceeding, the trustees were granted a seven-year extension. When that seven-year period finally ended, just recently, the trustees tried to extend their hold again. Fortunately, by this time I had purged all of the crooks and double-crossers from my life, and I had the situation handled by a team of lawyers who do have my best interests at heart. Last year, they fought the trustees in court and won back the rights to my royalties for me. After fifteen years, I *finally* received my first check for my own royalties in April 2011. That was just one example of the many ways Gordon continued to plague me long after I was free of him, and even six years after his death.

Then, before I departed music or America, I met someone who would change my mind about what was possible in my career and my country. I was still living in Las Vegas following my divorce, but I often traveled to Los Angeles on business. On one such trip, I was asked to meet with the producers of a film that was currently in development. A woman who worked for Joseph had contacted me about the project. She was the film's publicist, so I felt obligated to at least be polite about the opportunity. I allowed her to set up a call between myself and the film's producers and director. The film was a spoof, and I wasn't the least bit interested in doing it after reading the script. But no matter how adamantly I told her it was a waste of time, the publicist kept insisting that I had to meet with the producers to decline their offer in person. As I have shown time and again, I am extremely uncomfortable with confrontation of any kind, so I finally agreed to go to the meeting she had scheduled.

When I arrived at the office, I was met at the door by one of the film's producers, Jeffré Phillips. As we walked back to meet the others, he mentioned that he was my brother Jermaine's close friend, which set me at ease somewhat. The producers and the director were so animated and excited about their project that I couldn't bring myself to tell them that I didn't want to be a part of it. Finally, Jeffré noticed how edgy I was becoming. The meeting had lasted far too long, it was late, I was in a neighborhood I was unfamiliar with, and I had already sent my security home for the night. Jeffré was kind enough to intervene on my behalf and bring the meeting to an end. He invited me to go get something to eat at Mr. Chow, and although I declined at first, he wouldn't take no for an answer.

When we got to the restaurant and settled into a table, he addressed me with a frankness that impressed me. "Listen, this movie that we're doing is a spoof. We're just going to make fun of the character that we think you are. I don't think you should do it."

His words were such a relief after all of the pressure I had felt at the meeting.

As soon as we had gotten the question of the film project out of the way, we quickly fell into easy conversation and found that we had so much in common. It was as if we were meant to be friends. That he was close with Jermaine was a mark in his favor, as I hold all of my brothers in extremely high esteem and always compare all of the men that I meet to them, as well as to Joseph.

I was so struck by how close I already felt to Jeffré that I blurted out partway through our first conversation, "Oh my God, you're just like a brother to me."

Given that I had just escaped Gordon's clutches, it was then extremely difficult for me to trust new people. I was completely surprised to feel as comfortable around Jeffré as I did. He quickly became not only a friend, but my best friend.

Although we didn't end up collaborating on the film that originally brought us together, we were both interested in filmmaking. I told Jeffré when we first met that I wasn't interested in performing anymore, and I wanted to work behind the scenes. He had extensive experience producing films and television programs, and I liked the idea that we might write, direct, and produce our own projects, finally allowing me to step out of the limelight. We shared a similar philosophy about business and enjoyed each other's company, so we decided to become business partners. Even more important, I trusted Jeffré from the beginning, which I hadn't thought I would ever be able to do again. Together we formed Ja-Tail Films LLC in May of 1999.

When it came time to name our new venture, we brainstormed every combination of our two names, but nothing seemed quite right. We often discussed how we had met each other at the perfect moment when both of us wanted to reinvent ourselves. This realization led us to christen our venture Just Another Timely Adventure in Life. When we boiled the phrase down to the initials JA-TAIL, we had our business name.

For the first time in ages, I was enjoying my life and feeling good about the work I was doing. Jeffré and I began spending more and more time together. One day when he was at my condo, I found myself with a performance request that required negotiation. Jeffré had been in the music industry for many years, even working with Michael when Jeffré did marketing for Sony in the 1980s, and he offered to handle the deal for me.

I was incredibly excited about the business that Jeffré and I were building together and the many strides I was making toward a newly independent life. But I remained haunted by the aftereffects of Gordon's abuse. The emotional scars revealed themselves in many different ways, and I never knew when I was going to be struck by an attack of uncontrollable terror. Sometimes all it took was a phone call to put me over the edge. If I heard Jeffré get angry or raise his voice while speaking on the telephone, I would start shaking and crying. Once when he hung up and saw how upset I was, he was instantly alarmed.

"What's wrong?" he asked.

"You're going to beat me," I said.

"I'm going to beat you? What are you talking about? Why would I beat you? I have no right to do that."

"Because you're angry."

"No, I was angry with the person on the phone," he said. "But I hung up. I'm not angry anymore."

Jeffré is the most gentle, mild-mannered person

imaginable, yet I didn't believe him at first. No matter what Gordon's problem was with anybody else, he would always take it out on me. After years of abuse, I didn't expect anything else from those around me. So I had to recondition myself to expect a different kind of treatment. It took years of kindness and consideration from Jeffré for me to understand that I had nothing to fear from him.

Even once my mind knew I was safe, sometimes my body would still have a violent reaction to the slightest perceived threat. It wasn't just Gordon that I feared. I still saw potential danger everywhere I went. All it took was a pedestrian crossing the street in front of the car when Jeffré and I were stopped at a red light. My heart would race, and my palms sweat.

"Lock the door," I'd said to Jeffré. "Lock it! Lock it!"

Not until we pulled out into traffic again would I finally feel safe and my heartbeat return to normal. Intellectually I knew that I had no reason to react so violently, but there was no way to convince my body that it was finally safe.

Throughout all of this, Jeffré was an amazing source of support. I was extremely pleased with the results when he negotiated that one appearance for me, so I began bringing him in as my full-time business partner. He traveled with me when I went overseas to make appearances, and I began letting him in on more and more details of my career. Although he had extensive business experience, he had never managed anyone before, and I taught him how the process worked and how the money was handled. Once he knew the ropes, I gave Jeffré the contacts I considered cancer-free because they were not affiliated with Gordon in any way, and he took over all planning for my appearances.

Together, Jeffré and I took a step back and assessed my musical career as a whole. What we found was not encouraging. Although I had been making appearances without any involvement from Gordon for more than three years and was slowly rebuilding my reputation every time I arrived where I was supposed to be and delivered an amazing show, Gordon had done a great deal of damage to my reputation. Many promoters had previously wired money to him in advance of one of my performances, only to have him take the money without my even knowing about the show. My appearance fees had also substantially decreased. Gordon had driven them way down, in part because he was so interested in making a quick buck. Even more than that, he was determined to make my value be nothing. Thus, once he wanted to get rid of me, he wouldn't have to worry about my earning any money that wasn't going directly into his pocket. Jeffré and I set out to ensure that Gordon would not be able to damage my business life any further. We put out press releases across Europe, informing promoters that I was no longer working with Gordon and asking them not to do business with him if he approached them claiming to be my representative.

Overall, I was incredibly pleased with the way Jeffré and I were beginning to repair the damage that Gordon had done. Even more than that, I was absolutely thrilled to find myself living my lifelong dream of becoming a successful businesswoman and entreprenette. But it hasn't been easy. I got myself free, but Gordon's influence lingered within me, and it took a long time to heal.

22

❧

"FREE THE WORLD"

Although I was feeling apathetic about music, music didn't give up on me. When Jeffré called me on the morning of September 11, 2001, to tell me that the World Trade Center had been attacked, my first response to the tragedy was a song of hope.

I turned on my television and tried to absorb the breaking news about the first plane that had hit the North Tower. But I was at a complete loss. The reporter said that officials still didn't know if the event was a terrorist attack or a plane crash. As I watched my television in horror, the second plane crashed into the South Tower.

My first concern was my family. I cried hysterically, thinking that I might have lost them all. They were in New York City at the time, staying not too far from the World Trade Center. The night before, Michael had filmed his *30th Anniversary Celebration* for CBS at Madison Square Garden. During the show, he performed alongside all of my other brothers for the first time in more than a decade. At this big, exciting event for my family, nearly everyone had been there, including Mother and Joseph. I had longed to attend myself, but had been prevented by a scheduling conflict. I later learned that Michael was supposed to attend a meeting at the top of the World Trade Center at 9:00 a.m. on September 11, but he was too tired, and the meeting was canceled. Had he gone, he would have died in the attack that day.

I panicked as I attempted to reach any of my family members to make sure that no one had been harmed. I couldn't get through to anyone. Not one of the at least thirty family members in the extended Jackson clan answered his or her cell phone. With my family, I couldn't just call their hotel and ask for them by name, as they always stayed under different code names wherever they went.

I grew more and more frantic as I continued to call throughout the day. Finally, I reached Mother, who answered, gasping. I was never so happy to hear her voice.

"Mother, is everyone okay?"

"Yes, La Toya," she said.

I immediately felt the tension drain out of my body.

"What a tragedy!" she continued.

"I know, Mother, I've been crying all day. How are you guys ever going to get out of there? All of the planes are grounded. Do you want me to see what I can do?"

"No, that's okay, honey. Several tour buses are on their way from Texas to get the family. We're heading back to Los Angeles as soon as they arrive."

Now that I knew my family was safe, I was able to focus on the unbelievable events that had just occurred. Like the rest of America, I was devastated and terrified. Although everything was uncertain in the first moments after the planes struck, I knew that we were under attack and that life would never again be the same. In the next hour and a half, the chaos only increased, with the towers tumbling to the ground, and the news coming in that two other planes had crashed, into the Pentagon and a southwest-Pennsylvania field. As I continued to watch the horrible events unfold, I heard one of the news commentators speak words that hit me forcefully: "Oh my God, all those children that were in the nursery in the World Trade Center."

I burst into tears and prayed, *God, please save all those innocent souls who were in the building, and please forgive those souls who didn't know you, or who didn't believe in you as they should have. They know not better. And please watch over all those beautiful and innocent children, and open your arms wide, and receive them all into your heavens where they can live a peaceful eternal afterlife. Thank you, Jehovah God.*

These words provided me with some comfort, but they were not enough. The longer I watched the news on television, the more upset I became. As I stared at the television screen, transfixed in grief and horror, the lyrics to a new song appeared in my mind:

"We must bring an end to all discrimination and make a better place for children throughout the world, why should they suffer from our battles, they are our future, they are the voice of tomorrow, let's free the world."

As these words and their corresponding melody played in my mind again and again over the next few hours, they began to take shape into a song. The creative inspiration felt good, but writing the song did nothing to distract me from the sorrow I was feeling. I cried constantly as I watched the news coverage. The images showed such a chaotic scene, with all of the police officers, firemen, and brave citizen volunteers clambering over the wreckage of Ground Zero in search of survivors. I wanted desperately to be there in New York City, helping those brave firemen and police officers. Feeling powerless as I sat so far away at home in Las Vegas, I asked myself over and over what I could do to help. Finally, I saw a representative of the Red Cross on the news, urging people to donate whatever they could to help. I was happy to hear this because I knew I was blessed enough to do my part, so I instantly picked up the phone and made a donation. But it didn't feel like nearly enough.

Ever since I was a child, I had always wanted to be a nun or a cop or work at McDonald's. I had so loved the idea of being a police officer, so I could help those in need. As I saw officers from all over the country traveling to New York City to be of assistance, I wished I could join them. Of course, being a Jackson, I knew that I could never be a cop. But what I could do, as a Jackson, was to write music. We had all been raised to compose songs. Those words I'd heard immediately after the attack kept resurfacing in my head.

So I finally jotted the words down on a piece of paper. I wasn't thinking that these words might be the beginning of anything substantial. I was simply acting out of instinct.

That night, I couldn't sleep. I stayed up until dawn, watching the same coverage of the tragedy over and over. As I did, I continued to write, and the song began to finish itself. I heard strings so clearly it was as if they were being played in the room with me. Since I was a child, I had kept a tape recorder next to my bed, except for when I was living with Gordon, who obviously didn't want me to record anything that happened in our house. I grabbed my recorder now. I hummed the string part and the melody, as I heard them in my head, onto the tape. Then, I sang, "Let's free the world."

As the days passed, I keep hearing the same lyrics, melody, and music in my mind. But my fears prevented me from thinking that I could actually write and release a song.

If I do a song, it will just become a joke.

My grief and uncertainty made me feel the need to connect with others, and I found myself on several of my siblings' fan websites. This was the first time I had ever gone to these pages, but something told me to see what the fans were saying in this moment of communal grief. I was surprised to find the same message, again and again:

"What happened to La Toya? We haven't seen or heard from her in years! Is she still alive? She needs to write a 9/11 song."

At this time, I had been absent from the limelight in America for five years. Receiving such direct encouragement to write a song, especially after so many years, made me feel incredibly uplifted and inspired. This support began to give me confidence. I went back and listened to my new melody again and again, wondering if the kernel of a song was really there. I must have listened to those few bars of music a hundred times.

As I worked, I gained enthusiasm and confidence. I continued to jot down more notes. My vague thoughts were, miraculously, shaping themselves into a song.

I gathered my courage and called Jeffré, saying, "I have a song I'm ready to record."

Jeffré was shocked because I had told him, again and again, since we first met that I was finished with music and wanted to write screenplays and build our business instead. But once he grew accustomed to the idea, he was quick to support me, as usual.

Jeffré reminded me of a talented musician he was acquainted with, Peter Roberts, whose music he had played for me before. I was nervous about sharing my fledgling song with another musician and actually making my dream a reality, but I knew I couldn't give up now. Jeffré and I called Peter. He asked me to hum the melody on his answering machine, which I did. Within a few days, he had recorded a rough mix of the track. When Jeffré played it for me over the phone, I was floored. It was exactly what I had heard in my head. I could not have been more excited.

Peter sent the track to me, and Jeffré and I sat down

and completed the lyrics together. When we were ready, we called Peter and booked time in his studio to go in and record the song. I'm not sure who was more nervous, Jeffré or I. It had been so long since I had been in the studio of my own free will. I had thought that I was done with this side of my life forever. After having been ridiculed for years about my singing and dancing, I couldn't believe I was opening myself up to public scrutiny again. Jeffré was well aware that the stakes were incredibly high, and he didn't want me to fail. Not only because it would create a pall over our otherwise successful business venture, but also because he had witnessed how slowly and painfully I had rebuilt my self-esteem in the two years that he had known me. But this song was too important to ignore.

I will always feel so grateful to Peter for helping me bring "Free the World" to life. From the moment that I completed this song, I knew I had accomplished something special. I wasn't the only one who felt this way. *Access Hollywood* used it as the soundtrack to some of its 9/11 footage from then on, and finally I felt that I was able to give back in the best way that I knew how.

I had been nervous about letting the world hear my first original song in more than a decade, but the feedback was immediate and exceedingly positive. Fans started writing in and calling right away. Again and again, they asked the same question:

"Is La Toya doing an album?"

Up until that moment, I was ready to turn my back on the music world forever. I was tired of being ridiculed, and I preferred to expend my energy in areas where I seemed to be appreciated. But hearing such a glowing response to my new song, and feeling that it had been a powerful source of healing and connection during a painful and confusing time, was incredibly gratifying for me.

Surprisingly, it made me feel that I could do more with music still. As always, Jeffré was incredibly supportive. We booked additional time at Peter's studio and began piecing together an album, which we decided to call *Startin' Over*, in honor of my new beginning in life.

Once again I felt nervous, wondering if my first song had been a happy accident. I doubted if I would be able to write a whole album's worth of new material that listeners would respond to just as positively. As I embarked on the writing of new songs, I realized that it wasn't just the world that needed the restorative power of music in the wake of 9/11. I, too, had deep wounds that could begin to be healed by the words and music I composed. With Jeffré's encouragement, we began writing a handful of songs. Some revealed the horror of my life with Gordon, while others expressed the sheer joy I felt in every day that I was finally free to live on my own as I chose. Songs such as "Should've Left You," which addressed my longtime inability to escape Gordon's abuse, poured out of me. Often the songwriting was emotional and left me feeling exhausted and raw. But it was wonderful to hear the finished tracks. I was thrilled to turn Gordon's torture into a healing song that I could now use to reconnect with listeners who might be going through the same kind of abuse I had experienced. Maybe I could even change someone's life. For the first time ever, I felt empowered to write what I wanted to write and put out the songs I wanted to put out. Even better, I was doing it all without a single cent or accolade being stolen by Gordon.

The only problem was that the music industry was an entirely new landscape, and it was quickly proving to be quite hostile.

As soon as the record was completed in September 2002, Jeffré and I began making our first, enthusiastic preparations to look for a label to release it. We were optimistic about our prospects. I was a Jackson, I had released more than a half dozen albums over the years. Just working through our combined list of contacts would give us the opportunity to share my album with dozens of people, many of whom had opinions we trusted because of their experience and success in the business.

Jeffré sent out the album tracks to label executives we thought would be interested and began setting up meetings. Our enthusiasm was quickly put to the test. From the first time Jeffré sat down across the desk from someone, this is what he heard:

"La Toya Jackson can't sing, can't dance."

"She has no talent."

"She's damaged goods."

"Don't want to hear it."

"Don't want to hear it."

"Don't want to hear it."

Jeffré would not be discouraged. He had seen how hard I had worked, and he knew how much this meant to me. He, too, was as invested in the album as I was. So, he pressed the record executives for details.

"Well, what song of hers don't you like?" Jeffré asked.

Over and over again, he was met with nothing but blank stares. Nobody could answer his question because nobody had listened to the songs. These men were simply defaulting to the popular opinion of me at the time. And the larger trends in the industry were not in my favor either. Britney Spears was then ruling the radio with her fresh-faced-schoolgirl routine, and labels were clamoring for performers who were seventeen, sixteen, and even younger. At forty-six, I could not have been further from what they thought they wanted or could sell.

I suddenly realized how spoiled I had been in Europe where I did the bulk of my performing. Over there, age didn't matter in the slightest. In fact, it was an asset, as many of their biggest stars were sixty or seventy years old. I frequently performed with these entertainers on popular television programs and was struck by how much respect they received from the shows' producers and their fans at large. It was wonderful to see how these countries celebrated their elder entertainers, and I suppose that I began to take this attitude for granted because I spent so much time over there.

In America, the situation could not have been more

different. I was considered too old for the dance and pop music I was performing, and there was no discussion of the matter. Jeffré and I managed to remain hopeful throughout the first few meetings, certain that someone would actually give the songs a chance and hear how much they had to offer. But, finally, we had exhausted all of our potential avenues, and we had not found a home for the album. Still, we couldn't bring ourselves to admit defeat.

Next, Jeffré tried going to radio directly, in hopes that we could gain support for even just one track and create a popular groundswell that we could leverage into a record deal. The resounding response:

"We'll never play a La Toya Jackson song."

I had been ready to walk away from the music industry before this album, and now that I had approached it with renewed passion, I was being denied. Not only that, but my efforts were being met with general nastiness and a universal decree that my recording career was over. I had to digest this response for myself personally.

"I don't want to do this anyway, so this is a good way out," I said.

Jeffré shook his head no. He wasn't going to let me give up so easily. "Toy, we can beat them," he said. "Don't worry about it."

It took some convincing on his part, but I did believe in the music we had written and the vocal tracks I had recorded. So I came to agree with Jeffré that we should not give up on the album. But then, just as we were rethinking our approach to putting the songs out into the world, we were brought up short. As much as being a Jackson had clearly helped my career from the beginning, it also had its downsides. Only rarely wasn't one of my famous family members being ridiculed in the press for something. (Yes, I'm quite sure my siblings have felt the same way about me at times!) And in November 2002, we had to temporarily put the record on hold in the wake of a groundswell of negative publicity surrounding my brother Michael.

23

A DIRTY BUSINESS

I was finally able to reconnect with Michael in 2002. This reconciliation began with Mother. The more we saw each other when I was in Los Angeles and spoke on the phone when I was home in Las Vegas, the more comfortable I felt around her. We began to compare notes and uncover at least some of the truth beneath Gordon's treachery, and that helped me to free myself from his influence and begin to think for myself even more.

Rebuilding my relationship with Mother returned my whole family to me in an important way, because everyone in my family has always been joined through her. With nine siblings, many of whom were constantly traveling around the world with an extensive entourage of assistants and security guards, and staying under code names in hotels, we couldn't all stay in touch regularly. But because everyone spoke to Mother frequently, sometimes daily, we all kept up on each other's lives through her. Of course, we caught up with each other individually whenever we were able.

Because we grew up not celebrating any holidays or birthdays, Family Day was important to us all, and everyone tried his or her best to be there. These were always exciting and fun days for us. We would eat and play games, from Uno to charades, and catch up about everyday family life. We talked about how big the nieces and nephews had gotten, all of the new babies in the family, and how much we missed each other. Every time Family Day ended, it was sad for all of us, because our busy lives didn't allow us to gather often enough to show our deep love for each other. We always agreed to have Family Day more often and plan the next one soon. But once we exited the gates of Hayvenhurst, it was almost impossible to get all of us back for another day together. Often several months went by without a Family Day or any direct contact between family members because of conflicting obligations.

Because of the incredible demands of my siblings' schedules, it meant even more to me that they all put aside their busy lives to be with me on the first day of my divorce proceedings. This group reunion was a part of the reconnecting I also did individually with everyone on the phone. The one exception was my brother Michael, who was unable to attend my divorce proceedings, and I didn't talk to him for some time. Just after I escaped from Gordon, in the fall of 1996, Michael was launching his *HIStory* tour, a grueling, yearlong extravaganza that stopped in thirty-five countries. Because

Michael has devoted fans in every corner of the globe, when he went on a tour, he *really* went on a tour, staying out on the road for a year or more. Michael's popularity was so huge throughout the world that, from the time he was five years old until the day he passed, he could have toured the entire globe almost constantly and continued to sell out every show.

During this time, I spoke with Mother a great deal about Michael. I was absolutely thrilled to hear about his continued creative success and the family he was just then starting. In 1998, I met Paris when I was in New York with Mother, and the experience was incredibly special for me. Although I was disappointed not to see Michael, who was in the studio, it was thrilling to enter his hotel suite and have the nanny put such a tiny baby girl in my arms. I knew how much Michael had always loved children, and how devoted he was to his little ones.

Michael was an extremely conscientious parent and devoted himself to every detail of his children's upbringing. As soon as Paris was brought into the room, we were told that Michael wished the television to be off in her presence, even though she was just a baby. Michael was strict about what his kids were exposed to, allowing them to take in only educational programming. He also made sure that they never saw any of the news accounts about him. He never told me why he limited their access to the outside world so completely, but I've always believed it was because, while he knew their lives could never be completely normal, he wanted them to have the opportunity to know him only as their father. He didn't

want them to think of him as a pop star, or to associate
him with any of the negative words that were sometimes
used to describe him over the years. While I thought
he was wise to avoid hurting or confusing his children,
particularly with the many hateful lies that were spread
about him, I did worry that such a secluded upbringing
might make them vulnerable. As I was making sense of
what Gordon had done to me, I concluded that if I had
been less sheltered as a child and young woman, Gordon
probably could not have controlled me so completely.
But it's impossible to say for sure. As Mother and Joseph did for us children years earlier, Michael was doing
the best he could for his children under extraordinary
circumstances.

Michael was also particularly careful about the music
he allowed around his children. At that time, Paris was
allowed to listen to only one song, "Butterflies," which
singer Kolohe Kai had written for his own daughter. We
listened to it again and again in the hotel suite that day.
Paris clearly loved the song dearly, and every time it finished, she wanted to hear it again.

Although I didn't have any direct contact with Michael at this time, I was following his trials and tribula-
tions in the press and through Mother. He was locked in
a fierce battle with his record label, Sony. With billions
of dollars at stake, his foes were stopping at nothing to
defeat him. On the line was not just Michael's recording contract, which alone had earned the label billions of
dollars over the years. They were more concerned about
the ATV music publishing catalog. Michael had bought

this extensive collection of songs in 1985 in a deal negotiated by his then lawyer, John Branca, who himself
earned 2.5 percent of the catalog. Often referred to as
the Beatles Catalog, because the Beatles' many master-
pieces are among its most famous songs, it was a golden
egg for everyone in the record industry.

Michael had scored a coup when he bought the catalog for $47.5 million back in August 1985, particularly
because businessman Marty Bandier outbid him. But
the then owner of the catalog, Australian businessman
Robert Holmes à Court, was a Michael fan and decided
to accept Michael's lower bid if Michael agreed to attend a telethon in Perth, Australia, to raise money for
the Princess Margaret Hospital for Children. A savvy
businessman himself, although he was not yet thirty, Michael aggressively grew the catalog. He purchased the
work of hundreds of artists, growing the catalog until
he owned almost 750,000 songs, as others in the business
looked on jealously.

Industry insiders knew what most music fans do
not. Even for major pop stars such as Michael Jackson,
the real money in music is not in performing or selling
records, but in the licensing of songs. This is because
anytime a song is played anywhere in the world—in
a commercial, in a movie, on the radio, or in a public
space—a fee must be paid to whoever owns the license.
For popular songs by world-famous artists such as the
Beatles and Michael Jackson, licensing is big business.
As soon as Michael had the ATV catalog in his possession, greed began to drive those around him to want

more. In 1990, Branca tried to convince Michael to share equity in his publishing. Michael ended up firing Branca after music mogul David Geffen told Michael he thought Branca had too much control. In March 1991, Michael signed a fifteen-year, six-record deal with Sony that made him the highest-paid entertainer in the world, then he renegotiated the deal for an additional $700 million later that year. But this was nothing compared to the long-lasting value of the ATV catalog, which Sony wanted desperately.

Finally in 1995, at Sony and John Branca's urging, Michael merged ATV publishing with Sony's music publishing division. Sony became half owners of Michael's valuable catalog, and in exchange Michael was paid $95 million and retained half ownership. This not only meant that Michael would share in the label's profits, but that he also had to approve any moves the label wanted to make regarding the catalog. This power division soon became problematic because Michael was an artist first, and a businessman second. So, unlike his new partners, he was not motivated by an insatiable quest for profits. Often the decision that would have brought in the most money was not one that Michael agreed with personally, so he didn't allow it. For example, when Sony wanted to license Beatles songs for use in iTunes and other commercial ventures, Michael declined because he didn't think John Lennon would have approved, after he spoke with Yoko Ono about it.

All of these deals should have put Michael in an exceptionally strong position, professionally and financially. But Sony had played Michael. Branca, who by this point had been brought back in by Bert Fields, had not been clear with Michael about several alarming details of the contract. Only after he signed did Michael learn that the contract granted Sony the rights to his masters for much longer than he had thought. These masters would not revert to him until 2009. Michael died in 2009. Did he get them back, or did Sony keep them? Who knows?

This deception was not only a clear betrayal of Michael's trust, but it also created a problem for my brother. Like me, but to an even greater extent, Michael grew up with everything he ever wanted, plus the ability to earn all of the money he needed, and more, from an early age. He had no concept of money, and his legendary spending habits required a substantial revenue stream to keep his household afloat. With money he thought was due to him now going to Sony, and a $200 million loan past due, Michael needed to find another way to earn as much as he could as quickly as possible.

Being an international pop star with a recording contract with one of the world's biggest labels, Michael decided to turn his fortunes around by releasing a new album, *Invincible*, in October 2001. Only, just before the album dropped, Michael became suspicious of Sony. He began to fear that Sony purposely didn't promote his album because they wanted him to be so in debt to them that he would have to sell them his share of their collective publishing venture. He became so angry that he told Sony head Tommy Mottola that he wanted an early exit from his record deal with Sony.

Soon after that, Michael's album *Invincible* came out, and something strange happened. Those loyal fans who went to purchase *Invincible* found that it wasn't available in stores. The promotion and distribution of Michael's albums was the responsibility of just one entity, Sony. Here was one of the industry's most successful labels, which had ushered Michael's past albums into the world with fanfare. It was impossible to believe that they had suddenly lost their ability to promote and distribute an album, especially one for an artist as famous and adored as Michael Jackson. There could be just one explanation. At first, Michael didn't want to believe it. But he told me he'd ultimately concluded that Sony had purposely sabotaged his album so it would not sell. By doing so, they hoped to make Michael so financially desperate that he would be forced to sell his controlling half of the catalog to Sony, which was what they had wanted all along. My heart broke for my brother. Here he was being prevented from enjoying one of his great loves in life, creating music for his fans. His money worries were particularly concerning now that he had three small children to provide for, and he was also devoting himself to creating a legacy for them.

I was worried enough for Michael to begin with, and then I saw news footage of him in the fall of 2001 and the spring and summer of 2002 that made me realize just how dire the situation was. Like me, Michael was raised to be extremely meek and religious. He disliked confrontation and preached a message of love. He would rather experience hardship than react negatively, even to a person who was harming him. Yet, here he was speaking out against Sony in the most aggressive way possible and organizing boycotts of their products, which led to a dip in their sales that quarter. I watched on TV as Michael held a press conference in which he told his fans, and the world at large, just what Sony was doing to him. He was so frightened that he was going to be killed throughout this press conference that he wore a bulletproof vest. As he spoke, he became so upset by the injustice he was experiencing that he referred to Sony president Tommy Mottola as a racist and as the devil. Not only that, but Michael did something very unlike him. Michael publicly revealed that his good friend Mariah Carey, who had once been married to Mottola, had told Michael that she was terrified of Mottola. Michael had spoken to me about Mariah's confessions on many occasions, and I heard similar stories from others.

24

FAMILY REUNION

All of the difficulties Michael was experiencing in 2001 and 2002 gave me good reason to be concerned about his well-being. Then I was called to a family meeting that upset me. Michael was using prescription painkillers, and many in the family believed it was getting out of control. This was difficult for me to hear because I knew how emotionally devastated Michael must have been if he was having the problem they described.

For as long as I could remember, my brother had always been against any drug, even aspirin. Michael didn't believe in putting any chemicals in his body, and he was devoted to health food throughout his life.

When we both lived at home, Michael once became upset with me when he saw me take an aspirin, which was necessary to alleviate terrible menstrual cramps.

"La Toya, why are you taking that aspirin?" he asked. "That's a drug."

Even though Michael listened respectfully as I explained that I had no other choice in the face of such awful pain, I could tell that I didn't convince him. Once, sometime later, when he accidentally took an aspirin, he behaved as if he had been poisoned.

"Oh, no, I can't breathe," he said. "I'm dying. I'm dying."

"You're not dying," I said.

But he wouldn't listen.

"You're not dying," Mother said.

But he didn't believe her either.

Of course, his reaction was all in his mind, but Mother and I ended up rushing him to the emergency room, just to make him feel better.

Given all of this, Michael would never have taken a prescription painkiller on his own. But when he fell off the stage and injured himself while on tour, he was immediately rushed to a doctor, who injected him with painkillers. My brothers, who were on that tour with him, were upset because they couldn't figure out why he had been taken away like that and given such a high dosage of pain medicine. After his fall, Michael found it difficult to perform because his pain was so great. Because he had many dates left to complete, a doctor intervened and suggested that he continue to take pain medication.

"I refuse to do it," Michael said.

But there was no ignoring, or hiding, the fact that he could not perform otherwise.

"Please, Mr. Jackson," the doctor said. "This will

take away the pain. Let's just give you a little bit. If you don't like it, then we'll stop."

Of course, Michael couldn't stop, because he couldn't stop performing. A great deal of money was at stake, and this meant a great deal of pressure on Michael to keep the show going. So he agreed to take the painkillers, even though he was very much against them.

Then, as so commonly happens, by the time the original injury had healed and Michael no longer required the painkillers, he had developed a dependency. At first, my family was not worried. Because of Michael's lifelong abstinence from even over-the-counter drugs, everyone assumed that he would be the last person on earth to become addicted. But in 1993, he publicly admitted to having a problem and checked himself into a rehab facility.

Michael was extremely proud of himself for getting clean. But in recent years, chronic injuries from a lifetime of performing, and the tremendous stress of everything he was experiencing, caused him to turn to prescription painkillers once again. When it became clear that something needed to be done to help Michael, who was struggling with dependency again by 2002, we all rallied around him.

As my family members and I discussed the possibility of staging an intervention, I became frightened for Michael's health. The one universal code in my family is the avoidance of all direct communication about any subject that might be uncomfortable or upsetting. Because we do not want to upset each other or seem as if we are prying, we never talk about our feelings or confront each other. This emotional repression may not be the healthiest approach. But in a family as large as mine, I sometimes think it is necessary just to keep the many small conflicts that occur in any family from creating rivalries that would prevent anyone from ever socializing with anyone else.

That we all agreed that we needed to confront Michael made me realize just how serious his problem must have been. I was nervous about what might come of our plan, especially if Michael became angry or hurt. But the rest of my family and I were determined to help Michael, no matter what. Even if Michael didn't believe or want to acknowledge that he had a problem, I knew it was important for him to see that his family was there to support him. Because I had just come out of the shameful shadow of domestic abuse, I was aware that Michael might be feeling embarrassed or guilty about burdening his family with his personal issues. My main concern, as his sister, was to let him know that he didn't have to handle this alone.

When the day for the intervention arrived, we all met at Hayvenhurst. Along with a physician and a psychiatrist we had called to take part in the intervention, we loaded into two cars and two SUVs to make the trip to Neverland. I felt extremely anxious during the drive. I had not seen my brother in nearly a decade, and our first reunion was going to occur during an intervention that might push him away from me for even longer.

I had never seen Neverland. I knew it only as the ramshackle property that Michael had had such passion for when we filmed the "Say Say Say" video there many years before. I was awestruck as we approached the palatial estate that Michael had erected in its place. However, I was not able to enjoy my first impression of the grounds because we quickly faced an obstacle. When we arrived at Neverland, we were shocked to discover that the guards at the security gate would not let us in.

"We're the family," we said. "You have to let us in."

"No, you're not getting in," they said.

Well, we had come to help Michael, and we weren't going to let anyone interfere with our plan. So, members of the family decided that we would jump the gate, and the guards could just go ahead and try to stop us. Several of us crawled over the top of the gate and leapt down on the other side. When we landed on the grounds, someone pressed the button to open the gate for the cars and SUVs, then we ran for the main house as fast as we could. Everybody scattered around the house, looking for an entry point. Tito, I believe, found an open window, which he climbed through into the house. He opened a side door to give another sibling access, and finally someone opened the front door and we all came through the grand foyer of the house together.

I was even more apprehensive and excited now. Then, just like that, Michael came walking by, holding hands with Prince and Paris.

"Oh, hi," he said. "We were just on our way to the pool."

It didn't appear that he knew we were at the house until he saw us. It certainly didn't seem as if he wanted us barred from the grounds, which led to the question of who was trying to keep us out. As I knew from my time with Gordon, a person with an agenda could easily control access to an entertainer such as Michael or myself, who was otherwise isolated from the world. Often, the entertainer wouldn't even know that friends and family were being kept out and messages were being suppressed. Or, sometimes, nothing more ominous was at work than miscommunication. With a big staff such as Michael had, wires sometimes got crossed. Tragically, both of these factors made it nearly impossible to reach Michael with the help he so desperately needed at the end of his life.

On that day at Neverland, after Michael greeted us as a group, he suddenly noticed that I was there among the other siblings. His whole face lit up, and he raced over. "Oh my God, La Toya, I haven't seen you in so long. You look incredible."

We embraced and kissed and couldn't get enough of each other. I relished the moment of reunion, just as I had with all of my other family members. But it was a particular relief to see Michael and touch him and know that he was safe, after the many threats Gordon had made to harm him over the years. I was so happy to be reunited with my brother that I nearly forgot that we were there on a serious mission. Everybody was polite because the kids were present, and we didn't dare mention in front of them why we were there. It was wonderful to see what a proud father Michael was, and how much the two older children had grown since I'd met Paris as a baby.

After we all visited for a while, Michael called for his nanny. She took the kids off to play elsewhere in the house, and the family members followed Michael upstairs.

"I have to go check on Blanket," Michael said.

Blanket was only about three months old, and Michael wanted to make sure he was okay because the nanny was with the older children. It was absolutely amazing to see Blanket for the first time. He was just this tiny little thing, lying in his cradle. Michael didn't want Blanket to be alone, so we all sat and had the meeting in Blanket's room, which was where Michael was staying at that time to be close to him. While we spoke to Michael, he was also changing Blanket's diaper and taking care of matters regarding the house. When Blanket began to cry, Michael fed and burped him until the baby was calm and happy.

Once we were all settled in the room, we told Michael in the most gentle and loving way possible why we were there. We also informed him that we had brought along two doctors, who were waiting downstairs to speak with him. He said that he was done with doctors, and that he didn't wish to see them. Michael understood why we were there, but he began talking about what he was going through at the time instead.

"Certain people in this business are no good," he said. "They take things from you. They rob you. Don't ever trust them."

Then he turned and addressed me directly. "La Toya, you can't trust them. They're no good. They don't really care about us."

My mind immediately leapt to Gordon and the time
that Michael had phoned me years earlier to warn me
that I needed to get away from Gordon before he killed
me. I can't say for certain, but I believe Michael was
thinking the same thing, because he knew that Gordon
was linked to the Mafia, as, apparently, were some of the
men who were targeting him at this time.

Michael now addressed the whole group again.
"They just want to get everything they can out of you,
and milk you, and use you, and toss you away at the end
of the day."

He's so right, you can't trust anybody, I thought. But
I didn't agree with him out loud because I was trying
my best to remain positive and keep the intervention on
track.

One of the family members again brought up the
reason we were there.

"You guys don't understand, there's nothing wrong
with me," Michael said.

He did seem fine, better than fine, even. He was alert
and relaxed, and he looked good physically. Plus, I had
never seen him as happy as he was with his children. Finally, after several hours, he convinced us that nothing
was wrong with him. The nanny brought the other kids
back in, and it became more like a regular Family Day
than anything else. I don't believe that Michael ever spoke
to the doctors, but I'm not sure because I got caught up
visiting with everyone else. Overall, this was a wonderful
bonding moment for everyone in our family, even Michael, and I believe it brought us all closer together.

On the drive back to Hayvenhurst, the physician and the psychiatrist asked us to tell them what had happened, and how Michael appeared and acted. When we described the scene for them, they agreed that he sounded fine as well. All of the family members collectively decided that we trusted what Michael had told us. But we still wanted to be sure he really was okay. So we decided that all of the siblings would take turns staying with Michael at Neverland for a few weeks at a time, just to keep an eye on him. Unfortunately, we weren't able to follow through with this plan, and it would be several years before Michael finally got the help he needed.

I left holding an absolutely gorgeous picture frame containing a beautiful photograph of Paris. Mother and I had been admiring the frame back at Michael's house when he joined our conversation.

"Your frames are so beautiful," I said.

Michael picked up the frame and gave it to me. "Here, take it."

That was Michael, responding with his usual generosity.

As I thought back over the details of our reunion, I prayed that Michael and his family would remain safe. I hoped that I would see him again soon.

Unfortunately, the next time I saw my brother it was on a television news report, and he was gaining more publicity of the type that fueled public misconceptions about him.

When I first saw the images of Michael holding Blanket from the balcony of his Berlin hotel suite in late November 2002, I began thinking about what was happening beyond the perimeters of what was captured in those photos. It would be impossible for someone who never spent time with Michael to completely understand. Wherever Michael went in the world, his fans were so devoted that they would amass by the thousands and stand outside, chanting, "Michael! Michael! Michael! We love you! We love you! We love you!"

They shouted these words for hours, sometimes even all night, camping out to catch the slightest glimpse of him. Streets were closed down. Police were called to protect Michael's safety. City officials grumbled at the disruption he caused just by innocently coming to town.

On this particular day in Germany, the fans had a new chant:

"Let's see the new one! Let's see the new one!"

If Michael loved one thing almost as much as he loved his children, it was finding ways to please his fans. They were his life, and he always tried to show his gratitude to them. So Michael took hold of Blanket and held him out for the fans to see. Because Michael was always worried about his children's safety, he did so as quickly as possible. In his haste, he didn't appear to be holding on to Blanket securely. But knowing what a good father Michael was, I never for a moment doubted that he had a good grip on Blanket. He certainly didn't mean anything odd or upsetting by his behavior. He just didn't think about how his action would be perceived. The moment was misunderstood, and because he was Michael Jackson, the images and the negative headlines went around the world in an instant.

But, no matter how the media twisted the event, the reality was that Michael simply felt that his fans deserved to be acknowledged for their devotion. So, regardless of where he was, or how anxious he was about events in his own life, he always made a point to be pleasant and positive for his fans. As captured in countless photos, he always took a moment to peek out of his hotel window to wave and greet them. Once he had the kids, he always told them to wave as well. They were only allowed to be visible for an instant, in case something should happen, but he did want his fans to feel connected to his family.

Like myself, and all of the siblings, Michael had been raised by Joseph to be grateful to his fans and show them the respect they deserved. Many people wrongly assumed that because Michael was such a huge legend, and because he was shy of the press, he was unapproachable. This wasn't the case at all. Any fan could have a conversation with Michael. When he stayed in Las Vegas, he was known for wandering the hotel grounds late at night without any security or staff of any kind, stopping to chat with anyone who approached him. When he stayed at the Venetian, he often sat in their VIP room watching *Animal Planet* all night, while other guests gambled around him. Those who weren't intimidated by Michael's fame found that, when he had time, he often sat and talked with them for hours. Always concerned for their comfort and well-being, he commonly asked if they were hungry and offered to order them food or invited them back to his suite. He was also known to order pizzas for the fans who regularly stood at the gates of Neverland.

Michael wasn't only gracious because our parents had taught us to be. Michael was also incredibly lonely, as many entertainers are. Michael was, and still is, one of the most beloved pop stars in the world. He played concerts for as many as one hundred thousand people a night and attracted throngs of fans who screamed and cried and fainted and had to be carried away by paramedics. But all of this adulation, and noise, was followed by the deepest, emptiest silence possible. Every night when he walked off that stage, he went to his suite and sat there all alone. The high of performing was followed by isolation and boredom. With no friends to call on the telephone, and only staff members around him because they were paid to be there, it could be an incredibly bleak existence. And every day was just the same. I think that's why family was so important to Michael, because it took away that feeling of being so alone.

I know that, without family, I felt this extreme loneliness when I was with Gordon. I was performing on a much smaller level, but I still experienced that rush every night of being onstage, as everyone smiled back at me and wished they were in my position. It always felt nice to be out there, but the minute the show was over, I found myself back in my room. No one was there with me but Gordon, and even he left to enjoy freedoms that he didn't give to me. Then, it was just quiet.

On top of all this, I related to Michael for another reason. He also faced the burden of being incredibly misunderstood and facing persecution by greedy men who wanted to exploit him for all they could get and then leave him ruined and alone. From the moment I began seeing these parallels in our lives, after I got free of Gordon, I vowed to keep a close eye on my brother and look for any opportunities to help him, or to just let him know I understood.

25

∽

THE QUIET BEFORE
THE STORM

In the years after I left Gordon, I didn't want to attract any attention to myself. I hated the three-ring circus of negative publicity that Gordon turned my life into for years. So, when I had the opportunity to do so, I remained almost entirely out of the public eye in America. Some minor press surrounded my divorce, but I certainly didn't seek it. My frequent performances all happened in Europe and South America. My other creative endeavors and business dealings were happily done behind the scenes. Then, I got an offer that finally made me decide to end my silence.

We received a call in early 2003 asking if I would agree to appear on *Larry King Live*. I didn't want to do it because I was not ready to open myself up to public scrutiny and potential ridicule. But Jeffré felt that it was time for me to reemerge and finally show people my real personality, without Jack Gordon at my side forcing me to be someone I was not and to behave in ways that went against my beliefs. Furthermore, Jeffré was sure that *Larry King*, being a show that was seen in almost every country in the world at the time, was the perfect place for this public unveiling.

Finally, I agreed and appeared on *Larry King Live* on March 4, 2003. I wasn't nervous in the slightest, but Jeffré was a wreck. This was my first interview for an American news outlet since he became my business partner, and he was concerned about every little detail. We both knew that the public would be watching closely, since it was my first press in seven years. Jeffré wanted to make sure I looked good and every word was perfect. He was terrified that I would once again be misunderstood or become a joke to the public. Jeffré even brought our attorney to the set to observe everything, just in case the interview started to go wrong.

"Don't worry," I said. "When I go up there, I'm going to be me."

But worry Jeffré did. When we got to the set, he was sweating the whole time.

Larry made me feel right at home, and the show could not have gone better. People started calling in, and they didn't stop. They were calling from all around the world. Even Larry seemed a little surprised by the reaction.

"I've been doing this show for over twenty years," he said afterward. "We've never gotten a response for anybody like we're getting for you. And we've had presidents on here."

It ended up being their highest-rated show in three years.

During the interview Larry asked me about my new album, *Startin' Over*, and we spoke about it quite extensively. This conversation gave me the opportunity to create awareness about the record, even though I knew that all of the doors were being closed on me.

"When's it coming out?" Larry asked.

"Well, right now we have deals on the table. And we're considering which company we're going to go with."

Afterward, because Jeffré had been so anxious, I was curious to hear what he thought.

"Well, how was the interview?" I said.

"It was incredible, just incredible!" he said.

His words felt good, but what was even more gratifying was the immediate, incredibly positive response we got from the record industry. The very next day, people who had seen me on the show realized that I was on my way back up, and they started calling to talk to me about my new album. In the end, Jeffré and I decided that we both knew the industry extremely well, and that we liked doing what we wanted, when we wanted. Not liking how the record labels initially treated me, or my music, we decided that we could do just as well, if not better, for ourselves. We decided to start our own record label, Ja-Tail Records, so no one could control my musical destiny but me. We signed a distribution deal with Bungalo Records, a subsidiary of Universal Music Group Distribution, in 2004, an arrangement that has worked out extremely well for everyone involved. Since then, that same approach has helped us grow our business into Ja-Tail Enterprises, which now comprises seventeen individual companies.

This marked the beginning of a happy, if all too brief, period of calm and fulfillment in my life. I was proud of my creative and business endeavors, and I had been fully reunited with my family. We seemed to spend more time than usual together as a group that year, and almost once a month we found ourselves gathering for some family party or event. We had one such Family Day at Hayvenhurst in early 2003 that was particularly wonderful because much of the family was able to be there. Each Family Day had a theme, and an actual memo would go out to family members, informing them of how to dress. The theme of this day was Hawaiian, so everyone was dressed in tropical clothes and wearing flowered leis, except for Michael and his children, who apparently didn't get the memo. They arrived in a gorgeous black limo adorned on the inside with crests, which Joseph had bought for Michael as a present. I loved it!

This was the first time I'd seen Michael since the intervention at Neverland, so I was glad to be reunited with him and know that he had no hard feelings about that day. We had a wonderful time visiting, and Michael went upstairs to the gallery that Mother and Joseph keep. This is a huge room full of display cases featuring family memorabilia, such as Michael's white glove. The walls are lined with photos of the family throughout the years. Because of our long history in the entertainment world, it also includes many famous faces, such as family friends Marlon Brando, Katharine Hepburn, Cary Grant, Jackie O, and many others. But, for us, it's just the same as looking through an old family photo album would be for anyone else.

As we strolled through the room together that day, Michael stopped and pointed to an image of us with Paul McCartney on the set of the video shoot for "Say Say Say."

"Remember this?" Michael said.

Next, he stopped and pointed at a picture of him and me having fun at dinner with Yul Brynner. "Look at this, wasn't he great? We had a good time that day!"

Given our busy lives, and the time we had been kept apart, it was absolutely wonderful to have that quiet time with him, reminiscing together.

Soon after that, during the last week of April 2003, Jeffré and I were driving to lunch in Beverly Hills when we came upon a chaotic street scene. Cars were stopped in the middle of the road, with several hundred people mobbing the sidewalks and spilling out into the street. Paparazzi were everywhere. Clearly, something was happening to create so much excitement.

"La Toya, Michael's in there," Jeffré said.

"How do you know?" I said.

"Only Michael creates a crowd like this. I bet Michael's in there shopping."

Jeffré was referring to the Sharper Image on Santa Monica Boulevard in Beverly Hills, which we knew was one of Michael's favorite stores. We drove by slowly, trying to see through the crowd, and we caught sight of a man in a mask.

"That's Michael," Jeffré said.

"Oh, let me out," I said.

I was so excited by the possibility of having an un-expected visit with my brother that I leapt out of the car and let Jeffré go and park on his own. When I approached the store, it was total and absolute pandemonium. Everyone was trying to get a glimpse of Michael.

"Excuse me, excuse me, excuse me," I said as I pushed through the crowd.

When I got close to the store, I saw people pressed up against the windows, peering through the glass. All of the doors were locked, so I knocked on the door. The store's employees realized it was me and let me into the store. Michael was busy shopping, so he didn't notice I was there until I came up behind him and put my hands over his eyes.

"Guess who!" I said.

"La Toya!" he said, excited.

He turned around with the biggest smile on his face and immediately grabbed me and hugged me. We were both so happy to see each other, and it was wonderful to see the children, too. Jeffré had found his way into the store, and he and Michael greeted each other with a hug as well.

"I love your jacket," Michael said to me. "Take it off."

So I removed my jacket, which had a big crest on it, and let him try it on. Next, he noticed my shoes, which had large crests on them as well.

"Oh my God, I love those shoes," he said.

"You're not trying these on," I said.

We all laughed at that. Michael always loved my sense of style, and every time he saw me, he looked me up and down to see what I was wearing, then asked me where I got my outfit.

This whole time, the paparazzi were going nuts outside, trying to get our attention and take pictures, but we did our best to ignore them and just relax and shop around the store. Then, we all went into a private back room, with the kids and their nanny, and started watching *Gladiator* on one of the televisions. After we had been in there for about an hour, we decided to leave.

Without even being asked to do so, the kids put on their Spider-Man masks. I know that many people have misunderstood why Michael covered his children's faces in public and have tried to suggest it had some bizarre significance that it didn't have. Michael had his children wear masks only when they were with him out in public. He didn't want them to be photographed, so no one would know what his children looked like. He wanted them to have the freedom that he didn't have: to go out in the world and live a normal life. By keeping them masked when they were with him, he allowed them to enjoy that freedom when they were with the nanny or with someone other than Michael. I always believed this was a wise decision on Michael's part. The children not only understood their father's reasoning, but they actually loved the masks. It was like getting to play dress-up every day. At home, when it was time for them to go out, they would all run and get their masks, asking each other which one they were going to wear that day. Then they would excitedly put them on.

Once the kids were ready, we all walked out the back entrance of Sharper Image together. It was crazy when we went outside, with everyone shouting our names, trying to get a picture of us together with the kids. The limo was waiting for us and we all got in and drove away. We didn't have a destination in mind, but we wanted to escape the chaos of the street.

"Would you like to have dinner?" I asked my brother.

"Oh, I want to so badly, but I actually have to be in the studio in a little bit," he said.

So we just drove slowly up and down the streets of Beverly Hills, window-shopping on Rodeo Drive, then passing through the other streets in the neighborhood. Then we sat in the car for a while, visiting some more, before the driver took Jeffré and me to where he had parked. As the limo pulled up to Jeffré's car, I remembered something.

"Oh, I want to give Paris a gift," I said.

It was right before Easter, and I had bought a four-foot pink bunny earlier in the day because I knew one of my nephews or nieces would appreciate it.

Michael got out of the car with us so I could give it to him.

"She's going to love it," he said. "Come on, let's give it to her."

So we went back to his car together.

"Paris, Auntie La Toya has something for you," Michael said.

I will never forget the expression on her face, or how huge her eyes got, when she saw this huge pink rabbit. She loved it.

We all embraced and said our good-byes, and then Michael climbed back into the car. I was so happy to have run into him like that and get the chance to spend some time with him.

A few months later, I was asked to present a Best New Group award at the BET Awards on June 24, 2003. I received the call from a friend, Ron Weisner, who was one of the show's producers, and who had managed Michael in the early eighties. He also wanted me to help him get in contact with Michael because he wanted him to present James Brown with an award. He and I both agreed that, as much as Michael loved James Brown, he probably wouldn't do it because he never liked going to awards shows.

Then, the night of the show, Ron came up to me backstage with the biggest smile on his face. "I've got great news, La Toya. Your brother is here."

In my family, that doesn't exactly narrow it down, and I definitely didn't think he meant Michael.

"Who?" I asked.

"Michael. Thanks so much for helping me get him."

I was so excited to hear this, and I wanted to rush back and see him right away.

"Where's his dressing room?" I asked.

"We have him in an extremely private dressing room where no one can see him."

He pointed Jeffré and me in the right direction. When we got to the door, Michael's new security guard was blocking the doorway and not allowing anyone to enter. When he saw me, he introduced himself and then opened the door for Jeffré and me to enter. Now it was Michael's turn to be surprised. He didn't know that I was a presenter on the show as well. When I walked into his dressing room, he was so shocked to see me that we both laughed and exclaimed about what an amazing treat this was.

We were so elated to be together, and it felt just like old times. Michael was getting ready to present his idol, James Brown, with a Lifetime Achievement Award. As always, Michael wanted to look just perfect.

"How do I look?" he asked. "Do I look okay?"

"Yes, Michael," I said. "You look great."

"What about my shirt? Should I button it up one more, or leave it the way it is?"

"No, it looks nice the way it is. But you have a couple of blue threads showing." I removed the threads from his shirt for him.

"How does everything else look?" he said.

"Perfect, Mike."

"Are you sure? Should I take off one of these belts?"

"No, Michael, you can never have enough rhinestones."

Michael laughed. "Do you have a mirror that I can look in?"

"Yes, here." I pulled one out of my purse and handed it to him.

"Do you have any smell?" Michael always called perfume smell.

That was how it had always been before we walked out onstage when we were younger, whenever I was around one of the brothers' shows, or when we did our family show together in Las Vegas. So it was really nice to experience such a familiar moment of closeness with Mike once again.

"Do you have a camera on you?" Michael asked.

"Yes, Jeffré does," I said.

"Jeffré, please take a picture of us and make sure I get a copy."

We posed together, and I think it was one of the happiest photos we ever took. No one was in the dressing room with Michael, so we had a great one-on-one moment. This thirty minutes of quality time together brought us both back to our childhood. Neither of us wanted the visit to end. Michael kept saying how unique and different my outfit was and how it reminded him of the women who served Cleopatra.

Finally, it was time for Michael to surprise James Brown, and the audience.

"Mr. Jackson, it's time to get to the stage," his security said.

"La Toya, you and Jeffré come with me," Michael said.

We all walked through the backstage area together and stood in the wings with all of these different entertainment luminaries such as Steve Harvey around us. Quite a few big stars were there that night, but, as always, they were all mesmerized by Michael because he was the biggest star of them all. Michael had that effect on everyone from presidents to royalty, and even the biggest rock stars in the world. They all wanted to be around Michael, to get to know him, and to be his friend. It created a great deal of stress for Michael, but he handled it with grace and enthusiasm, like the true star he was. Growing up in show business, he and I were used to this kind of reaction from people, so we just kept our conversation going as if nothing were happening. I had already presented my award that night, but I was nervous for Michael. We stood to the side of the stage, and while James Brown was performing, Michael was so into him that he was bopping his head and tapping his foot on the floor, just as he did when he was a little kid and James would come to our house and sing for us there.

"La Toya, James is great," he said.

As Michael continued to listen to James, every crew member and celebrity standing around him was trying to get near Michael to meet him, talk to him, or just take a photo with him.

Then, a stagehand came over to Michael. "Michael, right at the end of the song, you're going to go onstage and put the cape on James Brown's back."

Michael was so excited! He was acting just like a little boy. I was so happy for him.

"La Toya, come with me," Michael said.

"No, Michael, you go!" I said.

"Please."

"This is your moment, Michael, go out there and do what you do best."

"Okay, but you stay here. Don't go anywhere."

"I'll be right here, watching, until you come back."

Michael instantly changed into his Michael Jackson, King of Pop, persona and took the stage. The audience went crazy as soon as they saw him. Even before Michael did anything other than walk out onto the stage, major entertainers were jumping up and down in their seats, clapping and screaming. I was clapping, too, and I had tears of joy in my eyes as I thought back to the little boy I had known in Gary, Indiana, who had such big dreams of being the greatest star who ever lived. And here he was, at forty-four years old, doing just that, and having been a superstar for nearly forty years already. I was so proud of him.

When Michael had completed the speech he made about James, he exited the stage to where Jeffré and I were standing, and we all went back to his dressing room together. Within minutes, James Brown, his wife, and his entourage came back to Michael's dressing room, where we all talked for about thirty minutes.

There was a small private closet, to which Michael excused himself and took me into, holding my arm as he did, so we could finally talk alone.

"I miss you, La Toya," Michael said to me. "I really miss you, and I love you, and I'm so happy I got to see you."

"I love you, too, Michael," I said.

It was a special moment. Unfortunately, as was always the case with Michael, he had too many demands on his time for us to be able to relax for long. We hugged and kissed each other, then exited the closet and rejoined the rest of the group. As Michael said his good-byes to everyone and started exiting the room, he stopped to look at me and wave good-bye. He had flown in for the show, and after a few hours, he had to fly out again. But I was extremely grateful for the little time that we did have together.

We had another happy occasion as a family that summer when Joseph had his seventy-fifth birthday party at Neverland. As with everything at Neverland, it was larger-than-life. The event was open to the public. About five thousand guests attended, including many celebrities. A stage was set up outside and several musical acts performed, including Jermaine. It was a fun day full of much laughter and the kind of shared jokes and stories that are common in big families. I would have enjoyed myself under any circumstances. But in the wake of my 1998 divorce, I was still very aware that, not that long before, I had thought I might never see my family again. Because of this, I truly appreciated the time that we had together that day. And with the troubling times that were ahead, it sticks out in my mind as an oasis of calm and enjoyment amid times of great hardship.

26

∞

THE CONSPIRACY
IS REVEALED

To this day, I can't see breaking news alerts on television without fearing that it is bad news about someone in my family. In the last years of Michael's life, my concern for his safety and well-being was so great that, upon seeing a breaking news teaser, I would sit paralyzed in front of the TV. I couldn't leave the house or do anything until I saw if it was about Michael, and if it was, that he was okay. In November 2003, I was at my home in Las Vegas when the news informed me of the latest devastating development in Michael's life. In this instance, I was first alerted to what was happening by a phone call from Joseph.

"Neverland is being raided," he said.

I immediately turned on the TV and saw the live coverage. Seventy cops were raiding Neverland to search for evidence in the wake of a second round of child-molestation charges against Michael. Terrified for Michael's safety, as well as his reputation, I started calling Mother and other family members to see if they knew anything.

"What's going on?" I asked. "What's going on?"

No one knew where Michael and his children were, or if they were okay. As much as I was concerned for his physical safety, I was also concerned for his spirit. I had no doubt that this was part of the campaign of hate against Michael that he had described when I was at Neverland the previous year for the intervention. I also knew that Neverland was in a prestigious neighborhood in an exclusive county, and that his neighbors didn't want him there. I wasn't sure who was behind this latest attack, but I was certain it was a direct assault.

Why are they doing this to him? I thought.

Within the hour, all of the family members who were in Las Vegas—Mother, Joseph, and Rebbie—met at my house to support each other and decide the best way to help Michael. The news was reporting that Michael's whereabouts were unknown, and that he was considered a fugitive from the law. It was incredibly upsetting to hear my brother described in this sensational way, as if he were some kind of violent killer. With Michael, who loved traveling and staying in the finest hotels around the world, it was impossible to guess even the country where he might be. We were all desperate to know his location. I kept calling more family members.

"Where's Michael?" I asked. "Is he okay?"

Nobody knew exactly where Michael was. Everybody in the family was calling his nanny, Grace, who was always with him. But nobody could reach her. Then we all began trying to call Grace's assistant, and just about anybody we could think of in Michael's inner circle, but we couldn't get through to anyone. I became increasingly scared for him. As we were sitting around discussing what country Michael might be in, we finally got a break. Randy called with good news.

"I found Michael," he said. "He's in Las Vegas."

We soon learned that Michael was staying in Villa One at the Mirage, which was, remarkably, less than five minutes from my home. Joseph went over to make sure Michael was okay. A little later, when Joseph was called away, Mother, Rebbie, Jeffré, and I went to see Michael. While we were there, Jermaine joined us.

At this point, the police were on TV saying, "Michael Jackson is a fugitive. We can't find him. He might have left the country."

The implication was that Michael was running from the law because he was guilty of the accusations against him. This made me so angry that I was sick, but I pulled myself together and tried to be as strong as I possibly could when I saw Michael.

We arrived at the bungalow and found Michael in his hotel room with Grace and his kids. He was dressed in this amazing, gorgeous outfit because he was supposed to be shooting a video or some other promotional materials that day. The terrible news out of Neverland had developed so quickly that Michael didn't even have a chance to cancel the day's plans.

Michael had successfully managed to keep the children from knowing anything about the allegations, or that the police were searching their home in a highly public fashion. But he was having difficulty pretending that everything was okay. Michael was incredibly upset, and even more alarming, the suite was a wreck. As soon as I saw the chaos, I knew that something bad had happened. Paris pulled Mother to the side and told her all about it.

"Grandma, Daddy got so angry that he threw the lamp down," she whispered. "Then, Daddy threw the food and turned over the statue. Daddy's never done that."

Mother and I reassured Paris that everything was going to be just fine.

Apparently, Michael had received a call from security at Neverland, telling him that the house was being raided, and he was unable to control his anger. He had good reason to be upset, too, given how brutally they attacked his home. He had many millions worth of art that was slashed from top to bottom. They cut open his mattress. All of these overdramatic gestures seemed designed to make it seem as if he was a criminal when he wasn't, and to scare him as badly as possible.

Michael was incredibly nervous, pacing every which way. I pulled him aside, where we could speak without the children hearing us.

"What's going on, Michael?"

"I don't know. I don't know."

"Michael, you have to surrender."

"No, I don't."

"You do," I said. "You have to surrender."

"No. They just told me, my manager, my attorney, they said I don't."

I couldn't believe that his closest advisers had given him such advice.

"Michael, you have to surrender," I said. "You can post bail, but you have to surrender."

He didn't believe me because he was going by what his people were telling him. He also didn't feel that he could raise the bail, which was $3 million.

"Michael, you only have to put up ten percent of that," I said.

"No. I have to put up the whole three million dollars."

I was growing increasingly alarmed about the advice he was receiving, but I remained calm. Without letting him see how worried I was about what might happen if he didn't turn himself in before the police found him, I tried to talk some sense into him.

He nervously started pacing again. I followed along with him, to keep talking.

"La Toya, I promise you, I don't know what's going on. I don't even know why they're doing this to me. I didn't do anything." He kept repeating these words again and again, in the most distressed tone of voice. "I didn't do anything. I didn't do anything."

"Of course you didn't do anything."

"I promise you," he said, as if I still didn't believe him. "I promise you."

Michael was clear that he was being framed in an

attempt to extort money from him. He couldn't believe a family he had tried to help was treating him this way.

"I've done everything for this little boy," he said. "He had cancer, and I made him believe he could beat it. And he got better. You don't have a clue, La Toya, what I've done. And they're going to turn around and do this to me."

It was absolutely heartbreaking to see Michael so distraught. I wanted to cry. But I couldn't because I knew I had to stay strong for him and for the children. And I had to try to talk him into at least making the best out of the situation that he could.

"Michael, I understand, but you've got to surrender," I said.

He remained adamant that he didn't have to do anything of the sort. He didn't believe that he was going to be arrested.

"La Toya, you're wrong," he said. "I'll call my attorney here on the phone right now."

Michael may have been reassured by what his attorney said, but I certainly wasn't. Then, all of the pressure finally overwhelmed him. He was so upset that he began to cry.

"I have to be honest with you," he said. "I'm even afraid to walk around in my own yard because I'm afraid they're going to kill me. I could never perform again because I know they're going to kill me."

"Michael, why are you thinking this?" I said.

"I'm afraid around my house because I don't know

what they might do. And security has caught some people on the property. They're watching me."

You're Michael Jackson, I thought. *Who in their right mind is going to kill you? The whole world knows you. People would have to be insane to even try it.*

It was as if he could read my mind. He became even more determined to convince me.

"They're watching me," he said. "They're watching me. They're watching me."

He kept repeating this over and over. Then he confided in me even more.

"La Toya, I'm being framed. All of this is a setup. You've gotta believe me."

I must have given him a look that suggested I still didn't believe him.

"And I know who's behind it," he said.

"Who, Michael?"

"La Toya, they want my catalog. They want my publishing. They'll do whatever it takes to get it. They're going to kill me. I hate my life. I don't even want the catalog anymore."

This was the first I had heard of his suspicion about such a plot. But I quickly came to believe him. I knew what it was like to have my life threatened by someone and not have my story accepted as true. Back in 1986, music producer Phil Spector tried to hold me prisoner in his house and subjected me to bizarre and terrifying treatment during a business meeting. When I told the story in my first book, everyone laughed it off. Years later, Spector was convicted of murdering another woman in a series of events that sounded disturbingly like what I had experienced.

I also knew firsthand what Gordon had been capable of in order to steal much, much, much less money from me. I had heard Gordon threaten Michael's life so many times that I immediately wondered if he was behind this. I wanted to know if this was what Michael suspected, so I pressed him for details. He went on to tell me he believed it was a whole handful of scoundrels behind the plot, who were coming in for the kill. He was clearly terrified.

"You'll see," he said. "It's all about my publishing."

What he described made Gordon look like a small-time crook. By this point, Michael's catalog contained almost 750,000 songs and was worth a billion-plus dollars. It was set up so that Michael and his estate would never have been broke in many lifetimes.

"This is nothing new," Michael said. "This has been going on for a long time. But they finally succeeded with this one."

It wasn't just the latest child-molestation charges that convinced Michael that they were closing in on him. As he told me more of the details and remained so adamant, I began to believe him. And tragically, in the end, it seems that he was right. Everyone he named that day was working to bring him down.

I think Michael told me because he knew that, after everything I had been through, I would believe him. Maybe he even hoped that I could help in some way because I had escaped from similar adversity. To my knowledge, he never confided in any of his other siblings. But Mother did let me know, after he passed, that he also told her that people were conspiring to take his life. It breaks my heart that we were not able to do anything to save him, and I am determined that those responsible will eventually be brought to justice.

27

◆◇◆

FACING DOWN ALLEGATIONS AS A FAMILY

While Michael and I were talking, the scene at the Mirage became even more tense and chaotic. It was now known that Michael was staying there, and helicopters began circling overhead, trying to get footage of him. Paris became excited about this.

"Oh, look, paparazzi!" she said.

Paris innocently wanted to go out and have her picture taken, while Michael was trying to keep her inside. This was a welcome distraction from the day's extreme tension. It was wonderful to see Michael try to be strict with his daughter, without scaring her about the seriousness of the situation, while also being charmed by her excitement.

"This is what I mean about her," he said, half laughing. "She always does things like that."

I smiled, thinking that Michael and Paris were just like any father and his preteen daughter, even though the circumstances were so out of the ordinary.

"La Toya, sometimes paparazzi are outside, and helicopters are flying around," he said. "And she will go out and wave at them to be friendly."

We laughed about this together, and I was happy to hear the sound of his laughter. We were trying to keep things as normal as possible for the kids, so we sat down and ordered lunch. We ate chicken fingers and soup and all of the foods they liked best. The whole time, we tried to keep the mood light, even though it was incredibly difficult.

Around this time, the management at the Mirage became concerned that the helicopters and paparazzi swarming the hotel were disturbing the other guests. In a gesture that I thought was extremely rude, they asked Michael to leave. The good people at the Green Valley Ranch were kind enough to offer him shelter instead. We gathered up all of Michael's and his children's belongings, and with the children and Grace, we all walked down a secret back passageway that led out the back of the hotel. The plan was for Michael to get in a car and go to his new hotel, where no one would expect him to be.

We all left the Mirage in a big caravan of cars. Because Michael didn't want anybody to know where he was, he had his driver start driving around and around the city. Only, a whole string of cars was following along behind him. Michael decided he didn't want us around anymore because it might draw attention to him and allow the paparazzi to know where he was. So the rest of the family all went to Mother's Vegas house. It was a terrible moment because we were all worried about Michael, yet we didn't feel that we could do anything to help him. But I was still convinced that if I could at least get him to surrender, that would be a good start. I got him on the phone.

"You've got to surrender," I said. "You don't understand."

Michael was still reluctant, but finally, the following day, he got in a private jet with the intention of going back to Los Angeles to surrender. But even then, he was still trying to avoid doing so if possible, and he spent several hours in the jet on the tarmac, uncertain of what to do. Proving that he could never feel completely safe anywhere, someone from the private jet company secretly filmed him and recorded his conversation while on the plane. Of course, Michael later sued, and won, but in that incredibly stressful moment, it was one more unpleasant and upsetting thing to worry about. He was facing one of the darkest hours of his life, and he had no one to advise or support him. After years of being exploited and robbed by attorneys and managers, he spent years with his nanny as his manager. Just think about that, in light of the types of decisions he was faced with and the vast sums of money that were at stake. It also explains perfectly how vulnerable Michael was to being influenced in his last days by malicious people who claimed to have his best interests at heart.

Finally, Michael arrived in Los Angeles, and the cops met him at the airport and took him to the police station. The moment was caught by news cameras and broadcast around the world, with the famous footage of Michael getting out of the back of the police car in handcuffs, which I thought was unnecessary and intended to make him look bad and guilty.

I felt relieved when Michael turned himself in because I knew that the best approach was to face up to what was happening, no matter how upsetting and untrue it was. But during the whole next year I never really felt better. I was worried for Michael, and worried about Michael. I could not shake from my mind our conversation at the Mirage and the look of fear, and passionate belief, on Michael's face as he'd said to me, "They're going to kill me."

I knew that it would be a long time before his name would be cleared, and that even then the damage could be lasting.

The following week was Thanksgiving. Much of the family gathered for Thanksgiving dinner on the ocean in Malibu. We tried to rally and be cheerful, but it was extremely difficult. It didn't help that, even though Michael wasn't with us, a paparazzi boat floated up, trying to get photos of the family.

After that, there was nothing to do but to support Michael and to see what came next. The allegations crystallized, official charges were brought against Michael, and the DA began making arrangements for the trial. This whole time, the most upsetting lies were being told about Michael in the press. We all just tried to keep our spirits up as best as we could.

To distract myself and feel that I could control at least one area of my life, I threw myself into my work

at Ja-Tail Enterprises and my new music. It took some
convincing on Jeffré's part, but I finally concluded that
it wasn't yet time for me to retire. I would prove all of
those nay-saying record executives wrong. Jeffré and I,
along with our record promoter friend Brad Le Beau,
came up with a plan to get my music heard and maybe
even have the last laugh.

We chose "Just Wanna Dance" as my first single,
then looked into having a CD single of the track manufactured in Santa Monica. We talked the plant into label-
ing the CDs with a stamp that read MANUFACTURED
IN THE UK. Instead of crediting the song to La Toya
Jackson, whom we had been told was damaged goods,
we decided to release it under my nickname, Toy. And
instead of decorating the cover with an image of my
face, which would instantly be recognized by music fans
around the world, we cropped out just one eye and created artwork that featured it in close-up.

When the packaging was complete, we started
submitting the song to dance radio. Without any additional effort on our part—no record-label pull, no
publicity campaign, not even a follow-up phone call—
the strength of the song landed it heavy rotation in the
clubs and on dance radio. Within the first few weeks,
the song charted, entering *Billboard* at number forty-
two. We were ecstatic. I had been right to believe in
my songs, and Jeffré had been right to believe in me.
The industry might have felt as done with me as I felt
with it, but apparently, clubgoers and dance radio listeners out there were still hungry for my music. The

next week, my song was at twenty-seven. Then it was at twenty-three. Finally, it topped out at number nineteen. This went far toward making me feel that I wasn't damaged goods.

When we saw that the song was slowing down, we concocted our first marketing tactic. We decided that "Toy" would call the club radio stations personally and thank them for playing her song. That's just what I did. We had worked out exactly what I was going to say when I got the first station's programming director on the phone.

"Hello, my name is Toy, and I just want to thank you for playing my song."

"Oh my gosh, Toy, we love your song," he said. "People are requesting it like crazy."

Because my song had come out of nowhere and been so popular, all of the programmers I spoke to were curious about Toy, and they had a multitude of questions for me.

"Now, Toy, are you Asian?" the first programmer asked.

"No, I'm not Asian," I said playfully.

"We see here that you're from the UK. Are you going to do a promotional tour?"

"No. Toy is just my nickname. My real name is La Toya Jackson."

"Oh my God! . . . You're kidding me!" he exclaimed. "You're La Toya Jackson? The real La Toya Jackson?"

"Yes," I said.

"What a great marketing plan," he said. "Because I'll be honest with you, I never would have played your music. Good job!"

Hearing this made me happy.

Each time, I let the radio programmer build up his story about how much he and the station's listeners loved my song before I revealed my identity. This made the payoff even sweeter when I witnessed them trying to backtrack after they'd learned that their latest hit song was mine. All the while, I knew that if we had told them the song was by La Toya Jackson from the beginning, we would have heard a resounding chorus of "Oh, we don't like it."

Nobody thought that I still had the talent or the guts to remain relevant to today's radio audience and club-goers. Everybody went ahead and wrote me off, so when I emerged with a hot new single, they were all floored. The editors of *Billboard* thought it was a brilliant marketing plan, and the magazine ran a full-page story on my radio coup.

In the wake of so much positive attention, and with our distribution deal in place, Ja-Tail Records prepared to release the album. Then, Michael's trial started, and we knew that, again, this would not be an appropriate time to release the album. I was ready to devote all of my attention to Michael and our efforts as a family to support him during his time of need.

28

❧

THE FINAL DAYS
OF NEVERLAND

Neverland was the culmination of everything Michael had worked for his entire life as an entertainer, and a powerful symbol of love for him. When his fame made it impossible for him, and eventually his children, to enjoy a normal existence in the outside world, the grounds gave him the opportunity to live a version of real life in his own world.

But Michael felt his sanctuary was ruined in the aftermath of the police raid in November 2003. The material damage done by the officers during their search could be repaired, but the spirit of the place was tainted for Michael forever. Michael voiced this conviction to me with a great deal of emotion the first time I visited Neverland after the raid.

As he contemplated what his enemies were attempting to do to him, and the criminal trial that was most likely yet to come, he vowed to me, "La Toya, when this trial's over, I'm never, ever, coming back to Neverland again. They've invaded my privacy. They've ruined my entire life. I hate this place. I can't stand it. I never want to see it again. Never. I'll never come back here."

Since I was with Michael when he first fell in love with the property during the "Say Say Say" video shoot, I knew how devastated he must be to walk away from his pride and joy forever. I also knew that when Michael made this statement, he meant it, because he was adamant once he made a decision. With all of this in mind, it was a bittersweet moment when I drove through the Neverland gate at the start of Michael's 2005 trial, knowing that whatever happened in the next few months, Michael would never set foot on the property again. At the same time that he made this promise to me, Michael also made it clear that I was more than welcome to visit Neverland, and hold events there, any time I wanted to do so. How sweet of him, as always.

Along with the rest of my family, I stayed at Neverland for the many weeks of Michael's pretrial and trial, and I came to see firsthand that the property truly was an exceptional place. At first glance, it appeared to resemble our family home, Hayvenhurst, only larger. But I soon realized that, behind his large golden gates, Michael had succeeded in creating a miniature replica of the real world on his three thousand acres of exceptionally manicured property. But this real world was also a magic kingdom. Upon driving beneath the Neverland arch, with its gilded crest and crown and a giant scroll that read MICHAEL JACKSON in black script, it was clear that this was a king's palace. Neverland was a living fairy tale, which Michael created to finally have a normal childhood and life for himself. Michael's gates were open to children of all ages and all races, to come and have fun any time they wanted. Whenever Michael heard about poor or sick children, it broke his heart to the point of tears, and he often invited underprivileged kids from schools, hospitals, and communities to Neverland. When they arrived, he had all of the amusement park rides going and offered them all the free candy, hot dogs and hamburgers, and anything else a kid or an adult could want. Michael threw these events monthly, sometimes weekly, to make as many children as possible happy.

One commonly saw an elephant or giraffe walk by with its trainer. Or an anaconda might be sweeping through the grass, past the man-made lake, with the most beautiful peacocks and flamingos in the water and the gigantic fountain at its center. I loved the elegant classical music that played everywhere on the property, immediately transporting visitors to a different world. I always listened to that in my room at home. Michael had this serene, heavenly music outdoors for everyone to enjoy!

What particularly struck me about Neverland, during the free time we had while waiting to go to court, was the day when Michael's children came running up to me, wide-eyed and overjoyed with excitement.

"Auntie La Toya, we're going to the beach today," they said. "Do you want to come with us?"

"Well, I don't know," I said.

Michael's children had no idea what was going on at this time, but we were waiting to go to court to hear the verdict, and I was thinking that the attorneys could call at any second.

"Oh, please, come to the beach with us," they said. "It'll be fun."

"Okay, what time are we leaving?"

"We're going to go in five minutes. Can you get ready in five minutes?"

I had on my pajamas, which is what I always wore while we waited to be called to court.

"It's a school project," Paris explained.

Prince and Blanket both had on their royal-blue swimming trunks with short, white terry-cloth robes with hoods. Paris was wearing a pink-and-white bikini. They were all carrying their brightly colored sand buckets and shovels for the beach.

How cute, I thought.

I was moved by how excited they were by this adventure, so I was smiling and laughing along with them, but the entire time I was wondering, *Now where are we going to go to the beach around here in the middle of the mountains?*

Well, just as the children promised, we left on our journey in five minutes' time. I soon realized, much to my delight, that the "beach" was right there on the property. This beach could be reached by the Neverland train, The Katherine—named after Mother—or one of the luxurious golf carts that were always available to cover the spacious grounds. Although no ocean or natural lakes were to be seen for many miles, we enjoyed the day at a pretty area of white sand with a beautiful pool of water.

When we arrived at the "beach," the children and their tutor set up their umbrellas. They lay out on their towels just like any kids relishing a day at the seashore. We even made sand castles with the buckets, shovels, and seashells we had brought along with us and had a nice lunch that the chefs had prepared for us. It was a delightful trip for all of us.

The next day, the children rushed up to me with another thrilling plan.

"We always go on field trips," they said. "We're going to the library today. We have to study."

As promised, they went upstairs to Michael's library, which was filled with row upon row of bookshelves, separated by aisles, with a tall ladder to reach the books on the higher shelves. It was tranquil and looked exactly like a university library.

For the children, this was the only life they had ever known, so these pretend field trips were a perfectly normal occurrence. For anyone else who visited Neverland for the first time, the experience was so exceptional that it was almost like living in a picture book.

At Hayvenhurst, we had a movie theater. No one else had a movie theater in their home at the time, so we would premiere the latest movies before they came out. Many entertainers, including Elizabeth Taylor, Gregory Peck, Marlon Brando, Jimmy Jam, Terry Louis, and

Spanky of *The Little Rascals* would attend our screenings.

At Neverland, Michael took this one step further and erected an exact replica of an AMC movie theater. Inside, signs listed all of the features that were being screened, and uniformed staff stood at attention behind the concession stand, ready to serve popcorn, hot dogs, sweets, and drinks. Although everything was free, they completed the transactions just as they would have at a regular movie theater.

Upstairs from the theater was the train station, where a bakery offered pastries. This train station had the grandeur of Union Station. The train would pull up to take passengers anywhere they wanted to go on the property. Another building contained a full video arcade with all of the most popular games. Videos were "rented" from a perfect re-creation of a Blockbuster video store. After they were viewed, the help could be asked to return them. Michael always liked having things that were the biggest, the best of the best, or one of a kind, which I found out firsthand when I walked over to his alligator pit, and there sat the largest alligator imaginable.

After the raid, Michael refused to stay in his quarters in the main house, so he chose to sleep in one of the property's many bungalows, which were lavishly decorated and just as comfortable as the world's finest hotels. All offered a DO NOT DISTURB sign, wake-up calls, and other such services. Inside each guesthouse were white slippers and robes adorned with the word NEVERLAND and its crest, as well as personalized towels, soap, pencils, pads of paper, and every other thing guests might need to make them feel at home during their stay. There was also a room-service menu, from which any item could be ordered at any time. I loved Michael for this because, growing up, we could always order what we wanted to eat from our chef, upstairs in our room, if we didn't feel like going downstairs to eat. Mike and I always said that when we got our own places, we would have a special menu to order from. He did just that when he created the Neverland menu.

Inside the main house, the dramatically decorated great room was a comfortable gathering spot that always seemed to attract whatever family and friends were staying at Neverland at the time. This room bordered the kitchen, which was as well stocked as the kitchen of any fine-dining restaurant, and usually staffed by a half dozen chefs, all dressed in uniforms topped with tall white hats. In front of the kitchen was a bar, where food was served. Items could be ordered from the regular Neverland menu, which was displayed on a tripod near the kitchen, and was also available in smaller laminated versions, like a restaurant's menu. The menus were adorned with an image of a boy sitting on the moon, just like the DreamWorks logo, but without the fishing pole. Michael told me that DreamWorks took that image from him. The menus featured any dish a person might desire, from a hamburger and french fries to foie gras, champagne and caviar, and, of course, dinner entrées. A board featured the day's specials, also like a restaurant.

The chefs could prepare almost anything that was requested at any time.

Every time Michael came home to Neverland from a tour, a vacation, or even just a day spent shopping or in the studio, all of the staff members lined up from outside the front door, all the way down the stairs, and along each side of the walkway. When Michael stepped out of the car, he walked between the rows of employees, who numbered about twenty-five, as they all stood at attention and addressed him when he walked by.

"Hello, Mr. Jackson," one would say.

"Welcome, Mr. Jackson," the next would say.

As Michael passed by them, he took a moment to acknowledge each employee with a greeting and a smile or a nod of the head. Once the trial got under way, I always marveled that he had the stamina to maintain this tradition and be so gracious to his staff, considering all of the stress he was enduring, and with his mind probably still back in court. But these rituals meant the world to Michael, and he seemed comforted by them at a time when his life beyond the gates of his home was chaotic and uncertain.

For Michael, the protection that Neverland offered was essential, even under the best of circumstances. With the fame that he achieved, he would never have been able to do normal things, such as enjoying a trip to the movies or the zoo, in the real world. So he created every possible source of entertainment he could desire for himself inside his own private world. That's why he called it Neverland.

"This is my world," he used to say.

As a member of Michael's family, I knew that such seclusion was necessary, and so the enclosed world of Neverland became normal for me while I was there. But I also knew that it must have been an exceptionally lonely existence for Michael at times. So, I was extremely glad that all of his family were able to be there with him during his trial.

29

THE TRIAL OF A LIFETIME

Just as on my first day in divorce court, the entire family rallied around Michael as he went through this difficult time. We planned to be there in court every day to show solidarity with Michael, and to let those who were persecuting him know that they didn't just face off against Michael. They were up against the entire Jackson clan.

So, in January of 2004 when the preliminary trial started, we all gathered at Neverland to stay for however long we were needed. Being together at Neverland felt a bit like the old days at Hayvenhurst, but even better, because after everything we had been through in our lives, we all appreciated our present closeness even more.

During this time, I had the chance to sit down and have a conversation with Michael that was more than a decade in coming. I was finally able, for the first time, to get him one-on-one, and I took advantage of the opportunity immediately. We were sitting close together on a sofa just off the foyer of the main house. I looked at my brother and gathered my courage to speak.

"Michael, I need to talk to you, because this has been bothering me."

"Okay." He smiled at me expectantly.

"I want you to know that what happened——"

"You don't have to say anything, La Toya."

"What do you mean? You don't even know what I'm going to say."

"You don't have to say anything. I know you. I know your heart. I know that he made you do those things."

I was shocked that, after all this time, he knew exactly what I was talking about.

"But I have to get it out," I said.

"You don't have to, La Toya. I know better. I know who you are. I love you very much."

To hear him speak those words of forgiveness filled me with such gratitude, but I still felt that I hadn't said enough. I kept trying to give voice to my apology, again and again.

"I just want to tell you," I said.

But Michael had clearly forgiven me long ago, and he didn't want to discuss it any further. He was just happy to see me, and to know that I was back in his life, and that we were all together as a family once again.

"I know you, and I know that you would never do anything to hurt me," he said. "I want you to know that I love you very much."

"I love you, too," I said.

Then, Michael looked right at me and spoke his famous phrase: "No, I love you more."

I started crying, I was so relieved and happy and overwhelmed. Then Michael hugged me to comfort me, and he started crying, too. We sat there for the longest time, just crying together, and embracing each other, and telling each other how much we loved one another and enjoying the feeling of being reunited at last. It was one of the most incredible moments of my entire life. I was so moved by hearing him say that he knew I would never turn against him or intentionally hurt him the way Gordon had forced me to do. It was just what I'd hoped for in that awful long-ago moment in Tel Aviv, that Michael knew me too well to be fooled by Gordon's evil plan.

But as I knew in the moment in Tel Aviv, and over the ensuing years, such forgiveness was almost too much to desire. I took responsibility for what I had done, even though forced by Gordon, and I would have understood if Michael had remained upset with me. So it was such a relief that he knew me so well. I later realized that part of what made Michael able to forgive me so easily was that he had his own manipulators and was aware of plots against him even as far back as the press conference, even though it would be years before he told me of it. That's why he knew what had happened without any doubt.

Michael's hatred of those behind the Neverland raid may have made it impossible for him to stay in his old room, but aside from making that change in his routine,

Michael was determined to keep life as normal as possible for the children. Every morning, when we left for court, he was sure to be incredibly upbeat with them.

"Daddy, when are you coming back?" they would ask.

"I'll be back later today," he would say.

He would kiss and hug them good-bye and keep his smile wide the whole time, until he got out the door and into the car. Only then would the anxiety and anger he felt over what he was about to endure show on his face, as he steeled himself for the day ahead.

On the first day of court, we all traveled together in a caravan of SUVs. Mother, Joseph, and all of the siblings except for Marlon were there.

The usual throngs of fans were waiting for Michael outside the courthouse, but they were even more animated than normal in their eagerness to show their support for Michael during his time of need. They went wild when he emerged from the SUV, screaming and shouting his name, as well as messages of faith regarding his innocence. Buoyed by their love and determined to show those who aimed to bring him down that he could not be broken, Michael jumped up on the roof of his SUV and began waving, blowing kisses, and flashing the peace sign. For a brief moment, he clapped his hands and did the slightest dance move as the adoring crowd cheered him on. Unfortunately, just as with so much else that Michael did, his intentions were incredibly misunderstood. This gesture was immediately leapt upon by the press and quickly criticized by many. Of course Michael meant no disrespect to sexual-abuse victims. But he knew that dirty businessmen with a vendetta against him had gotten the children behind the charges he was facing to speak their lies. He was thinking more about pleasing his fans, who were doing so much to sustain him during this difficult time.

The media storm that erupted following the first day made me extremely nervous about what was yet to come. Many nasty lies were written about Michael and spoken about him in court during this time. We family members all did the best we could to remain optimistic and keep Michael's spirits up.

After the pretrial, which lasted for several weeks, the prosecutors decided there was enough evidence to move forward with the case. But the actual trial was not scheduled to begin until January of the next year. Although it was a relief to have a break from the acute anxiety of being in court every day, it was impossible to relax during the time between the two trials. We all knew that Michael was about to face one of the greatest challenges of his entire life, with a barrage of exceptionally negative press for its duration. So I was particularly grateful that we were all able to gather as a family for a happy occasion in August. Michael's forty-sixth birthday was August 29, so we all planned to gather in celebration. In deference to Mother's Jehovah's Witness beliefs, we didn't call the event a birthday party and held it the day after Michael's actual birthday. We simply said that we were gathering for a dinner in Michael's honor. Even so, my sister Rebbie declined to attend because she felt the night's festivities were too much like a birthday party. But the rest of us felt that Michael needed something to buoy his spirits and take his mind off the troubles he faced, so we were all overjoyed to be there with him.

We all gathered at a restaurant in downtown Los Angeles, which provided us with our own personal chef and a private room where we could have privacy. Except for Rebbie and Marlon, all of the siblings were there, and it felt wonderful to be together as a family. I hadn't seen Michael since the pretrial. But I was well aware of his assassination fears, and I'd been researching on my own to put together the puzzle pieces of the conspiracy he had described. I was extremely concerned about his health and state of mind. I was eager to inquire about his well-being and see how he looked for myself.

"How are you feeling?" I asked him.

"I'm holding up," he said. "I feel good."

I didn't entirely believe him because I could see such worry in his face. I knew from my own experience with Gordon that people with a nefarious agenda tend not to stop until they have achieved their goal, and I was afraid that the upcoming trial might actually ruin Michael. If convicted, he faced a sentence of close to twenty years in prison.

But, as I have said, it was not our way to talk about feelings and other serious matters in our family, so I pushed aside my fears and did my best to enjoy myself. At this lovely dinner we all sat and talked and laughed and ate and just enjoyed each other, all together. It felt like a fun, bonding moment for all of us.

The night also offered the opportunity for a particularly sweet moment between Michael and Joseph. When Joseph first walked into the room, Michael noticed that his father was looking for a chair in which to sit.

"Joseph, sit here next to me," Michael said.

The two sat near each other and visited together for much of the night. This was a clear example of the comfort that Michael took from having his father nearby to protect him during this exceptionally frightening time in his life. I like to think that Michael was strengthened by the presence of all of his family members, but I know that Joseph was a special source of power for Michael.

At the end of 2004, I also had a positive experience in my personal life. Two years after completing my new album, *Startin' Over*, during which time Jeffré and I had done everything in our power to find a way to put it out in the world, we signed the distribution deal with Bungalo Records. The arrangement, by which they provide distribution for the albums we put out through our own Ja-Tail Records, gave me a great feeling of optimism that my music career and business life were about to blossom in all-new ways. With the distribution deal in place, we should have been incredibly excited to finally put out *Startin' Over*. But this all came to fruition just as Michael entered one of the most difficult periods of his life. I realized it was no time to push my own career forward, and I once again held my album. My main focus was on supporting my brother as best as I could, along with the other members of my family.

Michael's trial began on January 31, 2005, in Santa

Maria, California. Again, all of the family returned to Neverland to be in court with Michael every day. This time, we were determined to show even greater loyalty and unity than we had during the pretrial. We all rode to court together in one of Michael's tour buses. I was nervous on Michael's behalf as we approached what would inevitably be an extremely difficult and painful time for him. But I also felt honored to be part of such a strong family as we all climbed down off the bus together, especially because of the long years with Gordon when I feared I might never see my family again and, worse, that they might be harmed because of me. I hoped that Michael also felt the force of our family around him, and that we were helping to hold him up on this upsetting day. I had decided that everyone in the family should dress in all white as a symbol of Michael's innocence, so we all did. It looked great visually, and I think it worked on Michael's mood as well, helping him to feel as if we were projecting a positive message right from the start, and that he had a team of people with him who really loved and cared for him: his family.

We all planned to stand beside Michael in court every day during the trial. But when we arrived on the first day, we were told that there was not enough room for the entire family. We had been assigned a certain number of seats. I had never before heard of what, to me, seemed like an incredibly unfair rule. I believe that it was another subtle way in which those persecuting Michael were attempting to intimidate him and show him that they were in control. Oddly, the number of seats we were granted seemed to change every day, so we never knew exactly how many people were allowed to be there. Mother was present every single day, but the rest of us had to take turns.

Also there every day, although there wasn't always room for him to be in court, was Joseph. Like me, Michael had made peace with our father as he aged and began to have greater appreciation for Joseph's role in getting him to the heights that he'd reached in his life. Several times, Michael reached out and hugged Joseph or even held on to his father's hand as they walked into court together. I know how comforted I felt by Joseph's presence and words of strength in the first days after I left Gordon, and I believe that Michael felt the same way during his trial. He knew our father would do everything in his power to protect him from the dark forces then at work in his life, and Joseph did do his best.

As much as I wanted to be there for Michael, it was excruciatingly painful to sit and hear the lies spoken about him. I could not understand how Mother could possibly listen to the upsetting details day after day. What hurt more than anything else was the knowledge that the accusers were lying. I could almost see them patch the falsehoods together. The whole time, I was just hoping beyond hope that Michael's lawyers could convince the jurors that none of this was true.

If it was difficult for me to hear what was being said about Michael in court, I can only imagine how excruciating it was for him. When I looked at him as he listened to the testimony, he appeared so fragile. But I realized that he must be the strongest man in the world to be able to endure what was being fabricated about him and remain so composed.

When we were given lunch and other short breaks throughout the day, we would all go into a little room in the courthouse, or onto the bus, with Michael. I had a mission during these moments. I shared it with the siblings and made sure we all kept it in mind.

"It's important that nobody discuss business or anything of that nature at a moment like this," I said. "Whatever you do, do everything to cheer Michael up and make him happy. Try to get his mind off of what's going on."

Even with everyone doing his or her best to keep Michael's spirits up, he would sink into moments of despair. I continued to worry about his health because he didn't want to eat or do anything to take care of himself. We would plead with him to at least take his vitamins to keep his strength up, but sometimes it was difficult to convince him to do even this. After falling one morning, Michael was in so much pain that we had to take him to the hospital emergency room. He was wearing his pajamas, a white T-shirt, and a jacket that he grabbed on his way out of the house. Because it took him more time at the hospital than he expected, Michael found himself running late to be in court on time. He wanted to go home and change, but his attorney Thomas Mesereau, told Michael to come to court in his pajamas because he was almost an hour late, and if he didn't get there soon, they were going to put a warrant out for his arrest. This story about Michael's arrival in pajamas went all around the world and was seen as another example of eccentric behavior from Michael, but was nothing but a matter of bad timing.

Michael did receive one expression of support during this time that seemed to lift his mood. On one of the mornings that we were all traveling to court together on Michael's bus, Jermaine was talking on his cell phone to his longtime friend the prince of Bahrain. The prince asked to speak to Michael. He knew of Michael's trial, and after they spoke back and forth for a few minutes, the prince made Michael an offer: "You can always stay here if you want to rest and get away from all of the nonsense."

As I would later learn, that invitation was a life raft for Michael during an otherwise impossible time in his life.

As concerned as I was about Michael, I received news during this time that finally allowed me to relax in a way that I hadn't been able to in decades. Jeffré told me that Gordon had passed away from cancer on April 19, 2005. I immediately felt so much of the old fear leave my body. Then, I thought of his family.

"I feel sorry for his children and grandchildren," I said.

Although I immediately felt relieved, Gordon had faked his death before, so I couldn't believe that he had really died. I sent a security expert to the funeral to make sure that he was in the casket. The expert called me from the funeral home and confirmed that he had seen Jack

Gordon dead in his casket. Soon after that, Jeffré began receiving calls and e-mails from people around the world telling him to tell me they said congratulations because they had heard that Jack Gordon died. But as badly as Gordon had treated me, I continued to feel sorry for his children.

"May he rest in peace," I said.

After having always feared that Gordon would make good on his threats and kill me, the reign of terror had finally ended. I was free. My brother, however, was not.

Finally, in June 2005, both sides had presented all of their evidence and called all of their witnesses to testify in Michael's trial, and the jury began their deliberations. Every morning we woke up early, not knowing what the verdict was going to be, or if this was the day that we would finally find out. The court told us that once they called to inform us that the verdict had been reached, we had to appear in court within some impossibly short amount of time. So we all got half-dressed every morning so that we could all be ready to go out the door almost instantly. Then, we all relaxed around the house, talking and playing games, trying to make it feel for the children as if life were positive and fun. We were all worried about what was going to happen, but we tried to stay upbeat and say encouraging things to Michael whenever he emerged from his guesthouse. He was so nervous that he mostly stayed in his room alone, so I know he was glad that his family was there to be with the children. They still had no idea of what their father was enduring and thought that the family was simply there on an extended sleepover. They were still quite young at the time—Prince was eight, Paris was seven, and Blanket was only two or three. And they just adored their father, so he was careful to be as normal as possible around them. Also, they were not allowed to watch television, except for children's stations such as Disney and Nickelodeon that didn't show other programs that might include any mention of the trial. Michael didn't want his kids to be subjected to any of the lies that were being spread about him. So they actually thought this was a special time, like Family Day, only Family Month, and they loved having their grandparents and all of their aunts and uncles around.

Although we never doubted Michael's innocence, we were afraid that the verdict might not go in his favor. Michael had begun telling members of the family what they should do if he went to prison. So when we finally received the call to tell us the verdict had been handed down, the mood was somewhat somber. Michael came down the stairs. At the bottom, he waited as one of his dressers put on his bulletproof vest, then his blazer. As Michael prepared to climb into one of the waiting cars, I could tell by the drawn expression on his face that he was scared to death. I thought of the little five-year-old boy who had so much energy and couldn't wait to get onstage and perform, again and again, in front of tens of thousands of people. Those days were long gone. Michael had lost that energy from the wear and tear that this business puts on entertainers. He was so drained from the massive worries of his trial and the vultures who were out to get his publishing catalog, his estate, and everything he had worked so hard to achieve. I wanted to hug him tightly and cry for him, but I knew that would only make him even weaker, so I remained strong. I walked up and stopped him just before he took his seat in the vehicle.

"Michael, wait," I said. "How do you feel?"

"I'm okay."

I could see the pain and nervousness on his face.

"I want you to do something for me," I said. "I want you to think from the end."

"What do you mean, La Toya?"

"Think from the end," I said again.

"What does that mean?"

"Think as if it's already happened. You already know the verdict. You're innocent. So, whatever the end results are, you already know. Think from the end. Make it a good one."

He actually smiled then, which warmed my heart.

"Oh, that's great," he said. "I'll do that."

"Everything's going to work out," I said. "Just think from the end."

We shared a smile, but then Michael's expression darkened.

"When this is over, I'm leaving and I'm never coming back," he said. "This country has been cruel to me. I was born in this country, and they treat me so unfairly."

I tried to reassure him, but I knew that I could say or do nothing to right the wrongs that had been done to him. We got in the car to go to court. We didn't know what to expect, and we were all incredibly anxious. Michael had an even greater fear than the possibility that he might be found guilty. He was wearing a bulletproof vest, a habit he had adopted since the time when he went head-to-head with Tommy Mottola of Sony in 2001, and again in 2002.

"If I get off, I'm going to be assassinated," Michael said before the trial.

I was terrified that he might be right, knowing what I knew, and having been through the same fear with Gordon, so I could hardly breathe all throughout that morning. We were all incredibly nervous when we arrived at court, but it was impossible not to be moved by the amazing turnout of fans. As we entered the courtroom and waited to hear the verdict, we were all extremely emotional inside. But because everyone was watching us, we had to keep up our smiles for the public.

One of the jurors began reading the counts to let us know what each juror had decided. I was shaking and crying. Then, one by one, every count came back in Michael's favor. It was the most wonderful feeling of relief and happiness. But my elation faded when I looked at Michael. He had clearly been marked by the entire experience, and even having his innocence proven to the world was not enough to help him to recover. As we left the courthouse, his face was drained, and his expression was vague and distant. It was almost as if it had been too painful for him to endure everything, so he had buried his feelings so deep that he was now nothing more than a zombie. He was acting almost as if he had been found guilty. Rather than being happy and wanting to hold a press conference to comment on his innocence and express his gratitude to his fans, Michael wanted nothing more than to hurry into his waiting SUV. His face was a mask as he attempted to hide the fear he felt, certain he was going to be assassinated at any moment. Michael didn't think he was going to make it out of there alive that day. We had discussed it as a family inside, and we were supposed to go out through the back. A last-minute change of plans had us exit through the front instead, and we were all incredibly tense until we were finally in the waiting SUVs and on our way back to Neverland.

Although Michael didn't seem to have recovered in the least from the stress of the trial, he did share a tender moment with his family back at home. When we first arrived, Michael and I, along with several other family members, went upstairs together to a room where Michael could rest. He took off his coat and laid it to the side, then he began taking off his clothes and got into the shower. When he was done, he was so exhausted by the events of that day and the previous six months, he got right into bed.

"Wow," he said as he lay down.

Michael stayed there for the rest of the night, relieved to finally be able to rest and relax a little bit while Mother and me and a few of the siblings sat in the room with him and visited. We were all congratulating him and just enjoying him and how he could actually smile now. Other family members were downstairs toasting the happy moment. Michael's attorneys came by later to congratulate him.

Everybody was ebullient and smiling, except for Michael. Throughout the night, whenever I looked at him, I could see only the worried look on his face. Although the trial had not broken him, it had done grave damage. Michael had overcome one obstacle, but he knew more schemes were to come until his enemies got him for good. A crack had formed in his spirit. He had lost his will to fight. He had lost everything that had once sparkled and shone inside him. It was almost as if he were lifeless, and he was adrift and quite lost.

Michael had sworn that he would never return to Neverland after the trial, but he was so shattered in its aftermath that he couldn't stand to be anywhere in the entire country. He wanted nothing to do with America. He had a love-hate relationship with his publishing catalog. He didn't care about Neverland or his wealth anymore, except for the legacy it would provide for his children. What he cared about was his fans, and the way he and his music were received in the world, and he knew that his reputation would never entirely recover from the way it had been besmirched. This knowledge devastated him.

As soon as Michael received his passport back from the court, he left for Bahrain. For the next year and a half, he would just travel with his kids and the most minimal staff. He was almost like a vagabond. All he cared about was escaping from how cruel his homeland was being to him and all of the nonsensical mistruths that were being spread.

LA TOYA JACKSON

As much as I missed Michael and worried about him, I was glad that he wasn't here to hear what was being reported. Many of my other family members preferred to ignore what was being said, but I thought it was better to know, as painful as it was, so that we could combat it. So I sat and watched everything I could find about Michael in the news, and there was plenty. The worst was anything on Fox News, which was home to all of the female talk show hosts, from Diane Diamond and Lisa Bloom to Nancy Grace. These women had it in for Michael simply because they were listening to all the lies that were concocted during the trial. None of them knew him personally, so I can understand their point of view. Had they known Michael at all, they would have felt differently and been as supportive of him and concerned for his well-being as those who knew him. They talked about Michael as if he were dirt and tried to convince the world of all these lies. I'm not even sure why, except to boost their ratings. He was acquitted on all charges, and he had been driven into hiding with his children. They had no news of Michael to report, but Michael was news, and if you're an avid news watcher the way I am, you realize that most news is 90 percent bad and 10 percent good, and they really went for that 90 percent. They made up excuses to drag his name through the mud, and that hurt so badly. I heard one female reporter on Fox say, "I can't wait until they grab his publishing and give it back to Paul McCartney. He deserves it. Not Michael Jackson."

I didn't know why this matter was even their

322

business. Michael had bought the catalog after Paul McCartney had declined to purchase it on several occasions because he couldn't afford it. For all the trouble it was causing Michael, I'm sure he would have been glad to give it back at that time. Or that he might have wished that Robert Holmes à Court had never sold it to him. But that wasn't the point. I didn't understand how they could say that Michael didn't have the right to own something that he had bought with his own money—and not only that, but money that he had earned through his hard work.

During the time that Michael was gone, other than for the news reports, it was as if he had disappeared. He distanced himself from everyone in the family, and no one spoke to him. The only view I had of him was what I saw on TV, and these images always disturbed me because I could tell he was lost. Also, he had no true manager. His nanny, Grace, was running his business, along with one of her friends, who was handling his publicity. He was very much alone.

It was unclear what Michael would do next. He had vowed to never perform again because he was sure he would be assassinated onstage. Also, I think he felt as if the world had lost its faith in him, which wounded him deeply. He didn't want to go out and put his heart and soul into performing, and even risk his life for it, when he didn't feel that he would be appreciated. He did record some new songs during this time, but what he wanted was to go in a different direction entirely. Michael loved his work. His dream was to produce and direct movies, and to work with director Peter Jackson. Overall, Michael wanted to move into more of a behind-the-scenes role, as I was doing at the time in my own life. I hoped very much, for his sake, that he would find a means to do so.

30

❦

A NEW LEASE ON LIFE

In the aftermath of Michael's trial and flight from America, I obsessively watched television for any news of him. Whenever I was able to examine footage, I analyzed every detail, trying to gauge if he looked better or worse than he had the last time I saw an image of him. I was worried about his health, so I attempted to see if he had lost weight. I was concerned about his emotional well-being, so I tried to do the impossible and determine how he was feeling. I studied the expression on his face and, when the camera got close enough, the look in his eyes. I hoped that if I was vigilant, I might be able to find some way to help my brother and to ensure that the threat to his life, which he had spoken of so movingly back in Las Vegas in 2003, would not come true.

I began investigating the conspiracy Michael described to me on that day at the Mirage. Because of what I had been through with Gordon, I believed that an entertainer could be targeted for his or her money and power. I was convinced that Michael was being persecuted by those who would do whatever it took, even if it meant killing him, to get their hands on his portion of the Sony/ATV catalog and the riches it ensured. I was determined to find out all that I could so that, together, Michael and I might be able to stop it.

But, beyond that, I could actively do nothing for my brother in those days. I knew that he would want me to go on with my own life, and to be as happy and as productive as I possibly could. So, once again, I threw myself back into my career. It was the best way to momentarily distract myself from my concerns about my brother and feel as if something positive was happening in my life.

At the time of Michael's trial, Jeffré and I had decided that we would wait a year to release my new album, *Startin' Over*. But when we went back and listened to the songs again, we agreed that the music sounded dated. It had originally been written and recorded in 2002, and the industry had changed a great deal since then. *I* had also changed immensely in these years. For the fourth time, my desire to reconnect with the world through my music was temporarily put on hold. The album's title seemed more fitting than ever. Once again, as always seemed to be the case in my life, I was starting over.

In October 2006, I was presented with an exciting opportunity to live out a dream that had been mine since I was a young girl. For as long as I could remember, I had wanted to be a nun or a police officer when I grew up. My desire to serve as an officer of the law resurfaced in the aftermath of 9/11, when I longed to work alongside those brave men and women who helped those in need at Ground Zero. I never thought I would have the opportunity to do so. Then I received a call from the producers of the new CBS reality television show *Armed & Famous*. I could not have been more excited.

I had been approached by pretty much every reality television show there was. I had been offered my own show, and when I declined, the producers instead developed the Anna Nicole Smith show. I didn't care about being on television enough to do a show just for the attention. What I wanted was an opportunity to grow and challenge myself as a person. When I heard about *Armed & Famous*, I jumped at that opportunity with no hesitation.

I may have been up for a personal test, but I had a moment's pause when Jeffré told me about the details of the contract I would be required to sign. The basic message was that this was not a fictional show. This was real life, and the producers, network, Muncie Police Department, and the City of Muncie, Indiana, were not responsible if I was accidentally shot and killed in the line of duty while filming the show, or if I accidentally shot someone. As can be imagined, these were not exactly the types of conditions I was used to working under. Whatever happened while filming, I would have to take full responsibility. If I felt up for the duties involved, then they would be glad to have me, but I should not expect any coddling or special treatment. This was a serious commitment, and Jeffré had his concerns.

"Toy, please be careful," he said. "Don't let anybody shoot you."

"This is what I want to do," I said. "Please be supportive of my decision."

Jeffré has always been good about backing choices that are important to me, so he gave me his wholehearted—if nervous—support. I signed the contract and prepared myself to depart for a total of five weeks of police training and filming, seven days a week, fifteen hours a day. But first, I had to break the news to Mother, who was terribly worried for the duration of the show.

"Please don't do this," she said. "You're not strong enough to do this. You could get killed, La Toya."

"It's something I need to do, Mother."

I wouldn't let anyone talk me out of it, not that Mother didn't try, especially when she found out that my partner was a female officer.

"Why would they put you with a girl?" Mother asked.

Mother was so upset, as I was, that they had put me with a woman. During my first roll call, Chief Joe Winkle started partnering all the new rookies. I looked around the room for the biggest male officer I could see. I imagined that the chief was probably thinking that I was a little lady, and he should put me with a bigger officer to protect me. So when Winkle called my name, I knew he was going to partner me with this muscular guy.

"Jackson!" Winkle said.

I couldn't wait to see who my partner was, and I was smiling big.

"Yes, Chief," I said.

"You're partnering with Kesler."

"Thank you, Chief."

I scanned the room for a badge that read Kesler. After looking at every man's badge in the room, I didn't see him. I guessed that he was probably coming in to work in a little bit. Then I realized that a female officer was looking at me. Our eyes connected, and she nodded and smiled, as if to say, "Hello." I smiled back and kept on scanning the room. After our briefing was over, that same woman walked over to me.

"Hello, La Toya. I'm Officer Amy Kesler, your partner."

You gotta be kidding me. I'm dead, I thought.

I had hoped to have a partner who would make me feel protected on the street, and here I was teamed up with a pretty woman who was no bigger than I was. I knew I couldn't ask the chief to switch me because it wouldn't have looked good to do so on my first day on the force. I was sure I had made a huge mistake by becoming an officer.

Boy, was I wrong to worry. Kesler was one of the toughest female cops I've ever met, and she didn't take any mess. By my first night on the street, I knew I would be protected.

All of the officers called everyone by their last name, and I adopted their lingo while working on the force. Kesler was hard on me, probably because she saw how timid I was. Even though boot camp had toughened me up, it was one thing to lose a fight in training, when I knew I couldn't be seriously injured or killed, and another thing when I was confronted with the same situation in the streets. I didn't know what was going to happen. Although they had made the uncertainty of the job clear during training, Kesler made sure I really got the message and was wise to the streets. She didn't care who I was, what family I came from, or what I had done in my life. Her attitude was that this was the real world, girl, and out here I could get killed if I didn't know how to handle myself.

Kesler wasn't the type to let me lean on her, which she made clear right away. She watched my every move and didn't let anything slip. Every time I made a mistake, she pulled over the car and yelled me back into shape, until I was finally hardened to the ways of streets. Once I got the lessons she was teaching me, I was a totally different person. I was more focused than ever, my intuition was much stronger, and I was alert on every call.

I became, according to Kesler, the best partner she could ever have had.

Mother called me one evening to check on me while I was out patrolling the streets, and she asked if they had teamed me with a male officer yet. She was so upset when I said no that I had to put Kesler on the phone to reassure her.

If Mother had been given the opportunity to meet Kesler, or any of the other women on the force, I'm sure she would instantly have been reassured. What she didn't realize, and what I hadn't understood in the beginning either, was that these women were tougher than many of the men we knew. Since I was raised to be ladylike and taught that it was wrong to curse or even raise my voice, I immediately found that I was a bit out of my element. During one of the first meetings with the officers, I remained in my chair after everyone else stood up. I had always been accustomed to having a gentleman pull out my chair before I sat down or stood up from any table.

"Jeffré, could you get my chair for me, please?" I asked without thinking.

Jeffré pulled out my chair for me, but as he did so, he gave me a pleading look that asked me to think about where I was, and who these people around us were. But it was too late; the damage had already been done. Officer Debbie Davis, who is now the chief of police, immediately thought of me as a spoiled little girl. My partner didn't want to ride with me in the beginning because she feared her own life would be in danger.

"Oh, Toy, you're in for it now," Jeffré said with a laugh when he came to my room later that night.

After that, I became determined to prove myself. I had to complete all of the training, conditioning, and testing that any police recruit had to undergo. It was grueling, but I felt a great sense of satisfaction as I slowly progressed, growing stronger and more confident with each step. On December 5, 2006, I was sworn in as a real police officer at the Muncie Police Department by Chief Joseph R. Winkle and Mayor Dan C. Canan.

"Which do you like better, being a cop or being an entertainer?" Jeffré asked me.

"Being a police officer, by far," I said. "I can't even compare the two."

That show was instrumental in helping me to finally come out from the lingering shadow of Gordon's abuse. The instruction I was given taught me how to watch everything around me and pick up details that an untrained eye might not catch. These skills proved to be incredibly valuable in the wake of my brother's death, when I began looking for clues as to who had killed him and how, and during the preliminary trial of Dr. Murray, the man accused of involuntary manslaughter in my brother's death.

I received my training from professional officers who investigate crimes every day for a living, and I am a trained and skilled officer who has been at many crime scenes and arrested many people. If I had been naïve until I met Gordon, the experience of the show also reinforced the crash course he had given me in the worst ways of the world. Again, this helped me to see the circumstances surrounding my brother's death with an informed eye.

As much as I felt well prepared for the duties I was expected to carry out as an officer of the law, I had so much to learn even after I was sworn in and going out on calls at night. Having been as sheltered as I was my entire life, I was innocent of the ways of the world. Such naïveté had been acceptable before, but now that I was going to be investigating crime scenes and attempting to hold my own against violent criminals, I became aware that my lack of street knowledge might make my job difficult. My partner and I were talking about drugs in the squad car one day when I made an innocent comment.

"Marijuana smells like popcorn," I said.

"Wait a minute, who told you that?" she asked.

"Well, that's what I was told, it smells like popcorn."

"What kind of marijuana have you been smoking?"

I was feeling embarrassed and I didn't know what to say, so I simply smiled at her.

"Do you know what marijuana looks like?" she asked.

"No," I said without even having to think about it.

"Do you know what cocaine looks like?"

"Well, yeah, I've seen it in the movies. It's white. It looks like sugar, or powder, or flour."

"Oh my God," she said, realizing that this was no joke. I was as green as they came.

She phoned into headquarters on the radio, and we went right in so they could give me a lesson on drugs. We went into the evidence room, and they handed me a pound of cocaine.

"This is what cocaine looks like," my partner said.

"Wow," I said.

Then, they repeated the lesson with marijuana.

"So it doesn't smell like popcorn?" I asked.

A whole group of officers were standing around my partner and me, and they began to burn the different drugs, so I could get the sense of what they smelled like. It was important to be able to detect the different scents when we walked into a home.

I took a good long look at what they were showing

me. I definitely wasn't an expert by the time they were done with me. But at least I felt that I could tell the difference, when we went out on a call, between who was using illicit drugs and who was baking a cake.

Even though I had been trained, I was still incredibly nervous on my first night patrolling. Every time I left the hotel where we were staying, I didn't know if I would come back dead or alive. Jeffré didn't, either. One of the first nights I was out on the street, after we were done filming, the police van pulled up to the hotel with all of the talent in back, just as it did every night. On this particular evening, as Jeffré later described it to me, Erik Estrada got out of the van. Trish Stratus got out. Jack Osbourne got out. Jason "Wee-Man" Acuna got out. I didn't get out. He tried not to think the worst.

"Erik, where's La Toya?" he asked.

"She's at the hospital," Erik said.

"What do you mean, she's at the hospital?" Jeffré asked. "What happened?!"

"Don't worry, she's delivering a baby."

"Don't tell me she's in the hospital like that," Jeffré said. "You had me scared."

His biggest fear was that I was going to shoot myself in the foot while trying to pull out my gun. I'm not above admitting that I didn't know how to handle my gun well at first. But after being trained so extensively by the best of the best before being sworn in as an officer, I became good and knew how to use my gun well. Not as good as Jack Osbourne—who could be a sharpshooter if he wanted to be—but I was definitely better than the average person. After being afraid of guns my entire life and never having even touched one, I was smiling from ear to ear when I got my gun and badge from the police department. I had never before been so proud of an accomplishment in my life.

My gun was my protection, and I kept my hand on it at all times in the street, where it became my best friend. There were definitely moments when I thought I might have to use it, such as on my first pullover. My heart was pounding in my chest as I approached the car, not only because I was fearful that I might be in danger, but also because I wanted to be a convincing police officer who earned respect from the driver and my partner.

"May I have your license and registration?" I said to the driver.

When he opened the glove compartment to retrieve his registration, I saw a gun.

My heart leapt up into my throat. This was it, everything I had trained for and feared might happen was happening.

"Freeze, do not touch it," I said.

Luckily, the driver did as he was told, and I soon discovered that he had a license to carry the gun in his car. But for a moment I thought the worst possible scenario was unfolding, and that I potentially was going to have to harm someone. I don't know if I could have done so, even to save my own life, and I don't like to think about what might have occurred if I had not been able to bring myself to shoot in self-defense. At that point, it struck me that this was truly the real world.

I always had the feeling that anything could happen at any moment, and that I was always at risk. One night, I was used as a prostitute decoy, which meant dressing up like a hooker and standing outside on a corner while johns pulled over and tried to pick me up. I knew that backup was right around the corner, but I was still terrified that a man might force me into his car, or drive up and shoot me in the head just because he felt hatred for prostitutes, before they could get to me. I was also concerned with doing my job well, so it was important to me to be convincing enough to actually make an arrest. I was so happy when we did, and I was even happier to return to my hotel room in the evenings, still alive and in one piece.

My first thought when I agreed to do the show was that I would most likely get called out on domestic abuse cases. I looked forward to turning my horror-filled years with Gordon into a positive by using my firsthand knowledge of abuse to help women in need. But I was also worried that walking into scenes that so closely resembled what I had been through would bring my old life back in a visceral way that might be too much for me to handle. I wasn't on the force for more than a few nights before I had the opportunity to find out how I would react to my first domestic abuse call.

On most nights, my partner and I patrolled in our squad car, looking for suspicious activity while the radio kept us abreast of any situations to which we might need to respond immediately. We went on quite a few domestic violence calls during the time I was a cop, and

I quickly learned something about handling them. On my first few calls, when I entered the house, I instinctively assumed that the man was responsible for whatever beating or problem had occurred. I think I had this assumption because I'm female, and especially because I knew from Gordon just what type of violence men could so easily commit. But I quickly realized that I had to have an open mind, and I could not assign the blame to either party until I had heard the full story from both sides. As I became more experienced, I was able to more adroitly use my eyes and ears to uncover all of the evidence, while also using the investigative training I had received to question those involved. I had to be cognizant of everything around me all at once. While I was still speaking to the individuals, I was already quickly analyzing the facts, and watching their body language and their eye movements, to determine what was really happening. I was also keeping part of my attention trained on the scene around me. We were in someone else's home, and not only that, but someone who had done something that had caused the police to be called to this home, and often we knew that weapons were somewhere around us.

When I felt it was necessary, I would handcuff the person I was talking to, just in case, while being careful not to do anything to inspire him or her to have a violent reaction. As I snapped the handcuffs into place, I was careful to speak in a calm and assertive tone.

"I'm only doing this for now," I said. "You're not under arrest. But I am going to handcuff you, not only for your safety, but for the safety of everyone else in the room. And once we get the conversation done, I'm free to release you, if everything works out well."

Also for the safety of my partner and me, as we were preparing to check the rest of the house, I was asking myself a series of questions:

Who's in the next room?

Who's in the closet?

Who's hiding under the bed, or in the shower?

As much as my training allowed me to keep my cool and be objective during even the most emotionally charged moments, I could not help but become personally involved when it came to the domestic abuse victims. Often, I found myself wanting to nurture these women whose suffering I could relate to so well, but also to shake them out of their fear into action.

"Why are you letting this happen to you?" I said. "Leave him and start over. Do something better with your life. You're more worthy than this."

I knew the immense obstacles the women had to overcome to free themselves. It had taken me almost a decade of abuse before I reached my breaking point. But I hoped that my words could at least sustain them with a glimmer of hope in the midst of their horror. One woman inspired me to speak even more forcefully, though, because I found her situation so difficult to face. We were called to her house several times during my five weeks on the show, and every time she would lie through her bruises and tell us that her husband had never touched her. As much as she was conditioned to protect him, she couldn't erase the evidence against him, and we ended up arresting him on battery charges.

"Oh, it's okay," she said. "Please don't arrest him. I'll be fine. Please let him go."

I had spoken these same words to police officers in New York City, just a decade earlier, under much the same circumstances, and I could feel exactly what she was going through so intensely that I could not hold my tongue.

"I'm doing this for your own protection," I said. "I need for you to go and try to get help. I know that you're not going to do it tonight or tomorrow. But I need for you to really seriously think about what I'm saying to you and go get help, because this is never going to stop."

She wouldn't look at me the whole time I spoke, keeping her head down in shamed silence.

"From what I've been told, they've been here too many times to protect you," I continued. "And there might not be a next time. You might not be here. That might be the end of your life, and the coroners will be here with us."

I think she got the message then because she looked up at me with tears pouring down her face.

It was difficult to leave her house that night. Yes, we had arrested the husband who abused her, but I knew even if my words had gotten through to her, chances were that she was not going to have the courage, or the strength, to do anything to save herself before he killed her. That was a painful realization, especially because I simultaneously saw that I could so easily have been her. I felt incredibly lucky when I thought about how I had just barely managed to escape before it was too late.

Being a police officer gave me a valuable education in the ways of the world. Most cops on the beat have, quite literally, seen everything there is to see. Even in just five weeks, I came to understand human nature much better than I ever did before. I was shown, firsthand, all of the dark secrets that people hide. I saw a woman using drugs with her twelve-year-old son while her baby slept nearby. So, yes, by the time my five weeks were done, I was not quite the fresh-faced innocent who had seen drugs only in movies.

I was incredibly proud of the ways in which I became stronger and worldlier during the filming of *Armed & Famous*. The series premiere attracted an estimated 8.2 million viewers, but unfortunately, after the second show, CBS changed the night the show aired, putting it against *American Idol*, which was impossible competition, given that it was at the height of its popularity in 2007. The network only ran four episodes before canceling us.

I'm proud that I'm still a police officer today. It's a wonderful feeling to be able to help people in need. I always tell people, if I could go back in time, I would have started my career in law enforcement a long time ago. I also have to thank everyone in Muncie, and the wonderful officers of the Muncie Police Department, for treating me as an equal partner and teaching me skills that I will take to my grave. Thank you, especially, to

Officer Amy Kesler, for teaching me strength and how to be a cop on the street.

Luckily, I was busier than ever in all of the other areas of my life. After the filming of the show, Jeffré and I quickly returned to building Ja-Tail Enterprises, and I began making appearances around Europe again. I had almost fully repaired the damage that Gordon had done to my reputation, and I was able to work as much as I wanted to, and at my original rate, which was an incredible relief for me.

Before long I had the chance to be a part of another television program that offered me a new personal challenge that was too exciting to resist. The show was *Celebrity Big Brother*, which had actually approached me every year it was in production to ask if I would be interested in taking part. I had rejected their offer so many times that Jeffré had stopped asking me when the call came in and simply declined on my behalf. But in September 2008, when they began casting a new season, I had a change of heart. The thought of being locked up in a house with no television or contact with the outside world was no big deal for me; Gordon had forced me to live like that for years. And I had also lived in seclusion, out of fear, for the first six months after I left Gordon. So that was the easy part. The hard part—living with a handful of other celebrities I didn't know for twenty-three days—was so overwhelming that I almost couldn't bring myself to accept the offer. That anxiety made me certain that I had to do it. For as long as I could remember, I'd lived a life of such seclusion and shyness that I was never forced out of my comfort zone. Even though I grew up with so many siblings, we were all raised to be exceedingly polite and nonconfrontational, and so I had no experience dealing with strong personalities, other than Gordon.

Mother always said that I didn't know what people were capable of because my siblings and I always got along so well. We never argued or fought or anything of that nature. No one in our family liked disruption, so we were always a quiet group. I think a part of this had to do with being Jehovah's Witness, as well as being polite, kind, soft-spoken, and everything else we had been raised to be. According to Mother, unlike us, certain people could not be with others for too long before having to start a fight. I had seen such behavior firsthand, but not in a way that impacted me personally. So I felt that this show would break me out of my shell and make me a more confident person with better interpersonal skills.

When I first arrived in the house, I was extremely shocked because of all the fighting among everyone who lived there. At times I feared that I wouldn't make it until the end, but I had no choice but to stay and find ways to coexist with those who were impossible to get along with. As the days passed, I began to learn the different personalities around me and understand how people thought and behaved in extremely varied ways.

I learned to be more sensitive to other people and

comprehend their motivations in a deeper way. When coupled with my experience as a cop, which taught me so much about the world in which people live, I feel that my television experience has enlightened me in so many different ways. It has almost been like getting a college degree in humanity. I know that I have gained skills that I use in business and everyday life, and I feel so incredibly grateful for these opportunities I have been given.

Most people go sit in a room and speak to a therapist they don't really know, and that person is supposed to help them repair their lives. I didn't want to do that. I wanted to build my strength by being in situations where I was forced to overcome my shyness and fears and gain the power I never had. Although I'm still a work in progress, I've come a long way.

31

⸙

THE FINAL DAYS

I was so worried about Michael's having disappeared from America, and not knowing if I would ever see him again. I knew that he still employed a large staff at Neverland, so I thought he might return one day, but I didn't know for sure.

Then, in mid-2006, I heard that Michael had laid off the majority of his staff and closed down the main house at Neverland. In my mind, that confirmed that Michael was never coming back to America, unless there was a family emergency. I was extremely concerned for Michael. Knowing him as well as I did, I was aware that he was stubborn once his mind was made up. Michael was becoming extremely secluded, like the eccentric entrepreneur and Hollywood luminary Howard Hughes. Michael had gotten rid of his entire entourage—including his attorney, accountants, and managers—and was just traveling around with his chil-

dren and his nanny, Grace Rwaramba, who was acting
as his manager. This worried me a great deal. I knew
well from my own experience that if the wrong person
came into his life when he was in this vulnerable state,
that person could easily have the power to destroy him.

Then, on Christmas Day 2006, James Brown died.
As I was grieving his passing, it occurred to me that Michael would probably come home for James's funeral
because of their lifelong friendship. On December 27,
2006, I heard that Michael had landed in Las Vegas. As
I had thought, the death of his idol, James Brown, had
prompted him to return home to give a eulogy at the funeral in Augusta, Georgia. It was the first time Michael
had set foot in the United States in eighteen months.

Once Michael was in America, although I was not
immediately reunited with him, I began to receive word
of him again through Mother and the more frequent
news reports that I saw on television. My soul was at
least a little at peace knowing that he was back home,
and that I could now reach him. I was determined to try
my hardest to help him overcome his mental suffering
and pain, while playing the big-sister role by looking out
for his well-being, and making sure no one was able to
get into his life and take advantage of him anymore.

Unfortunately, I was not able to protect him as I had
hoped. When Michael returned to America, he found a
new manager. In early 2007, Jermaine introduced Michael to Dr. Tohme Tohme, who was later revealed to
be a man with a troubled past who had misrepresented
himself as a successful investor. But the personal con-

nection was enough to make Michael trust this virtual stranger as a close adviser.

While Tohme has since described his relationship with Michael in the most glowing and affectionate terms, I could see that Tohme was employing some of the same techniques that Jack Gordon had used to isolate and control me. Tohme has said in interviews following my brother's death that he "built a fence around Michael to keep people out." This was true; he kept my family away from Michael completely, no matter how hard we tried to reach him. Tohme has suggested that he did so to protect my brother from aggressive predators who wanted to take advantage of Michael and steal his money. But it was Tohme whom I was apprehensive about trusting. As soon as he began acting as Michael's business adviser, he fired key people who had been close to Michael for years. He claimed these were cost-cutting measures, but Michael began telling people that he feared Tohme was trying to isolate him so that he could control him. It seemed to me that, just as Gordon once did to me, Tohme was separating Michael from others. Michael didn't have access to any outside perspective or support from those who might have advised him that his new business adviser didn't seem to have his best interests at heart. Once Tohme shut out the rest of the world, he would be able to steer Michael toward business ventures that were profitable for Tohme and his friends.

During this time, a window briefly opened in which a trusted, longtime family friend, Leonard Rowe, was able to get close to Michael again. Leonard had pro-

moted the "Victory Tour" for Michael and the brothers
and had also worked with several of my other siblings
over the years. Although Leonard and Michael had not
been in touch for some time, I knew that they always had
great affection for one another. As Leonard detailed in
his own book, *What Really Happened to Michael Jackson*,
he contacted Michael in January 2009 as the representative for a concert promoter who was willing to offer Michael $15 million to perform a single show. Michael was
understandably intrigued by the deal and asked Leonard
to fly out to Los Angeles to meet with him in person. He
also put Tohme in touch with Leonard to help facilitate
communication regarding the meeting.

Everything seemed to be moving along smoothly
until Leonard arrived in Los Angeles and attempted to
get in touch with Michael regarding their agreed-upon
meeting. Leonard was not able to get through, no matter how he tried, and finally concluded that Tohme was
avoiding him. When the two men did eventually meet
about the proposed concert deal, Tohme said that he
could not accept any offers until Michael completed negotiations for a $300 million deal that was then in the
works.

Any savvy business adviser might put a $15 million
deal on hold while negotiating a $300 million agreement,
but Tohme's explanation was far from the whole story
in this instance. As was later revealed, the contract provided that Tohme's monthly salary of $100,000 would
be paid by AEG, the concert promoters who were trying to get Michael to commit to the $300 million deal

Tohme had mentioned. This meant that Tohme was far from an unbiased business adviser who could counsel Michael about the best path forward, personally and financially. As Gordon did with me, Tohme began committing Michael to deals that favored Tohme's powerful friends, who, I can only imagine, lined Tohme's pockets and extended his influence in return. The way I see it, Tohme could not be trusted to give Michael unbiased advice about which deals to pursue as long as AEG was paying his salary.

At this time, the president and CEO of AEG Live, Randy Phillips, told Michael that if he did not agree to re-hire his onetime business manager Frank DiLeo, whom Michael had fired back in February 1989, the entire deal for the London concerts would be canceled. Michael was in desperate need of the revenue these concerts would generate and could lose everything if he didn't do them. Michael was not in a position to argue with Phillips. I assume Phillips knew this, and since he had set DiLeo up with this extremely lucrative position, he had the potential to influence the advice DiLeo gave Michael.

Although Michael was receiving far from unbiased business advice at this time, he did have a moment of clarity in March 2009, when he contacted Leonard and asked him to take over as his business manager. Michael even sent a letter to Randy Phillips, dated March 25, saying that he should please extend every courtesy to Mr. Rowe. Michael told Leonard that he absolutely could not come home penniless after doing the London concerts to which his AEG deal had committed him. He was deeply concerned that those whom he was doing business with were planning to take advantage of him, and that by the time they were done with him, they would own everything, and he would not be able to provide for his three children. Leonard was extremely moved by this request from his longtime friend, and he immediately agreed. When he pressed Michael for details about his AEG contract so he could begin to help, Michael confessed that he didn't even know what he had signed because their attorney had drawn up the contract. Michael told Leonard, my mother, and several other people that he had said he would perform only ten shows in London, and AEG had gone ahead and sold out fifty performances without his permission. I have never been shown a signed contract in which Michael agreed to the fifty shows, and I wonder if such a contract ever existed.

When Leonard next met with Michael in Los Angeles on April 14, 2009, he brought Joseph along to the Carolwood house with him, allowing for a reunion between father and son following three years in which they had not seen or spoken to each other. Leonard expressed concern to Michael that AEG was paying him in dollars, which were much weaker than the pounds they were taking in for the tickets for his shows. Plus, they were allowing tickets to be scalped, which would create ticket sales for which Michael would not receive any payment, which could cause him to lose millions of dollars in revenue. Michael and Leonard signed a letter addressed to Randy Phillips that identified Leonard as Michael's financial representative. It was not a moment too soon.

That spring, a series of moves by Michael's advisers made me question their interests. Tohme had all of the furniture removed from Neverland and entered into an agreement with Julien's Auctions to sell it off between April 22 and April 25, 2009. Michael must not have known anything about these happenings because when I informed Mother and she called Michael and told him, he began to cry.

"They can't do that, Mother, they have no right," he said. "They just came into my house. They told me they were putting everything in storage."

After Michael died, Tohme said that this was a storage arrangement, but I wonder what Tohme's intentions were at the time.

As has since been reported by the *Today* show and other news outlets, Michael began confiding in a trusted spiritual adviser, June Gatlin, in the spring of 2009 that he feared Tohme, who had put himself between Michael, Michael's accountant, and other representatives. Michael told Gatlin that Tohme controlled his money and kept him away from his family and friends. Michael spoke to this woman of wanting to replace Tohme with someone he could count on. Michael even went so far as to sign a letter on May 5, 2009, revoking Tohme's authority to represent him. This was undoubtedly an act of courage for Michael, who was not able to stand up for himself unless pushed to the absolute limit, and who had been beaten down. This was Michael's attempt to take back his life. Sadly, Michael was not able to enlist his family to help, as I was during my moment of need, and he remained vulnerable to Tohme and others.

In mid-May, Joseph called Leonard in a panic, asking him to please meet him, Michael, and Mother at a meeting with Randy Phillips and Paul Gongaware, also of AEG, at the Beverly Hills Hotel. Both Mother and Joseph told me that Joseph and Leonard stood up to Phillips at Michael's request, confronting him about the ways in which AEG was taking advantage of Michael in regard to the London shows. Joseph became so incensed that he stood up from his chair and began yelling at Phillips.

"I'm not going to stand around here and let you steal from my son!" Joseph shouted. "You've done it all your life, and you're not going to do it now."

As Joseph spoke out so vehemently, Michael began laughing. He was so happy to have his father there to protect him from the vultures that were closing in on him.

Although Michael was animated at times during the meeting, Leonard was struck by something alarming in Michael's discussion of the upcoming London shows. Leonard knew that Michael was a total perfectionist when it came to recording and performing, as I would be the first to confirm. Michael agonized over even the most minuscule decisions until he got them just so, and this attention to detail was what made his every accomplishment as an entertainer so incredible. However, Michael seemed completely indifferent to the many particulars that he should have been preparing for the upcoming

London shows. Leonard felt it was almost as if Michael knew that, for one reason or another, he would never perform those concerts.

Unfortunately, soon after the meeting at the Beverly Hills Hotel, Leonard was slowly pushed out of Michael's inner circle. Phillips has said that he was following Michael's instructions not to work with Leonard. But I don't believe it because the notes I read of Michael's are clear that he felt that AEG was controlling his life, and Leonard has adamantly denied Phillips's claim. Such an instruction would be in clear conflict with Michael's wishes as expressed by the agreement I was told he and Leonard had signed, and Joseph was also unhappy about Leonard's being removed. Even more alarming, Phillips was bringing in DiLeo, over whom Phillips had an influence that he didn't have with Leonard. At first, Michael asked Leonard to work in conjunction with DiLeo, which Leonard tried to do. This didn't work, as it seemed DiLeo and the others wanted Leonard out. But without Leonard, Michael was in the dark about many of the details of his business life.

At the one meeting that occurred between the two men, Leonard apparently tried to enlist DiLeo to help him with what he felt was the most concerning matter at hand, Michael's health. DiLeo wanted to talk only about the issue of ticket scalping in London. After that, Leonard was given less and less opportunity to talk to Michael. Although DiLeo supposedly replaced him as Michael's manager, Leonard has repeatedly told me that he never received a letter of termination from Michael, and I've never seen a letter appointing DiLeo.

From that moment on, Leonard didn't again have the opportunity to get close enough to Michael to gauge his state of mind or health. He also did not have the opportunity to intervene on Michael's behalf in regard to his painkiller dependency or his financial dealings. Losing Leonard, in my mind, severed Michael from the last business relationship dedicated to his well-being and making sure he was healthy and protected.

As I learned about these happenings from Joseph and other members of my family, the revelations were extremely painful for me. It was difficult for me to know how serious Michael's condition really was because I didn't see him in person during these months. Finally, on May 14, 2009, I spent time with Michael for the first time since his 2005 trial. The occasion was a family dinner that was held to commemorate Joseph and Mother's sixtieth wedding anniversary.

With my mother and Rebbie being strict Jehovah's Witnesses, anniversaries were the only special occasions they could celebrate, so we wanted to make a big deal of the event and be sure the entire family was there.

Everyone in my family loves Indian food, so for the event we rented out an Indian restaurant in Beverly Hills that is frequented by much of my family. When I entered the restaurant, I saw Michael talking to his kids and Jermaine. Before I could get any words out of my mouth, Michael's eyes widened, and a big smile spread across his face.

"Oh my God, La Toya!" he said. "Hi . . . you look great, it's so good to see you."

He was so full of compliments, as always.

"I love your belt," he said. "Your hat is so cool."

I kissed him on both cheeks and embraced him tightly.

The extreme happiness I felt about seeing Michael was quickly replaced with alarm when I got close to him, because he was excruciatingly thin. He had always been a light eater, and slender as a result, but this was something different. When I hugged him, I was even more upset because I discovered what little bulk he did have on his frame was actually only an illusion created by the layers of clothing he was wearing to make himself appear more robust. As soon as I had the opportunity to pull him aside, I did my best to determine what was wrong with him. I fear that I must have sounded like a nagging mother, but I could not stop questioning him, no matter how many times he tried to tell me that he was well.

"Michael, are you okay?" I asked.

"Are you healthy?"

"Are you fine?"

"How are rehearsals going?"

Michael insisted, again and again, that he was well and that the preparations for his London shows were proceeding positively. I was still concerned about him because he had this worried look about him, as if the life were just draining out of him. Part of me thought that it was due to his rehearsals, because he appeared to be happy other than for that. Michael had always been secretive about his personal life, but I knew something was wrong with him without his saying anything. He was my brother, and I knew his personality well. Also, I had never forgotten the conversation we had back in 2003 at the Mirage, when he first revealed to me his belief that he was going to be murdered. I knew that he was trying to uphold himself for his children, but those who were trying to devour him were beginning to succeed. I could do nothing in the midst of this joyous family party but take my brother at his word. As the night progressed, I was overjoyed to see him at least relax enough to enjoy his time together with all of us, including his nieces and nephews. Michael stayed at the event for several hours. When it was time for him to leave, he approached me.

"It was so wonderful seeing you, La Toya," he said.

I was still so concerned about him, and his well-being, and this Dr. Tohme, who I feared was taking over his life.

"Michael, let's get together and talk," I said. "I want to see you more."

"I would love that more than anything," he said.

We hugged tightly and kissed. I straightened the jacket he was wearing.

"I love you, Michael, and I'm so happy to see you and the kids."

He looked me directly in my eyes with the most beautiful smile and uttered those famous words of his: "I love you more."

Michael got to the doorway, stopped, turned around,

looked at me once more, smiled, and waved good-bye, as if he knew it was the last time I would see him alive. And it was.

Three weeks later, on June 7, Michael was supposed to attend my first ever surprise birthday party, which Jeffré organized for me. Michael not only confirmed that he would be present, but he also expressed how excited he was about attending. His head security guard, Brother Michael, had even called to find out when I would be arriving, so Michael could get there just before me and be a part of the moment of surprise.

Because Michael would be in attendance, Jeffré was thoughtful enough to set up the whole party to make sure that Michael would be comfortable. A private back room was made available so that Michael could enjoy time with family away from the prying eyes that followed him everywhere. Michael's own photographer was hired to document the day's festivities so Michael would feel completely comfortable around him. Of course, I didn't know any of this until I was already at the party, and Jeffré informed me that Michael had not been able to attend at the last minute.

Although it meant so much to me that the rest of my family was there, especially Joseph, who had driven in from Las Vegas just for the event, I was disappointed that I didn't see Michael. I wanted to have him near me on that day so I could assess his health and at least know he was safe for those few hours. Unknown to me, that party was to be the last carefree moment I would enjoy for some time.

32

THE WORST DAY OF MY LIFE

I always dreaded seeing the words BREAKING NEWS
on my television from the day that Michael told me he
was afraid for his life. In the spring of 2009, I grew increasingly concerned for my brother's life. Whenever
I saw the familiar graphics scroll across my television
screen and heard the telltale music, informing me that
something earth-shattering had happened, I immediately feared it would be upsetting news about Michael.
Then I would be relieved to hear that it was something
else.

On June 23, 2009, I saw those dreaded words pop
up on the screen while I was watching CNN. My heart
raced until I learned that the breaking news was actually
the death of television announcer Ed McMahon.

Then, on June 25, 2009, I saw those same words on
CNN once again, and again my heartbeat quickened.

What is it now? I thought.

I soon learned that the breaking news was the sad loss of actress Farrah Fawcett. I mourned the passings of Ed McMahon and Farrah, who had both given the world so much with their talents. But my main feeling was an immediate sense of relief that, as far as I knew, my brother was at that moment safe.

I called Jeffré, who was staying in Las Vegas at the time, and informed him of Farrah's passing. Just as moved as I was, he turned on his television to learn more. After we discussed Farrah for a little while, we began talking about death more generally, and we discussed the way in which famous people always seemed to die in groups of three.

"I wonder who's going to be next," I said.

This statement of the most innocent variety, spoken without really thinking, would soon come back to haunt me in the most upsetting way possible.

After Jeffré and I hung up, I spent the rest of the morning watching the news on Farrah. Although I was truly saddened, it wasn't a big surprise, because everyone knew she was battling cancer. While watching the coverage of Farrah's life and feeling sympathy for the pain her family must have been going through, I received a call from Joseph a little after noon.

"La Toya, get over to Michael's house *right now*," Joseph said.

"What's wrong?" I asked, concerned.

"A fan called and told me Michael's sick."

I was immediately filled with panic, and my hands shook as I began dressing. I was preparing to leave my house as quickly as I could and drive the three minutes to Michael's nearby home, Carolwood. I called Jeffré back to alert him to Joseph's call and to see if he had heard anything about Michael's condition from the fans or anyone else we knew.

"La Toya, Michael's just doing this to get out of his shows," Jeffré said.

This immediately eased my mind because I knew that it could well be true. I had been told that Michael didn't want to do the London shows, which were scheduled to begin in just a few days. Michael was known, within the family, to have faked illness and injury in the past to avoid commitments that displeased him, and I felt better as I assumed this was the case now. I was so certain there was nothing to be alarmed about that I slowed down the pace at which I was getting ready to venture out in search of information.

Then Joseph called me again. "A fan just called me and said there's an ambulance at Michael's house."

Joseph passed the phone to a friend, who told me that the fan was now telling Joseph that Michael was on his way to the hospital.

"Forget going to the house," Joseph said to me. "Go to the hospital. They say he had a heart attack, and I hear that he's on his way to the hospital."

When I heard these words, I was so distraught that I almost dropped my phone. I couldn't breathe or think or move.

"Hurry up and get over there," Joseph said, panic audible in his voice.

I called Jeffré back to tell him the latest.

"Calm down until you get to the hospital and find out what's really going on," he said.

This was asking me to do the impossible, but I knew I had to hold it together for Michael.

"Have you heard anything about it?" I asked.

"No, but I'll check the Internet to see if I can find anything."

While Jeffré went online, I turned on my speakerphone function and finally got myself dressed to go over to the UCLA Medical Center, which was where they had taken Michael. When Jeffré spoke again, I could tell by the tone of his voice that something was terribly wrong.

"La Toya, just relax until you get over to the hospital. But I did find a statement online from the paramedics that said, 'Mr. Jackson was not breathing when we'—the paramedics—'got to his house.'"

My legs literally buckled beneath me, and my vision blurred as my entire body was instantly drenched in sweat. I was in such acute shock that I felt I might actually drop dead. I couldn't speak.

All I could do now was to get to Michael as quickly as I could, and to pray.

God, please don't let this be true. Please give me strength to get to Michael.

I pulled myself together, but I couldn't get ready fast enough. I was having the reaction I always had when I heard any bad news. My entire body was shutting down, and I felt so weak that I could barely move. But I knew that such a response was not going to help Michael, so I fought through my panic and forced myself to be strong. The whole time, I kept praying and talking to myself out loud.

"Okay, La Toya, calm down. Michael is going to be fine. It's just an act."

But somehow, I knew this wasn't true, and the more I said it, the more nervous I became. All I could hear was the fear in Michael's voice as he told me, "They're going to kill me for my publishing catalog and my estate."

I was still trying to put my shoes on as I rushed downstairs and got into my car. Even though the hospital was only two minutes away, the drive seemed like an eternity.

As I drove, I kept trying to call Mother, but her phone rang and rang with no answer. I was so desperate to talk to her that I just kept calling her, again and again, as I panicked in the next moments. Finally, Mother's assistant Trent answered her phone. He told me that he was in the car with her, driving her to the hospital.

I was crying and breathless to the point where I could barely speak.

"Trent, is everything okay?" I asked. "Please tell me it is."

But he wouldn't answer me, and his silence made me cry even harder and more uncontrollably.

"Trent, is everything okay?!" I asked again, this time more forcefully. "Is he better?"

I could hear Mother speaking in the background.

"Trent, who's on the phone?" she asked in a tone of voice I had never heard from her before.

"La Toya," he replied.

The next thing I knew, my mother snatched the phone away from Trent and screamed as loudly as she could into the phone:

"HE'S DEAD!"

"NOOOOOOOOOOOOOOOOOO!" I said, also screaming my loudest.

A torrent of sobs shook my entire body, which stopped working altogether. I was so weak that I could no longer grip the steering wheel of my car or apply enough pressure to the gas pedal to keep the car moving. Horns honked as my car slowed and drifted to the side of the road, nearly causing several accidents before it finally came to a stop. Although I was less than a mile from my house, I didn't have a clue where I was, where I was going, or what I was doing. I rolled down my window and stuck my tearstained face out into the street.

"Please drive me to UCLA," I said to a woman who was walking down the sidewalk. "I can't drive."

She looked at me, knowing something was horribly wrong, but hurried away.

"Please!" I cried to the next man who drove by me. "I have to get to Michael. Please help me. I'll give you anything. Please! Please! Please!"

The cars in his lane, and my lane, kept honking their horns for us to drive on, as I kept pleading and crying. He didn't stop to help me, either. He just drove away from the honking horns and the traffic jam I was causing. I finally gathered my composure enough to realize that the only way I was going to get to the hospital, and to Michael, was to drive myself there.

When I arrived at UCLA, I had no idea where I was going. Michael was at the Ronald Reagan UCLA Medical Center, but I didn't know where the building was. With every second that passed, I was growing increasingly distraught. I didn't think I could stand any more of this torture. I pulled up to a security-guard station and pleaded with one of the guards.

"Please drive me," I said.

He clearly recognized me, but apparently the news about Michael had not yet gotten out. "That would be against the rules, Miss Jackson. I can't leave my post. I'm sorry."

I took a deep breath and willed myself to keep driving. Finally, I arrived at the correct building. My car was still rolling as I jumped out and started to run toward the front doors. The valet clearly recognized me.

"It's okay, it's okay," he kept saying as he took control of my car for me.

I continued to cry harder than I had ever cried before as I hurried, my knees buckling with every step. As I ran through the automatic sliding-glass doors, a nurse saw me and immediately grabbed me.

"This way," she said.

"Where's Michael, is he okay?" I asked anyone that I encountered.

Nurse after nurse just stared at me with a glazed look.

Finally, another nurse came up to me and grabbed my arm. "Come on, we'll take you to where he is."

"Is he okay?" I asked. "Is he dead?"

"No, La Toya, he's not dead."

"He's not? Oh my God. Thank you. Thank you." I grabbed the woman and hugged her as hard as I could. "Thank you, oh, thank you."

Suddenly, all of my fear and grief evaporated, and I felt normal again. I actually felt better than normal. I was euphoric, as if I had just woken from a terrible nightmare to find myself safe in my own bed. I couldn't wait to see Michael and do everything that we too often put off in life until it is too late: hug him and hold him and tell him how much I loved him, and how proud I was of him and all of his accomplishments, and that I had no doubt that he was the absolute best at everything he did, and that I wanted to spend much more time with him in the near future.

And tell him never to scare me like that again!

In those terrifying moments when I thought I had lost Michael forever, I had realized how devastating it would be to lose any member of my family. I never wanted to experience that type of excruciating pain again. And now that it had been lifted from me, I realized that I must be extremely careful never to take life for granted.

While I was thinking of all this, I finally reached the area where my family was. I was feeling so much better, expecting to walk into Michael's hospital room and hear him say, "Hi, La Toya, how are you? You look great!"

Even though I was going to be as excited to see him as he was to see me, I was going to lay into him to never worry us like this again.

Then, I spotted Mother. All three of Michael's children—Prince, Paris, and Blanket—were sitting on her lap, screaming and crying. Frank DiLeo stood nearby, watching the whole scene, which immediately made me uncomfortable because I still associated DiLeo with Gordon and the old days.

Seeing how upset the kids were as they sat on Mother's lap, I knew something was terribly wrong.

"Mother, what's wrong?" I said. "Michael's okay, right? The nurse just told me he's not dead."

Mother wore a rigid, pained expression on her face that I had never before seen. She wasn't crying at all. She was being strong for the children. Her assistant Trent stood nearby.

"Trent, how is he?" I asked.

"He's gone," Trent said.

"Are you sure?"

"La Toya, *Michael's dead!*" Mother said resolutely, and I knew it was true.

I leaned against the wall, but it wasn't enough to hold me up. Quickly, before I had time to realize what was happening, I dropped to the floor and just lay there. I felt as if I were dying. I was choking on my tears, screaming, unable to breathe, gasping for air.

33

TRYING TO MAKE SENSE
OF THE TRAGEDY

When I finally realized that Michael was dead, my immediate thought was not

How did Michael die?

but

Who killed Michael?

My mind leapt to the many times that Michael had predicted this moment to me in no uncertain terms.

"La Toya, I'm going to be murdered for my music publishing catalog and my estate," he had told me again and again.

Michael believed there was a conspiracy. I vowed right then to find out if Michael's prediction had come true, and if so, who was responsible.

I pulled myself together because I knew I must be a good example for his children. I took Blanket from Mother's lap and began embracing him.

"Please, can we go see Daddy?" he said. "We want to go see Daddy."

Paris had become hysterical. "Dr. Murray is the best cardiologist in the world," she screamed. "He's the best. He's the best. I don't know what happened. He's the best. He's the best."

I helped Mother to calm Paris down until she was finally crying quietly. But we could do nothing to comfort her.

A little later, Paris broke my heart for the second time that day.

"Auntie La Toya, I want to die," she said. "I want to be where Daddy is. I don't want to live anymore. I just want to die. I don't want to be here anymore."

I said, "Paris—"

But I stopped short. I didn't know what to say at this exceptionally painful moment. This was my first experience of trying to explain death to a child. It was also my first time of losing someone in my immediate family, and I was filled with that sensation of extreme helplessness that the loss of a loved one can cause. I knew that I could do absolutely nothing to bring Michael back, or even to explain his loss to his young, distraught daughter. I had no words for her except to say, "It's going to be okay. It's going to be okay."

But Paris had much that she needed to say, and I learned a great deal about Michael's final days from that conversation.

"Daddy was always cold," she said. "Daddy was always freezing. He would sit and fall asleep by the fireplace. He would always cry. And we would watch to make sure everything was fine."

I didn't say anything that might interrupt her because I wanted to know more.

"He was always freezing. And he needed a doctor. And then, they turned the lights out. We were in the dark."

This final statement got my attention. Nurses in the room were trying to console the children as well, and I didn't want them to hear this.

"Paris, come here," I said. "They turned the lights out?"

"Yes, and they cut the phones off."

My mind was racing as I formulated what this could mean. *Okay, are these threats? If you don't do what we say, we're going to turn your lights out. Was he being controlled with intimidation? A show of power, like some of the ways Gordon manipulated me and broke my spirit?*

Paris was crying and crying. I felt so bad for her because she was taking it so hard. Prince also took it hard, but he was trying to be a strong young man. I could feel the hurt in his heart, and I felt completely helpless for the first time, knowing that I couldn't bring his father back. Paris knew that Michael had wanted her to be strong, but she was so heartbroken that she was having difficulty.

"Daddy told me that I have to be strong," she said. "Because he told me, 'You're going to have to take care of Prince and Blanket if something ever happens to me.

You're going to have to be the mother if something happens to me, Paris.' "

That made me wonder how much Michael had told them, and if he had let them know that he was fearful for his life. Gently I tried to determine how much she knew.

"When did he say that, Paris?"

"Last night, before he went to rehearsal. Prince and I were arguing, and Daddy said, 'Stop fighting with your brother. I'm not always going to be here, and you're going to have to be the lady and watch over them.' "

As Paris relived the memory, she seemed to realize that this had been the last moment that she saw her father alive, and she began to cry harder.

"Please, Auntie La Toya," Paris said, interrupting my thoughts, "I want to go see Daddy. I just want to go see him. I need to see him one more time."

"Paris, I don't think that's a good idea," I said.

I looked to a nurse who was standing nearby for guidance.

"Excuse me," I said. "She keeps crying that she wants to see him."

"That's very normal," the nurse said.

I didn't want them to see their father that way, but the nurse assured me that it could be therapeutic for the children. "It's closure for them," she said. "Once they see it, they will understand."

So two nurses escorted Blanket, Paris, Prince, and me down to the room where Michael was. Mother didn't want to see him because she knew it would be too painful.

When we walked into the room, Michael was lying on a gurney with a white towel over his face. I walked over to him and removed the towel. It was painful to see how incredibly skinny he was. Michael had always been thin, but nothing like this; he was just skin and bones. But other than that, he looked so peaceful, as if he had just closed his eyes to go to sleep. I was filled with so much love for him that I found myself kissing him, and stroking his hair and his face. The whole time, I was devastated by the belief that he had died because of greed, and that he had been aware of his end as it was happening. I knew that it didn't need to end this way, and because I felt so awful that I hadn't been able to do more to save him, I made a promise to my brother right then and there.

"I'm going to find out who did this to you," I whispered in his ear.

Then I was so filled with emotion that I was moved to express it out loud.

"I love you so much, Michael," I said.

We all held hands around him and prayed, then we each took turns addressing him.

"I miss you, Daddy," Paris said. "I love you so much."

She removed a red string bracelet that she was wearing and put it on Michael's wrist.

"Daddy, I want you to have this," she said. "I want you to keep it with you."

Prince then said a few words to his dad, as did Blanket. We all continued to speak to him and tell him how great he was, and what a wonderful father he was, and we also said prayers, until the kids felt comfortable leaving him alone. Even the nurses, who didn't know Michael personally, spoke about what a special person he had been and all of his amazing accomplishments in life.

The children had been crying uncontrollably before that moment, but when we walked out after we were all done, they were surprisingly calm. Having the chance to say good-bye had helped them. It was still difficult for me to even look at them because I felt so terrible for them. They had lost their father, and he was all they had in this world. As much as I was grieving for Michael, I felt even worse for them.

My grief was already turning into anger. I was dying to see this Dr. Murray who Paris had mentioned. I had no idea who he was, but I knew he must have answers, and I wanted them. As we were walking back to the waiting room, I began inquiring about Dr. Murray. He had been there at the hospital the entire time.

I cornered Dr. Murray and made him speak to me.

"Come here," I said. "I want to talk to you right now. What happened to my brother?"

His response struck me as nothing but evasion and excuses.

"No," I said. "You're going to tell us what happened."

I had never been so forceful with anyone in my life before this, but I didn't care, my brother was dead. I never did extract any information from him, as the scene was so chaotic. More family were coming in to visit, as well as my old childhood friend Kathy Hilton, and her sister Kyle Richards, who arrived at the hospital to comfort me and say their good-byes to Michael. As I was walking back to see Michael with Kathy, she gave me some thoughtful advice.

"Honey," she said, "you should collect all the notes. Everything that you see that he's written down, collect it. Collect it. Collect it."

Her own mother had recently passed, and so she knew that Michael's papers would provide crucial information to whoever possessed them, and she wanted them to be in the right hands. Her advice proved to be even more valuable than she could have known.

34

※

THE INVESTIGATION
INTENSIFIES

Even if Michael hadn't confessed his assassination fears
to me, so much suspicious activity surrounded his death
that I am quite certain I would quickly have had questions about the circumstances of his passing. Almost as
soon as the family began to gather at the hospital, we
received panicked phone calls from Michael's head security guard, Brother Michael.

"We all have been fired," he said. "And we can't stay
around here too much longer. You have to get to the
house as soon as you can."

"Who fired you?"

"Tohme Tohme."

Brother Michael vowed that he would not leave until
someone from the family arrived to make sure nothing improper occurred at the house. I was alarmed by
Brother Michael's call because it seemed strange to me.
The members of the staff who had been at the house at

the time of Michael's death most likely knew something about how he had passed, yet they were being sent away before the family had a chance to speak to them and before the police investigation was completed. The police had soon arrived and had been there all day, investigating the situation while we were at the hospital. We were not allowed to go to the house until the detectives said it was okay. So the family caravanned back to Hayvenhurst after leaving the hospital. I had been trying to get someone from the family to go over to the house all day, to keep an eye on the place, but no one had been willing to do so. Finally, the family elected Jeffré and me to go.

Jeffré had flown back from Las Vegas with my sister Rebbie as soon as they heard the news about Michael, and they went directly to Hayvenhurst. At about 11:30 p.m., Randy, Jeffré, I, and Ron Boyd, a police officer and a family friend, arrived at the Carolwood house. Thirty minutes later, Mother and Trent showed up, then Janet arrived as soon as her plane from New York landed in Los Angeles.

The house was directly across the street from where Elvis Presley had lived in the 1970s. As we pulled up to the huge wrought-iron gates, I noticed that they were still adorned with Christmas wreaths with red bows. Michael always liked keeping Christmas ornaments up all year because they made him happy. Seeing these decorations made me face all over again that he was gone, and this realization left me awash in grief.

I called Brother Michael's cell phone to let him know

we were at the gates. Within seconds, the gates slowly opened to reveal the majestic seventeen-thousand-square-foot mansion that Michael and his family had called home since December 2008, when they had spent their final Christmas together there.

I had never visited the house before, but as Brother Michael ushered us in, I felt Michael's presence and smelled his cologne everywhere. That smell will never leave me. Lit Christmas garlands were wrapped around the banister going up the stairs, as well as around the fireplaces. I immediately noticed that the house was extremely hot, even though this was a mild night in late June.

"Why is the house so hot?" I asked.

"Michael always kept the heat on because he was freezing," Brother Michael said.

Is this house so hot only because Michael was freezing, or did someone turn up the heat to try to keep his dead body warm, so it looked as if Michael died closer to the 911 call than he really did?

Brother Michael began to describe what had been happening at the house as he led us upstairs to the right, to Dr. Murray's room, which was the room in which Michael had died. At the same time I was questioning Brother Michael.

"Did anything suspicious happen last night?" I asked.

"Not that I saw," he said.

Outside the door, on the top of a dresser, was Michael's unfinished meal, what looked like a bowl of soup and the crumbs from a sandwich. As we entered the room in which Dr. Murray worked, Brother Michael pointed out the side to the right of the bed, where Michael had died just a few hours before. At the sight of the mattress, and the thought of what had happened here, the edges of my vision went black and my body began to weaken. But I forced myself to be strong because I needed to have my wits about me to find out everything that took place here when Michael died.

On the floor next to the bed was Michael's pajama top, which the paramedics had cut off when they were trying to save him. About four feet away from the foot of the bed was an IV stand with an IV bag on it, and in the corner next to the dresser, three large, green oxygen tanks stood in a row. My eyes immediately started searching the room from floor to ceiling, just as I had been trained to do as a police officer. My first question was whether the room had cameras that might yield useful footage of what had happened, but there were none. I tried to look beneath the surface of the room's appearance. In my mind, all I could hear was Michael's anguished voice:

"La Toya, they're going to kill me for my publishing and my estate," he said again and again.

Staring at the bed, I could almost feel Michael's pain, knowing that only hours earlier he had lain in this bed alive. Because of the drugs that he was receiving, he was too weak and frail to do anything to save his own life. I looked around with a suspicious eye.

Then, Brother Michael stood back as he pointed in the direction of Michael's actual bedroom.

"Michael didn't allow anyone in there," Brother Michael said.

The room, which was to the left of the entry to Dr. Murray's room at the top of the stairs, was a complete wreck.

"This room is a mess," I said. "Was it always like this?"

"I don't know," Brother Michael said. "We were never allowed upstairs. I've never been in this room before."

While the rest of the house was immaculate, this room had been torn to pieces. Everything in the room had been turned upside down. It looked like a garbage dump, or as if several burglars had been in here. Suitcases were ripped open, dressers were turned over, with papers and clothes hanging out of them and scattered across the floor.

The mess is too much to have been the police's doing. So who did this, and what were they looking for?

I surveyed the room and tried to make sense of what I was seeing. *Michael has been dead for hours. I find it hard to believe that no one has been in his room, knowing how much cash and jewelry he keeps in his house.*

Then, I remembered Kathy Hilton's advice. As I have said, all of us children were taught to write down our thoughts, and throughout his life Michael was a compulsive note taker. I had never, ever seen anyone come as close to writing down *all* of their thoughts as

Michael did. He wrote them on walls, on mirrors, on any surface where he could find room to write. Although he had lived at Carolwood only since Christmastime, his bedroom was littered with Post-it notes that documented his thoughts during the last days of his life. Among the notes we read were:

I hate John Branca.

John Branca stole lots of money from me and continuously double & triple billed me.

I hate Tohme Tohme.

Randy Phillips & Dr. Tohme are not flying with me. NO! NO! NO! EVER!

Call Joseph.

Get Joseph's help to get these people out of my life.

I don't want Frank DiLeo back in my life.

I only agreed to 10 shows.

Tell Tohme Tohme to give me back my cars.

AEG is pressuring me to go see Dr. David H. Salvit for a physical.

Together, we all reviewed hundreds of notes, papers, and documents. Just by reading these notes, we learned so much about whom Michael feared. His notes only strengthened my conviction that I must do everything to bring this information to light, as did the letter the family later received from the estate ordering us to return anything we might have taken if we wanted to avoid a trip to court.

I was extremely glad that the family went to the house that first night because all of the family members were ultimately ordered out by the estate. We were not even allowed to organize Michael's possessions or set aside any keepsakes for his children. Still, to this day, I don't know what happened to any of the belongings that were in Michael's Las Vegas house or the Carolwood home.

35

A FAMILY LOSS

As painful as it was to lose Michael, his death caused a secondary cost to me that was nearly as devastating. Over the past thirteen years I had reestablished the close bond I had enjoyed with my family up until I was thirty-one, when Jack Gordon took me and kept me away from them for just a few months shy of a decade. I was incredibly upset to feel our connection weakening as we all responded to Michael's death in very different ways. We had never lost a loved one from our immediate family before, and as with all families who go through this, we each had contrasting opinions about the best ways to handle our grief and eulogize Michael.

Michael was the world's biggest pop star. The entire globe was watching us for the proper way to move forward, and everyone had his or her own opinion about the most appropriate way to bury Michael, including the fans; media; international leaders, dignitaries, and royalty; and our own extended family and friends. This all put more pressure on us than is usually felt by most families who undergo the loss of a member. As everyone watched our every move, it did nothing to help existing tensions within the family during our shared grief.

The disagreements began as soon as we met to plan a memorial service for Michael. Everyone had a different opinion about what Michael's wishes would have been. I would never have disagreed so passionately with members of my own family if I didn't believe I knew exactly what Michael would have wanted. We had had similar tastes since childhood, and we always shared a passion for the crests that so often adorned Michael's outfits and belongings. I recognized that Neverland was intentionally designed and run like a palace, and I understood that Michael would have wanted his final send-off to be just as regal.

First, we had to think of the proper place to hold a service of this magnitude. We couldn't have it at a church because Mother is Jehovah's Witness, and it would have gone against her beliefs to associate with the church. To hold the volume of people from around the world that we expected to attend, it would have to be at a venue of the size that only Michael could pack within minutes of the service's being announced. The Los Angeles Police Department had estimated that more than 1 million people were coming to Los Angeles to attend Michael's memorial service. Even in death, Michael's presence could improve the economy of any struggling town, just as when he was alive, traveling the world, and attracting crowds everywhere he went.

"Let's have it at the Washington Monument!" Jermaine said.

"You're absolutely right," I said. "It's the perfect place to have it. Michael would love that."

The rest of the family was not on board with this suggestion. But we all knew that we needed a venue that would be large enough for the King's popularity.

"What about the Los Angeles Coliseum?" I said. "It seats one hundred thousand people. I know we can't get everyone in there, but at least we would be able to include a decent amount of fans."

Jermaine agreed with me, but the rest of the family didn't because they felt it would take too much time to prep such a large venue.

Several brothers mentioned that AEG had contacted them to have the service at the Staples Center. AEG had offered to pay for all of the expenses associated with the memorial and would show a simultaneous transmission of the service at the Nokia Theatre, a property AEG also owns, across the street from the Staples Center. I was suspicious of the offer, wondering if AEG was only thinking of the money and the publicity the service would generate. But, with so much going on, I let it slip by without paying too much attention to it. I was just happy to know that one of the many details of the burial was solved. But I feared that my intuition was right when I heard that they were planning to charge the public an admission fee to go to the funeral.

"NO!" I said. "We are *not* charging the public to go to Michael's memorial, that's *ridiculous*! It's *embarrassing*. And it's not right! We're not doing it."

My family was against the idea as well. That, at least, was something on which we all agreed.

"Michael has been exploited his entire life," Joseph said. "He won't be exploited in his death."

We told AEG we wanted to give tickets away, rather than selling them, and they agreed not to charge. They created a website with an online registration, and after more than 1.6 million fans registered, they randomly picked names to give away 8,750 pairs of tickets. Then, 11,000 winners were admitted to the Staples Center, and 6,500 winners were admitted to the Nokia Theatre. So that part of the memorial all worked out well. But I later heard that AEG charged the media $5,000-plus for box seats at the memorial, and $30,000 to $50,000 for news trucks to park on their property on the day of the memorial. They also had the exclusive rights to film the memorial service and broadcast it to the world. I imagine that earned AEG a substantial profit in licensing fees from the many networks throughout the world that broadcast it. Plus what they also made from the concession stands and merchandising the day of the service.

LAPD officials were concerned that, with only ten thousand officers on their entire force, they were unprepared for this type of crowd control. So they made it clear that those who didn't have a ticket should not come to the area that day. They blocked off most of the streets surrounding the Staples Center to keep control of the crowd.

Once we chose the location, we began to plan the details. I wanted a procession of gilded, horse-drawn carriages to make its way to the Staples Center, where a fanfare of horns would signal the arrival of Michael's body, as if he were a king, which he was, after all: the King of Pop. I wanted a beautiful gold casket to be carried between rows of uniformed guards like those at Buckingham Palace. Overall, I wanted the effect to be presidential because I knew it was what Michael would have chosen, and it was just the way he was seen in the eyes of his countless fans. I wanted the entire audience of twenty thousand at the Staples Center to be seated as my brothers carried in Michael's casket, and then have the announcer say "Please rise for the king."

I knew Michael would have wanted an open casket. His designer, Michael Bush, had dressed him impeccably, and with great style, as always. Michael's longtime hair and makeup person, Karen Faye, did an amazing job. He looked incredible, and so peaceful, as if he were just sleeping. After the service, I wanted his body to be preserved like that of Vladimir Lenin, at the Kremlin in Moscow, because I knew that Michael was so passionate about his fans that he would have wanted them to be able to visit him and see him long after he was gone.

But being Jehovah's Witness, Mother definitely didn't want anything at all showy. She preferred a closed casket and a relatively simple service. The rest of my family deferred to her.

"Nothing's too good for Michael," I said.

"Who do you think he is?" Rebbie said.

"He's a legend. He's the biggest entertainer in the world."

"No, he's not," she said. "He's your brother."

"It should be like the service they had for Princess Diana," I said.

"Are you insane?" my family members asked me.

"No, I'm not. It's what Michael would have wanted."

It was incredibly upsetting because I felt that I was fighting for Michael's wishes, but was silenced at every turn. Only Jermaine agreed with me, and in the end we were overruled.

A few hours before the service at the Staples Center on July 7, 2009, the family had a private viewing. Although Michael was not a Jehovah's Witness at the end of his life, in deference to Mother and Michael's deep, lifelong faith, the family memorial was a Jehovah's Witness service, including the songs that were sung and the prayers that were said. A few days prior, Paris once again showed what a brave and thoughtful girl she is.

She had made a special request of me during our fitting for the clothes we would wear to the memorial: "Auntie La Toya, I would like to give Daddy a half of a heart necklace. I'll have one half, and he'll have one half."

I knew that this was important for her, so I made sure we got the necklace and gave it to her before the private viewing, which she and I attended with Rebbie and Randy. No one else wanted to see Michael after he had passed.

Paris stood there by her father's casket, and she just cried and cried and cried. Finally, she took off half of the necklace.

"Daddy, this is for you," she said. "I have this part of the heart. And I want you to have this other part and carry it with you."

It was such a beautiful, sentimental moment.

She tried to wrap half of the necklace around Michael's neck. But we couldn't lift him, so we weren't able to slide it over his head.

"Let's try this," I said, wrapping it around his wrist instead.

Paris seemed happy with this, and then she put two colored stones on his chest. My heart went out to her. She was weak, yet strong; determined to see her father and share a heart with him, her half of which she will cherish forever. We left that evening, then waited to view him the following day.

Although I regret deeply that Michael's memorial service was not grand in the way that I believe he would have wanted it to be, I do feel that Paris had a large part in helping the memorial do justice to Michael. In the midst of the biggest luminaries in the entertainment world, she knew she had something important to express about the father she so loved.

"Auntie La Toya, I want to speak," she whispered to me during the service. "I want to say something about my dad."

"Whenever you're ready, let me know," I said.

"Auntie La Toya, I'm afraid to. I don't want to right now."

An hour went by while she sat silently, crying, and listening to the words being spoken.

"Okay, Auntie La Toya, I'm ready," she said.

Of course, just at that moment, Stevie Wonder had been announced to sing. I suppose it's a sign that Paris has inherited her father's sense of dramatic timing.

"You can't go now," I said. "But when we're on-stage, you can speak."

When Paris finally did take her turn at the microphone, she spoke simply and purely.

"Ever since I was born, Daddy has been the best father you could ever imagine," she said between tears. "And I just want to say I love him so much."

When Paris spoke those words, I think it humanized Michael for the world in a way that had never been done before. This moment made me extremely happy that people were finally able to see Michael as everyone in his family had always seen him: a devoted father who did everything in his power for his children, even agreeing to an impossible contract with greedy businessmen. As we all knew so well in our family, Michael wasn't weird. He wasn't Wacko Jacko. He was caring, kind, and fun-loving.

Most of the brothers wanted Michael to be buried at Neverland, even though he had vowed to never return there again. I knew Michael had lost the love he once had for Neverland. He had grown to despise it because of what it later represented for him after the police raids that were launched against him there: corruption, jealousy, maliciousness, and most of all *greed*. It was no longer the perfect, beautiful park he had created it to be, but a vision of the loss of his livelihood and reputation. Because of that, I was adamant about not placing him there, especially after his children told me that he wouldn't want to be buried there.

We had several meetings before we found an appropriate resting place for him. It wasn't easy to find a location that was secure enough for Michael. I wanted a place that was private and safe for him. After making a few phone calls, I went out to Forest Lawn in Glendale with Randy and Rebbie to look at locations. I desperately tried to convince my mother to come along with us, but she couldn't bear the thought of any of us planning to bury our brother—and her son—in the ground indefinitely. She finally agreed to come for the ride, but she stayed in the limousine when we looked at the grave sites. We viewed many different interment properties and sarcophagi, but I felt best about putting Michael in the mausoleum. It was extraordinarily beautiful, almost angelic, with cathedral ceilings and marble throughout. The sun's golden rays dazzled as they fell through the stained-glass windows located directly behind where Michael would be placed and beamed right onto his final resting place. What I valued most was that it was absolutely secure, and all visitors had to be on a list and then buzzed in to enter. This level of security was a necessity because it was being rumored that many were looking to steal Michael's body.

36

❧

INSIDE THE CONSPIRACY

While we were dealing with all the details of Michael's memorial service, AEG was discussing with my brothers the possibility of taking over Michael's show at the O2 Arena in London.

"AEG wants us to take over Michael's show," my brothers said. "They want us to take over all the dates that Michael was playing."

"Don't you see?" I said. "They're distracting you from what really happened to Michael. Michael hasn't been dead for twenty-four hours, and they're already speaking to you about doing his shows. That's never going to happen! It's all just to sidetrack your minds."

In my opinion, AEG was trying to ensure that no one in my family, or beyond, would focus on the details of Michael's death. Well, I did, and I saw a big cover-up. When I said I believed Michael was murdered because he was worth more dead than alive, I did so because

Michael had told me on several occasions that he knew he was going to be killed, and because everything I'd seen made me believe he was right.

First of all, I was surprised that AEG didn't express greater concern about Michael's death. They had put a tremendous amount of manpower and money into preparing for the London shows that Michael didn't live to perform. This made me think that the deals in place at the time of Michael's death meant that AEG stood to make more money with Michael dead than alive.

Let's think about this for a moment. Fifty of Michael's shows had sold out in four hours, generating roughly $85 million, which would have to be reimbursed after he died. AEG had reportedly spent $35 million prepping for what would have been the biggest concert in the world. And, apparently, before they even had the chance to put together all of the proper insurance policies, the performer they had spent all of this money on died under the care of the doctor they had supposedly hired to watch over him and make sure he was in the best possible health to do these shows. And they were allegedly paying this doctor $150,000 a month to do so.

Under those circumstances, I found it perplexing AEG had little to say after Michael died. I figured they would be out fighting to uncover what happened, and calling for an investigation. But perhaps they had a reason not to make a lot of noise about the performer's passing, and the money that was lost because of it. Maybe they feared that they wouldn't make the money they thought through the shows, and that they would do better after his death.

Let's start with AEG Live, which filmed Michael's last three rehearsals—including the final rehearsal on June 24, 2009, mere hours prior to his death—according to several full-time daily workers with the show. Before the film was theatrically released, Randy Phillips gave TV interviews stating that AEG had one hundred hours of raw footage, making it sound as if all of this footage was of Michael. It wasn't. They weren't able to film many hours of Michael rehearsing because he often didn't show up. That's one of the reasons that the O2 show was pushed from July 8 to July 13, and had Michael lived, it would probably have been pushed again. The sale of the rehearsal footage more than made up for any money lost on the shows, and that doesn't take into account distribution, ticket sales, or back-end participation for the film.

All of this made me increasingly suspicious. Why would AEG film Michael's rehearsals when they had no agreement in place with him to make a concert movie? And did they own the footage, or did Michael, as I suspect? If Michael owned it, how did AEG have the right to sell it, and would his children get the share of the profits from the sale that they deserved? When AEG found themselves in possession of the last footage of the legend performing on the nights before he passed, wasn't it a little heartless of them to immediately make plans to create a film that would allow them to profit from that material?

Plus, I find it odd that AEG did a deal with Sony to help them distribute *This Is It* when they own Regal Entertainment Group, which includes sixty-seven hundred movie screens at Regal Cinemas, United Artists Theaters, and Edwards Theaters, making it the largest motion picture exhibitor in the United States. Wouldn't AEG have made more money by distributing the film exclusively through their own theater chains? Why bring Sony in, unless some larger deal was in the offing, perhaps involving Michael's catalog?

I haven't seen *This Is It*, but Jeffré has, and he and other people who worked closely with Michael during the rehearsals have told me that it doesn't show a single complete run-through of any song. The editing is apparent because Michael is wearing several changes of clothes for each song during the film. Throughout Michael's life, he could always practice an entire set without a break. Now he couldn't get through a single song without stopping. *Michael was sick, and they had to know it!* All of this makes me more convinced that Michael was not well, and that he probably could not have done those shows. AEG was working closely with Michael at the time. It's hard to believe that they didn't know the poor state of his health and do something to intervene on his behalf, what with all that was financially riding on those concerts.

This Is It has earned more than $500 million throughout the world. Court documents indicate that as much as 90 percent of the film's back-end net profits go to Michael's estate, with his children as primary beneficiaries to a trust controlled by Mother. But John Branca and John McClain control the estate itself, and therefore any deals that could generate the money that would go to Michael's children. The remaining 10 percent goes to Sony, which is a company Michael had stopped doing business with at the end of his life.

Another matter that I don't understand is how the production credits played out on this film. Shouldn't Michael be a producer of *This Is It?* Yes, he should! Yet, his name was listed only under the credits for choreography, and for original concert production creation and direction, and both of these cards were shared with someone else. Even Michael's music supervisor and choreographer got producer credits on the film. Why? At the same time, John Branca, John McClain, and Frank DiLeo are also listed as producers on the film.

It is extremely interesting to me that many of those who received producer credits on the film were people whom Michael had at one time fired and told me that he didn't want to work with again, including Sony, John Branca, Frank DiLeo, and Dr. Tohme Tohme. Those who got producer credits also included AEG, whose behavior when they sold out fifty concerts in London after Michael only agreed to perform ten had upset Michael.

These were all business relationships and deals that I could not imagine Michael allowing to occur had he been alive. And the film was only the beginning of the many ways in which people have profited off Michael's death.

After Michael died, the $85 million collected in ticket

sales needed to be reimbursed. But AEG gave fans the option of getting a refund *or* receiving the actual commemorative concert ticket, inspired and designed by Michael. AEG said the ticket had special 3-D images on it and would become a collector's item. AEG was able to keep the money from all of the fans who chose to keep the ticket.

Finally, who named the tour *This Is It*? Was that some kind of a sick joke because "this is it" for Michael Jackson's life and career?

That's not all. I think that most people would have reached out to the family of the performer who died, expressing their condolences about their loss, and saying how great it was to work with him. Well, that never happened either. Randy Phillips of AEG has avoided me. As far as I know, no one from the circle of people who surrounded Michael when he died—Randy Phillips, Paul Gongaware, Kenny Ortega, Frank DiLeo, Tohme Tohme—has said a word of condolence to any of my family members. Michael said it the best in his song "They Don't Care About Us" when he sang, "All I wanna say is that, they don't really care about us."

Also, there's the money Michael's music has earned just from June 2009 to June 2010. According to ABC News, as of June 21, 2010, in the year after Michael died, his estate generated $1 billion. I know that my eyes have been opened wide as I've watched all things Michael fly off the shelves since he passed. Many of these were things that I can't believe Michael would have released.

It was no big secret that Michael was in liquid-cash

debt when he passed. He owed what has been reported as more than $400 million. I know that Michael loved to shop and spend, and I believe he was in heavy debt, but I'd love to see where that figure of more than $400 million comes from, to understand if it's a real number or an exaggerated sum. Even if he did owe that much, with just the bits and pieces of Michael's estate that I know of, there seems to be a great deal of money out there to take care of that debt. In the first year after his death, according to the Nielsen SoundScan, Michael sold 33 million records worldwide, at a 25 percent royalty rate. So, based on a blended worldwide retail sales price of $11 per CD, that would garner $363 million—at 25 percent royalty, roughly $90.75 million for the MJ estate. On the digital side, roughly 26.5 million Michael tracks were downloaded worldwide, which brought in roughly $34 million. Michael's ringtones alone sold 3 million units worldwide, at $2 per unit, which equaled $6 million in profits, of which the estate most likely saw $2 million. Global digital performances earned roughly $4.5 million. Michael's personal music publishing company, Mijac, through which he licensed his own songs, was valued at around $150 million, which means it brought in about $25 million a year. Since Michael's death, it's probably earned almost double that. Michael's estate owns 50 percent of the Sony/ATV music publishing catalog, which is valued as a $2 billion company. If 50 percent of that were sold, $1 billion would go to Michael's estate. That 50 percent should bring in $100 million a year to the estate. The estate also did a deal with Sony for a guaranteed $200 million to $250 million to release ten Michael records through 2017, and that money should be pretty much free and clear. Plus, the estate made another deal with Ubisoft and released a dance-oriented video game of Michael, which I'm sure made millions. Then there was the deal for a Las Vegas Cirque du Soleil show based on Michael's music, which is also bound to make millions. These are only the business ventures that I am aware of, and even just with this amount of money out there, it seems as if Michael's estate should be able to get out of debt quickly. So why hasn't it?

As I have said, no one from my family sits on the estate's board. All we ever hear is that Michael was in debt and the estate is broke. But the executors haven't shared bookkeeping or other records with my mother. I'm so concerned that, after Michael worked his entire life with the intention of leaving everything to his children, they are going to have nothing. I'm worried that just as Michael predicted, he has become the target of those who wanted to gain control of his empire. And I'm going to continue to fight until justice is served.

Many of my family members have been reluctant to create trouble by launching an investigation into Michael's death.

"You can't bring him back," they said. "He's dead. Just let it go."

My immediate response was to let them know that I can't let it go. Michael's children deserve to know the truth. My anger has fueled my investigation ever since

Michael's death. The more details that have emerged about Michael's passing, the more determined I have become.

In the weeks after Michael's death, Mother was acting as the executor of his estate, as I believe Michael would have wanted her to, and as it should still be. Not until a few weeks later, in July 2009, did John Branca and Joel Katz show up at my brother's house and present us with Michael's will, which we had never seen, and I had never heard anything about. The will named John Branca and John McClain as executors, with no member of the family represented on the board of trustees.

"Isn't this something?" I said when I saw the will. "How do we know that's not fake?"

I was shocked that it was Branca with a will, because Michael wouldn't have worked with Branca again, and I believe that he was pushed on Michael in the last days of his life. Besides that, the will was dated July 7, 2002. Michael had fired Branca in 2003, so I found it difficult to believe that Michael wouldn't have changed his will after that. I also find it interesting that Barry Siegel, who was another executor named on the will, immediately removed himself and wanted nothing to do with the will.

This meeting was the first that Mother learned of the will, and I had always assumed that she would be the executor of Michael's estate, especially as she had custody of his children, who were the main beneficiaries of the will. That was also the first time Branca saw Mother after Michael's passing, and I didn't hear him offer her one kind word. He simply showed her the will and informed us, Michael's family, that Michael's will provided that he and John McClain would be the co-executors and that not a single member of the family would be a part of the board that would run the estate.

Then, when the will was before a judge, DiLeo and Branca sat together, which made me wonder how they were connected in relation to the estate. I felt, as my mother and father did, too, that a family member should be a part of, or on the board of, Michael's estate. During a court break, we were asked to discuss a few matters concerning the estate. Well, these guys remained adamant about not letting a family member be a part of the estate. Although I am usually quiet and soft-spoken, I became so enraged at the sight of Joel Katz, John Branca, and Howard Weitzman, I had to speak up.

"If this was your son's estate, you would not allow *us* to handle it without *you* having any part of it," I said. "You would say, 'No, you're not going to handle my son's estate with us not being a part of it.' None of you would allow this to happen. And you know it."

"La Toya, sit down and be quiet," Randy said.

"Ah, ah, La Toya, let me handle this," said Londell McMillan, who was the attorney representing my mother.

At that moment, I began to wonder what was going on with Londell. After all, he had just shown Mother, Randy, and me an affidavit from Branca's former secretary that alleged that Branca was double-billing and sometimes triple-billing Michael.

Londell had told us that the secretary was willing to

go before the judge with the documents to prove her allegations, if it should come to that. And now he was urging me to back off.

"No, it's true," I said. "Would you let me handle your son's estate and you have nothing to do with it? And he's the biggest entertainer in the world?"

I went to each of them in turn, pointing at each as I did so.

"No," I said.

They didn't say anything, but who would tell me I was wrong?

Of course, my words did no good, and the executors got their way. Once this judge signed off on the estate as established in the will its executors had presented to the family, they could run it however they wanted. Since Michael's death, I have estimated that well over a billion dollars has been earned from Michael's music and merchandising, yet the executors continue to tell Mother that the estate remains in the red because they're still paying off Michael's debts. Like so many other things surrounding Michael's death, this leads me to have so many questions.

37

A LEGEND IS LAID TO REST

At the same time that I was beginning to investigate Michael's death, I was extremely busy with all of the matters that must be attended to when someone dies, especially a person of Michael's eminence. My family gave me the great honor of being the informant on Michael's body, which meant that I was designated to look over his body between his death on June 25, 2009, and the day that he was finally laid to rest in a private family service on September 3, 2009.

During these months, I was still having difficulty coming to terms with the loss of my brother. Even though he had been telling me for nearly six years that he was going to be murdered for his publishing catalog and estate, and I feared for his life throughout that time, I couldn't comprehend that he was really gone. I was incredibly distraught to have actually lost him, and I was filled with a deep desire to be close to him. I went to visit Michael at the funeral home where his body was being kept as often as I was able during these months, to spend time with him and begin to process my terrible loss. In all, I went to see him on nine or ten different occasions. It was the first time in many, many years that I could actually be alone with my brother whenever I wanted to be. There was no Gordon controlling me, and no one controlling Michael. There were no planes to be caught, no concerts to be performed, no fans clamoring for a sighting of the King of Pop. There was no security, no family even, just me and my brother, just the way it used to be when we were in our teens and twenties back at Hayvenhurst, having sleepovers in my room that we used to call camping out.

Although my brother had passed, he was still Michael Jackson, so there was constantly the risk of something happening to his body. Perhaps overeager fans could not let him go, or someone with a more malicious purpose would try to get access to cover up some aspect of his death.

After the service at the Staples Center, I got a call saying that Michael's body had been stolen from his casket. Then I started hearing the same rumor on television. I thought back to one of Michael's favorite actors, Charlie Chaplin, whose body was stolen in 1978 in an attempt to extort money from his family. I was nervous that this might have happened to Michael, too. I called the funeral director at Forest Lawn, where Michael's body was being kept. I asked him where Michael's body was and told him I would like to see it.

I called Jeffré to go with me, and we rushed to Forest Lawn. As I waited thirty minutes for the funeral director to get the casket, I became even more worried. When he finally rolled in a casket that was tightly wrapped in what looked like silver Saran Wrap, I fought back tears. It looked so final. Even worse, his body might not even be in there. As much as I didn't want to be faced once again with the fact that he had passed, I was hoping his body was there.

The attendants started unwrapping the plastic wrap. When the gold casket beneath was revealed, they unlocked it and opened it slowly. I was going crazy, wondering if his body was going to be in there, and what I should do if it wasn't. As the top of the casket lifted about one-fourth of the way up, I saw Michael's beaded-pearl jacket. Slowly, they revealed Michael's full body. I was relieved that his body was in there, but I still couldn't believe that my little brother was dead. He looked so peaceful. I turned to the funeral director.

"May I stay and visit with him awhile?" I asked.

"Take your time," he said.

As soon as he had left the room, I cried my heart out to Michael.

Throughout the summer, I heard on several more occasions that Michael's body had been kidnapped out of his casket. Each time I raced over to Forest Lawn to investigate, and the report was always a false alarm. But on one occasion, it took the attendants seven hours to produce his body.

"Why is it taking so long?" I kept asking.

The delay was so great that I actually left and came back after they finally called me to tell me that the body was ready for me to view. Although everything seemed fine when I finally laid eyes on him, I have always wondered what the delay was all about.

During another of my visits to Michael's body, Jeffré asked me, "How does it feel to be able to have access to see your brother, any time you want, after not being able to see him regularly for so many years?"

"It's a nice feeling," I said through tears. "But it's too bad that it had to get to this point before I could see him all of the time like this."

Whenever I arrived at the mortuary, the attendants brought out Michael's casket for me. I sat there with him, usually for an hour, telling him everything I had been given too few opportunities to say to him in life.

"I'm going to find out what happened," I said. "I'm going to make sure that I let your children know what really, truly happened to you."

Finally, all of the details had been arranged, and the time for Michael's burial arrived. I had to face that it was really time to say good-bye. The night prior, almost ten weeks to the day after Michael died, I went to the funeral home one last time. I could hardly comprehend that this was my last opportunity to be with my brother, and I sat there for a few hours. I didn't want to ever leave because I knew that the next day he would be buried, and then he would really be gone.

But one last difficult moment still had to be withstood in the ongoing investigation into Michael's death.

Just before Michael was buried, I was contacted by the Los Angeles County Coroner's Office.

"We have to see Michael's body again," they said.

"Again?" I said.

They told me that they needed Michael's palm print, which they did not have, and several additional hair samples. I was against disturbing Michael's body again because I felt that they had been given more than enough opportunities to get everything they needed. But when their request had to be granted, I insisted that I be there to oversee the proceedings.

So a few days before Michael was laid to rest, a lab tech, a photographer, and a police officer came out to Forest Lawn. I met them in the viewing room, and Scott Drolet, supervising vice president of Forest Lawn, and an assistant wheeled the body out. It had been nearly ten weeks since Michael had passed, so everyone was wearing surgical masks. I opened the casket with Scott, and Jeffré stepped between Michael and me because he wanted to protect me from seeing something that might disturb me.

"Let me look at him first," Jeffré said.

He was afraid that the skin would have changed colors or that bruising would have set in. But he saw that Michael looked so incredible, it was as if he were sleeping.

"Toy, come see him," Jeffré said.

I walked up and looked down at Michael's body, and it was good to see him, but also excruciatingly painful and sad.

We had to lift Michael's body up in the casket and hold him in a seated position for the lab tech to get her samples. I didn't want them to see his body or get pictures of it with the cameras they had brought.

"Why do you need to take pictures?" I asked.

They told me that they were going to take pictures of the hand they fingerprinted, but I was still suspicious. So I covered Michael completely with a white sheet and only revealed each individual part that they needed to see. First, they wanted new samples of his hair.

"Why are they doing this all over again?" I asked.

Again, they would not be dissuaded. So I pulled the sheet up over Michael's head and face, tight around his ear, so that only the tiniest segment of his hair was exposed long enough for them to pull off a strand. As soon as they were done, I covered the area right back up.

Michael was wearing black gloves, which were duct-taped around his wrists to make them stay in place, beneath his beautiful white-pearl-beaded jacket, so we had to remove all of that. Again, we covered the back of his hand with a sheet, so that only the palm was visible. They photographed it, then they rolled black ink over his palm. Because it had been almost ten weeks since Michael had died, they couldn't get a print in the middle, so they kept pushing his palm down and forcing it until they finally got a good one.

The whole time, I never took my eyes off them once. I'm sure they were wondering why I was being overly protective. But I didn't trust anybody, and with good reason, too, as far as I was concerned. After the lab techs finally left, I presented my theory to Jeffré.

"You know what's going on, right?" I said.

"What?" he asked.

"What they're going to say is he injected himself with propofol. He grabbed the bottle and did it himself. That's why they want his full palm print."

"You're right. You have a good point."

"I wouldn't be surprised if his palm print is found on the bottles, making it look like he killed himself."

At pretrial, Dr. Murray's defense did indeed suggest that Michael took the drugs and injected himself, which just absolutely infuriates me because it's so unlike Michael.

I then redid Michael's hair and fixed his clothes one last time. I put his signature sunglasses just so, on the neckline of his jacket. I replaced the items Paris had given him at the private viewing before his memorial at the Staples Center—the heart necklace around his right wrist, and the colored stones above his left breast, next to his heart. I knew Michael would like that, and so would Paris. Even though his body was not going to be exposed at the family memorial, I wanted to make sure that everything was immaculate and looked just right. It was an honor to be able to show my brother this kind of care, but it hurt me deeply to be there with him that day. September 2 was my last chance to have private time with him. This was really the end. This was the end of the end. After this, I would never see him again.

Once again, I stroked Michael's hair and spoke to

him of how much I loved him and how determined I was to find justice for him. Scott came in the room just then.

"La Toya, we're about to leave," he said. "We have to put Michael's body away."

They closed the top of the casket and started to lock it.

But I couldn't let go. "Could I just see him one more time?" I asked through tears.

They agreed and opened the casket back up.

I began to sob uncontrollably.

"Michael, I love you so much," I said. "Rest in peace, and I'll see you again one day."

I kissed him on his forehead and turned to go. Then, I stopped in my tracks, turned back to him, and said, just as Michael used to, "I love you more." That was the last time I ever saw him. I almost couldn't bring myself to leave. But I knew I had to walk away and finally I did.

I will never forget Scott Drolet, who took such extraordinary care of my brother, as if he were his own son, and who was always extremely accommodating and allowed me to see Michael for as long as I wanted. I will always love Scott for that.

The next day, September 3, a private memorial service was held for the immediate family members and friends. So many things went through my mind at the service, which was incredibly painful to sit through. Even though I had been given those ten weeks to face my loss, there was no coming to terms with it. Michael was my brother, and I loved him dearly, and it's so unbelievable that he's gone. As difficult as it was for me to comprehend my grief, I was even more concerned about Michael's children. The day of the private burial I sat with Blanket to make sure everything was fine, and Mother was on the other side of him. On the outside, his grief was not overly extreme, but what disturbs me is what's going on inside him and his brother and sister, because it's not discussed. Knowing my family's dislike of discussing anything remotely troubling or emotional, it might never be, unless I do it myself.

After the ceremony was complete, Michael's body was carried to its final resting place as the rest of my family moved off to attend the repast. But I still couldn't bring myself to leave. I had said my good-bye the night before and finally forced myself to really let go. But now, I was concerned that the casket might not actually get put into his tomb. Even more than that, I was suspicious that Michael's body might not be in his casket at all, and I was determined to make sure that it really was. So I made Scott promise to be an eyewitness.

"Please promise me you'll do me a favor and make sure Michael's body is in that casket, because I don't trust any of these people," I said.

"I promise you," he said. "I promise you."

I later called Scott, and he promised me he would stay all night at the site where Michael was being buried, until he had seen the casket sealed into the tomb. Now that I think back on the situation with greater clarity, I wish that I had demanded to see Michael's body one last time in those final moments, just to be sure that he was really there. But it was such an emotional day, and so much was going on, that I let the opportunity pass. I will always regret that decision because, now, it is too late, and I will always have my doubts about whether Michael is actually buried in his tomb.

The mausoleum we chose is an exceptional resting place for the exceptional talent and individual that Michael was. A long hallway leads to an aboveground tomb that holds Michael's casket. On either side are walls of stained-glass windows, which catch the light in the most beautiful way during the day, so that it just beams down from above onto where he lies. A small gate allows access to the tomb itself. On either side are walls of stacked tombs in which the rest of the family members will eventually repose. All of the Jacksons will be together, once again.

38

〰

EYEWITNESS ACCOUNTS
OF A COVER-UP

Many people approached members of the Jackson family after Michael's death to reveal concerns about his final days. Leonard Rowe reached out to me after he saw me say on television that I believed Michael was murdered. He called a mutual friend to let me know that he needed to speak with me, so I called him back. During our conversations, he told me that AEG had put Michael in an awkward position to encourage him to sign their contract. As I knew, at the time that Michael made the deal, he had vowed that he would never perform again because he feared he would be assassinated onstage. So I knew that the contract must, quite literally, have been irresistible to Michael for him to agree to do even ten shows. To convince Michael, AEG presented him with a contract that promised him the world, or nearly that much, including a house in Las Vegas, and enough money to basically settle his debts. Also, in advance of the shows, they took over the substantial expense of keeping Michael's household afloat. But after the recoupment of expenses, Michael might not earn a profit from the concerts, and suspecting this, Michael had called in his old friend Leonard Rowe.

The promoters might not have made much of a profit either, with such a high payout guaranteed to Michael. However, when he passed, they stood to earn the significant payout from a life insurance policy they had taken out on Michael, and their share of the $500-million-plus in profits from the concert documentary *This Is It*, which was rushed out in the wake of Michael's death. The executors of the estate itself, which included Michael's share of the valuable Sony/ATV publishing catalog and could net $300 million to $500 million a year, also stood to profit from a percentage of any deal done on behalf of the estate. Michael's legacy was especially valuable at just that moment because of the excitement the promoters themselves had generated to sell out the tickets for Michael's London shows. In its wake, Michael-mania was at a fever pitch it hadn't been at since the *Thriller* era in the 1980s. So, when he died, the possibilities for what the estate could earn from licensing profits alone were beyond belief. It does not sit well with me that no one in the family is a part of the estate's management in order to be able to watch over it for his children.

Not only was the contract troubling, but Michael was increasingly isolated at the time that he signed it, which prevented him from getting advice from anyone who might help him to understand the ramifications of what he was about to sign. As I learned from Joseph after Michael died, during the final weeks of Michael's life, Joseph became increasingly concerned about Michael's health and safety. Because of this, he went over to Carolwood several times to try to see Michael, and security would never let him in. Once Joseph became so agitated that he threatened to crash his car through the gates to get to his son, but he was still denied entry.

I have recently learned that Michael was also trying to get in touch with Joseph in his final days. Apparently, Michael gave Paris and Prince the following instructions again and again:

"Call Grandpa, he'll know what to do. He'll help me. Call Grandpa, call Grandpa."

Unfortunately, the message never reached Joseph, and although Michael actually tried to call Joseph on the day before he died, he was not able to get through.

Through the generosity and thoughtfulness of so many people who cared about Michael, including his fans and those who were rehearsing with Michael in his final days, I have been able to piece together an idea of what his last night was likely like. Michael's fans have been particularly helpful in providing useful information. Because they were so loyal to Michael, they knew his habits extremely well and were struck by the deviation from the norm on the nights just prior to, and the night of, Michael's death.

Every day, many of Michael's most loyal fans stood outside the gate of whichever house Michael was living in at the time, in whatever country he was in. That June,

Michael was busy preparing for his London shows. His fans knew what time he left for rehearsal and were always waiting outside the gate to greet him. Every time Michael left Carolwood, he told his security guards to stop the car so he could roll his window down to talk to the fans.

"Hi, how are you today?" Michael would ask as he shook their hands.

"So, how are you guys doing today?" Michael would say as he posed for photos.

"Oh, thank you," he would say as he collected whatever gifts they had for him.

The fans were there so often that Michael had come to know each personally in these friendly exchanges. He even had photos in his bedroom that had been taken of them in his house. And as I mentioned earlier, he sometimes ordered pizzas to be delivered to them at the gates.

When Michael was finished speaking with all of his fans, he drove off. The fans immediately jumped in their cars and sped to the Staples Center, to arrive there before Michael did. Then they jumped out of their cars and stood outside and waited for Michael so they could do it all again. And Michael did. Patiently, and with the exact same warmth as before, Michael greeted them a second time. Then, when his rehearsal was over, the fans were at the door waiting for him a third time. After Michael visited with them a third time, he left. Again they got in their cars and raced back to Carolwood, to go through the whole ritual a *fourth* time, when Michael stopped one final time on his way into his house. Then they would stay out there all night and wait to do it again in the morning.

According to the fans, when Michael was on his way to rehearsal on the day of his death, as he drove through the gate at Carolwood, he did not roll his window down and talk to them. That was totally out of character for Michael. I've never known Michael to behave in that way to a group of fans who had been so devoted to him. Michael would close himself off like that only if it was an uncontrollable crowd, and even then he would still have tried to talk to the fans that he could. Then, when he arrived at the Staples Center, he didn't walk over to his fans.

"No, you can't go over and talk to them," one of the guards told him.

But this seemed strange, given how friendly Michael always was. So the guards finally relented, just a little bit.

"Well, you only have two seconds," the guard said. "It has to be very short."

"Why?" Michael said. "These are my fans."

When Michael finally approached his fans, he was apologetic, but seemed nervous.

"They won't let me talk to you," Michael said in a lowered voice.

The fans noticed that a security guard was standing close while Michael talked to his fans, even though that hadn't happened before. Because Michael was so devoted to his fans and made it such a point to stop and greet them, security was accustomed to standing to the side and letting Michael take his time with them.

"No, you're not talking to them today," security said, pulling Michael back from his waiting fans and herding him inside.

That night, June 24, 2009, Michael's last night of rehearsal before he died, his usual routine was again interrupted. Although he was already late, security took Michael into his dressing room at the Staples Center. A number of men involved in his business dealings, who had never before been there during rehearsals, were waiting that evening for Michael to get there. Michael and the men remained in his dressing room for several hours while the dancers and the other assorted staff and crew rehearsed.

I don't know what was said in that room. But I believe that the men realized that Michael was not going to get on that stage in London and was never going to perform again.

Possibly they had concluded that Michael was not well enough to do the shows and that he would not pass the physical that Lloyd's of London demanded take place by their own physician prior to the performance. Unless this new doctor declared Michael fit enough to perform all fifty shows, the tour would be canceled. If Lloyd's didn't insure, AEG would be out millions of dollars. All they would be able to do then was stand in line to sue Michael, who was in financial difficulty at the time and already had several lawsuits directed against him.

Alternatively, Michael, being the incredible, extremely professional performer that he was, may have felt able to do the shows but had decided not to and said that at the meeting. It would take an extreme situation to push Michael to stand up for himself, but as had happened with Gordon and me, perhaps Michael had his breaking point. If he was pushed too far, he might have snapped. In that moment he would have been extremely fierce, the implied message being:

"I'm Michael Jackson, and you can't tell me what to do."

I do know that Michael was threatening not to show up for rehearsal or do any shows until they canceled the forty shows that he hadn't agreed to perform.

After leaving the meeting, Michael went to the stage, and although he was supposed to be leaving for London in the next few days, he didn't perform the rigorous rehearsal that might have been expected, especially from a perfectionist such as Michael. He quickly ran through two songs. He was being filmed, but he didn't appear to be performing like his normal self at all during those numbers, and then he left. I believe that Michael knew at that moment he was going to die soon.

These filmed songs form part of the documentary *This Is It*, and Michael does not appear to be himself. He did appear strong enough to perform, but some of those who were at that rehearsal have a different story. Apparently, Michael's hairdresser felt Michael was too ill to go onstage and tried to intervene on his behalf with Frank DiLeo.

"Frank, we've got to get Michael to a doctor," she said. "He's sick."

"There's nothing wrong with him," DiLeo said.

One of Michael's choreographers at the time was also concerned about Michael's health because of how skinny he was. The choreographer didn't feel Michael was behaving in his normal fashion and wanted to get help. In the last week of Michael's life, he lost fifteen pounds, according to his costume designer. I have been told that on the day after Michael died, he weighed only 112 pounds, although it has incorrectly been reported that he weighed 136 pounds. In spite of the many layers of clothing he wore to rehearsal, he was constantly freezing.

"He's sick," the choreographer tried to alert people. "He's so tiny. We need to get him to a doctor."

"No, he's not," the choreographer was told. "He's going to do it."

When Michael left his final rehearsal on the night that he passed, he managed to deliver a covert message to some fans through tears.

"You've gotta help me," he whispered. "You've gotta get me out of here."

Then security ushered Michael into his waiting vehicle. As usual, the fans sped to Carolwood to get there before Michael arrived. They did so, as always, but this night was different. According to the fans who stayed outside Michael's house every night to watch him come home from rehearsal, on the night of June 24, 2009, the last night before he passed, when he arrived home from rehearsal, the security measures at the house were much different from on any other night when Michael returned from rehearsal. A line of roughly ten men were lined up on both sides of his gate. Normally, he had only the two or three security guards who were with him, and the one who was in the post inside the yard. But this night was different, security was everywhere, and again Michael's car didn't stop on the way inside the gate.

I received another report of Michael's last night one evening while I was at dinner with Jeffré and my nephew Taj, when a fan walked right up to me.

"I need to talk to you about what happened that night," she said.

"Who are you?" I asked.

"Toy, listen to what she's trying to say," Jeffré said.

"But who are you?" I said again.

"I'm a fan."

Then, in a hushed voice laced with emotion, she told us what she had seen.

"I stand outside the gate, and Michael has the same routine every night. After he comes home from rehearsal, he goes upstairs, and about twenty minutes later the light in a room goes off. The night that he died, the light stayed on all night. I got worried. The light never went off. I didn't get it. I didn't understand what had happened. It was very strange."

Jeffré and I exchanged a look but didn't say anything so as not to discourage the fan from talking more.

"Oh, and security was acting strange," she said.

I knew I needed to speak to several other fans regarding that night, and when I did, their stories were the same.

What I heard during Dr. Murray's pretrial only

added to the uneasy feeling I had about Michael's death. As I learned, Michael's head was turned to the left, and his eyes and mouth were wide-open, as if he were dead. Even so, the doctor and one of the security guards, Alberto Alvarez, gave him chest compressions while he was still on the bed, instead of calling 911. I find it hard to understand how a trained doctor, and another adult, didn't know that they should move Michael to the floor and resuscitate him on a hard surface. Then, they removed the IV bag from the stand, and they began to clean up, putting away bottles of medicine and several needles. Not until *after* that stuff was hidden did they finally call 911.

I try not to torture myself by imagining Michael's last hours, but it's inevitable, given what I've learned. I believe that when Michael walked in that house that night, whatever it was that greeted him, he knew that his end was upon him. And as soon as he had passed, some of the very people he had expressed suspicions about now controlled his estate.

With as much love as Michael showed the world, he died not with his family or fans, but surrounded by the very people whose motives he questioned. The thought tortures me. When my search leads me to become frustrated or frightened, I am sustained by the desire to put this right. There is still so much to be learned and so much to be revealed.

The following day, June 25, everyone prepared for rehearsal as normal. However, as Kenny Ortega has said under oath, Randy Phillips went to Michael's house to pick him up for rehearsal that morning. This was strange, as Michael usually rehearsed in the evening and didn't generally ride over to rehearsal with Phillips. I was told by someone who was at Michael's house that Randy Phillips was also at the house when Michael came home from rehearsal the previous night, although Jef-fré and I saw an interview in which Frank DiLeo said that he and Randy Phillips arrived at the house immediately after Michael passed because Dr. Murray called them right away. I eventually asked the investigator on the case if they had secured the surveillance tapes of Michael's property. When they told me that they had, I asked if they could tell me who entered and exited all entrances to the house, just before and after Michael's death. They told me that they could when they had a chance to look at the tapes. Although I have explained how important it is for us to know who went in and out of Michael's house, I have never been given access to or any information about what can be seen on those tapes. And now, the surveillance video is apparently unaccounted for, except for four minutes of Michael entering the gates around 12:30 a.m.

As soon as Michael passed, the doors at the Staples Center were locked. Then, I was told by people who were there at the time, the promoters walked around and gathered everybody's camera, and all of the footage that had been shot. Much of the film that became *This Is It* actually belonged to Michael's personal cameramen, which makes it even more upsetting that no one close to him had a role in its production or release. People from AEG removed the film from everyone's cameras, as well as footage from the cameramen's computers. In my opinion, this was because they knew that they were going to make a movie out of this footage, and if anyone had any footage of what happened at that meeting the night before, they wanted it. They had just learned that Michael had passed. Yet, it seems as if they were already focused on the profit to be made.

In the wake of Michael's death, I am amazed by how quickly that film came together from only three days of shooting Michael, which makes me wonder if a film of some kind was already in progress. If nothing else, its release was in poor taste. That's why I have never seen the film myself. To me, it is further exploitation of my brother and his memory.

Other than Michael's extreme emaciation, and the toll this took on his health, he was remarkably healthy. His system was clean of drugs, except for the propofol and other drugs that were in his body in such high dosage the night he died.

I learned a great deal during the pretrial of Dr. Murray, who has been accused of involuntary manslaughter in my brother's death, but who I believe is the fall guy for a much larger plot. It was excruciating to sit there every day and hear what was said. Some of the details of that night were so painful to imagine, such as that, even with all of the security and adult staff members in the house that night, Dr. Murray called Prince to come help him resuscitate his father. According to several different witnesses, Paris was screaming hysterically. Of course she was. She will be haunted by this image for the rest of her life. I cannot imagine any good reason why they were allowed to witness what they saw.

As upsetting as the testimony was, I listened carefully because I knew it could prove valuable in my tireless pursuit of the truth. Also, I wanted people to know that I had my eye on them at all times when we were in court. The trial is set to begin in the fall, and it will not surprise me if Dr. Murray is found guilty of negligence and given the minimum sentence, or allowed to walk away, never having served any time, or even having been handcuffed. This will convince the public of the story that Michael's death was a simple case of malpractice. Again, I will be there in court every day, determined to achieve real justice for my brother. I'm not done with my investigation for the truth yet; I've only scratched the surface. I will never give up until I unveil the truth and justice is served.

39

❧

STARTING OVER AGAIN

In the meantime, while my investigation into Michael's death never ceases, I have begun to put my own life back together. Sometime in 2010 I finally began to do so, at Jeffré's urging, as he was concerned that my entire life was becoming consumed with Michael's murder, and I was constantly sad about it.

"Toy, you have to get on with your life," Jeffré said. "You have to get back to your life."

Since founding our company in 1999, Jeffré and I have continued to grow Ja-Tail Enterprises. Early last year, we added a new venture that I am particularly proud of—representing other artists. After everything that my brother and I endured at the hands of greedy managers, it is a great pleasure for me to protect and nurture our artists.

Just recently, I have also returned to making personal appearances, largely overseas. This experience is always bittersweet for me now, as Michael's legend continues to live on in Europe in a way that it simply does not here in America. All over Europe, everywhere I turn, there is nothing but Michael merchandise. His estate has licensed everything it could possibly sell, and every item that I see is just another reminder of how the estate is making decisions I don't believe Michael would approve of, and that the family can't evaluate to determine if they're in the children's best interest.

Despite all of this licensing, I could not even have a few of Michael's personal photos of him and me, just to have them hanging up in my house so I can be surrounded by happier memories of my brother.

"Absolutely not," I was told.

I become incredibly sad whenever I think about everything that has been taken from the family. My family, the Jackson family, will never ever be the same. A piece of all of our hearts is gone forever, and we are no longer whole. There hasn't been a Family Day since Michael passed. Everyone still has strong opinions about the estate, the people controlling it, and what happened to Michael. Every day since Michael passed, I have watched my mother trying to be strong for not only her family, but also for Michael's children. But anyone can see the strain on her, and that she's quickly fading away. The worst part is that the trustees have never asked the children if they want anything that once belonged to their father. I can't imagine that the trustees ever will. I know Paris would love to have some keepsakes from her father, or anything, for that matter.

Michael's estate has begun selling off large numbers of his possessions at auction, including everything from his furniture and memorabilia to his handwritten notes. Because I miss my brother so much, I want a few mementos of him, and with the family denied access to his personal belongings, I have sent Jeffré and others to auctions several times on my behalf to buy pieces that Michael and I picked out together, pieces that have significant sentiment for me. I cannot bring myself to go in person because I feel too embarrassed that I am being forced to purchase my own brother's possessions.

Healing from Michael's death has been extremely difficult, especially given how it has divided me from many members of my family. They do not support me in my fight, but if I have to stand alone, I will. I don't blame any of them for their actions following Michael's loss. I love them all, and I always will. I know that we all must respond to our grief in our own ways. I hope that we can repair our relationships down the road, when time has begun to heal the severity of our wounds and I have proven that I had a good reason not to just let Michael's death be, as some wished that I would. Even without their support, I feel that I am fighting for Michael as a Jackson, and on their behalf. I am simply doing what anyone would do for a loved one, trying to find out what exactly happened to my little brother, in the hope that justice will be served. I owe it to his children, his fans, and most of all to him; because Michael cannot start over.

ACKNOWLEDGMENTS

TO MY JA-TAIL FAMILY:

A very special thanks to Jeffré Phillips, my coauthor and best friend, whom I have been most fortunate to work with for so many years. You have proven yourself in many ways, and you continue to prove yourself with your brilliance. Thank you for your continuous support and your undying devotion to seeking the truth. You were very sound in helping me produce this project, and I thank you for this and for all of your concerns for my family. I love you with all my heart.

Richard and Jamie Boyd, you both have been truly wonderful and your input makes Ja-Tail complete.

Ron Labuzan, you're a great addition to Ja-Tail.

Courtney Benson, it's a pleasure having you on board. I only have one thing to say to you: tequila shrimp.

Juliette Harris, thank you for seven years.

Ian Marsden and Jamie Garcia, thank you for my Internet presence.

Michael Morris, thank you so much for your friendship and your expert legal guidance over the past decade. You've protected me in many of the best deals of my career, and I thank you for always having my best interest at heart. Gary Torrell, thank you for your undying fight and thank you so much for the win! Stephen Moeller, Janette Richter-Addo, and everyone else at Valensi Rose, PLC, thank you.

Wayne Johnson, of Wayne Johnson & Associates, thank you for all your corporate expertise over the past twelve years. I wouldn't have my companies without you.

I thank you all for being the MOST INCREDIBLE team ever and thank you for helping me start over.

TO MY JA-TAIL COMPANIES:

Ja-Tail Publishing Company (www.jatail.com): Thanks for publishing this book.

Ja-Tail Records: Thank you for releasing my music.

Celebrity Branding Group (www.cbgbrands.com): You guys are great. Let's continue to change the branding world.

La Toya Luxurious Collection (www.latoyaluxuriouscollection.com): Thank you, Julie Pruett, for helping me create the wonderful fragrance for SIMPLY LA TOYA.

ASAP (Auto Spa Amazing Products) (www.autospaproducts.com): Tunch and Serra Goran, thank you for helping the world stay green. ASAP is the best car product in the world, and I'm so proud to be an owner of a company that will make a difference in the world.

TO SIMON & SCHUSTER AND GALLERY BOOKS:
Jennifer Bergstrom, you are a TRUE PLEASURE and an easy person to work with! Thank you for publishing my book and allowing me to tell my story. I appreciate you for many reasons, and you are a true gem. Jeremie Ruby-Strauss, thank you for being a wonderful pilot on this book. Without your strong push, we would never have made our deadlines. Jennifer Robinson, Emilia Pisani, Elisa Miller, Stephen Fallert, and everyone else at Gallery/Simon & Schuster, thank you for giving me this opportunity to speak the truth in this book.

TO THE MUNCIE POLICE DEPARTMENT:
Thank you so much for making my dream of being a police officer come to fruition. Being sworn in by then chief Joe Winkle and former Muncie mayor Dan Canan—that was the proudest moment of my life. Officer Amy Kesler, I love you so much! You are truly the best partner anyone could have. Please always be safe on the streets, because I'm not there to protect you. Chief Deborah Davis, thank you so much for making me tougher. I'm so proud to know that you're now the Chief of Police—you deserve it! I look forward to coming back and working the streets soon under your direction. Lieutenant Al Williams, thank you for your kindness; you are a true sweetheart. Officer Jamie Brown, Officer Scott Odell, Officer Damon Stovall,

Officer Temple, Officer Joe Winkle, Officer Jay Turner, and every other officer in the Muncie Police Department, you are all the best officers in the world.

THANKS TO:

Tanya Bass. Lacrezia. Florence Anthony. Marva Lee for always listening. Dolores Cardelucci for telling it like it is. To anyone else I may not have been able to mention by name, of course I also offer my deepest thanks as well.

SPECIAL THANKS TO:

Joseph and Katherine Jackson for your unconditional love. I love you both so very much. Thank you for the life you've given our family. You both have been wonderful and understanding parents.

Randy Jackson and Tony Whitehead for rescuing me. It was the most frightening and the happiest moment of my life. I will never forget either one of you for that.

My entire family and all my nieces and nephews, I love you all so very, very much!

Scott Drolet at Forest Lawn for showing such warmth and kind love. You were hands-on in making sure that every little detail was perfect! You cared for Michael as if he was your baby. I truly thank you for that, Scott.

Michael Bush, thank you so much for dressing Michael in the way you knew he wanted the world to see him. YOU DID A MAGNIFICENT JOB!

Karen Faye, thank you for making Michael look so incredibly great. WHAT A FABULOUS JOB with his hair and makeup. He loved you for that.

Prince, Paris, and Blanket, whom he lived his life for: he loved you and wanted only the best for you. So let's continue to make him proud.

Rob Kaplan and Steve Fisher and everyone at APA, thank you for your belief.

Leonard Rowe, thank you for your continuous fight as to what you witnessed.

Paul Ring, thank you for always being there for Ja-Tail Records.

Kathy Hilton, thank you for your forty years of friendship with Michael and myself. I will always love you!

Brian Oxman, thank you for your fight and continuous drive toward justice for Michael.

Majestik Magnificent, thank you for always checking on me and being a good ear after I left Gordon and until this day.

Christine Fahey, you are an angel and a doll. Your heart is pure. I wish more people were like you. I love you, Chris!

Donald Trump, what an experience I had working with you. Thank you for allowing me the opportunity to create more awareness of my charity, AIDS Project Los Angeles. What a joy it was to raise $65,000 for them during my work on *Celebrity Apprentice.*

All the media and networks that have been there for me in a positive way, thank you for helping me start over.

This book would not have been possible without the editorial help of Sarah Tomlinson. You are truly a gifted person. Thank you for always being there when I needed you.

FOLLOW LA TOYA AT:

www.twitter.com/latoyajackson
www.jatail.com
www.latoyaonline.com
www.myspace.com/latoyaonline
www.youtube.com/latoyaonline